THE HELL'S KITCHEN® COOKBOOK

THE HELL'S KITCHEN® COOKBOOK

RECIPES FROM THE KITCHEN

GRAND CENTRAL
Life & Style
NEW YORK · BOSTON

Grand Central Life & Style
Hachette Book Group
1290 Avenue of the Americas
New York, NY 10104

www.GrandCentralLifeandStyle.com

Printed in the United States of America

Q-MA

First Edition: October 2015

10 9 8 7 6 5 4 3 2 1

Grand Central Life & Style is an imprint of Grand Central Publishing.

The Grand Central Life & Style name and logo are trademarks of Hachette Book Group, Inc.

The Hachette Speakers Bureau provides a wide range of authors for speaking events. To find out more, go to www.HachetteSpeakersBureau.com or call (866) 376-6591.

The publisher is not responsible for websites (or their content) that are not owned by the publisher.

LIBRARY OF CONGRESS CATALOGING-IN-PUBLICATION DATA HAS BEEN APPLIED FOR

ISBN: 978-1-4555-3569-9 (hardcover) / ISBN: 978-1-4555-3568-2 (ebook)

THE HELL'S KITCHEN® COOKBOOK

CONTENTS

INTRODUCTION: **HELL'S KITCHEN IS HOT!** 1

CHAPTER ONE: **HELL'S KITCHEN: WHERE CHEFS SET FIRE TO THEIR PASSIONS** 2

CHAPTER TWO: **BRINGING HOME HELL'S KITCHEN: WHAT YOU NEED TO KNOW TO COOK LIKE A PRO** 8

CHAPTER THREE: **STARTERS** 30

CHAPTER FOUR: **ENTRÉES** 80

CHAPTER FIVE: **SIDES** 168

CHAPTER SIX: **DESSERTS** 192

CHAPTER SEVEN: **MENUS** 240

CONCLUSION 254

INDEX 255

INTRODUCTION: HELL'S KITCHEN IS HOT!

HELL'S KITCHEN **IS AMERICA'S LONGEST-RUNNING CULINARY COMPETITION ON A BROADCAST NETWORK** and is and one of the hottest dining tickets in LA. As the country's appreciation for all things culinary has broadened over the past decade, *Hell's Kitchen* has been both a mirror and a catalyst for food trends. It's no coincidence that food has become sexier since *Hell's Kitchen* has come onto the scene, and the show is obsessed with what's in—from small plates to molecular gastronomy, pop-ups, and food trucks. If it's hot, *Hell's Kitchen* has it covered!

Winning *Hell's Kitchen* is an incredible feat of stamina, persistence, and skill. Throughout each season, contestants must survive grueling challenges and emotional struggles to make it to the final face-off in the most important night of their cooking careers. Starting with the first episode's lineup of chefs presenting their signature dish and continuing with the battle of the sexes that rages throughout the season, we witness the contestants' ups and downs as they sweat through dinner service for a hundred guests who demand perfection. Additional challenges—from the "Blind Taste-Test" to "Taste It, Make It" to surviving the elimination rounds—push contestants to the max.

Hell's Kitchen elevates entertainment to culinary education, giving viewers a backstage, uncensored view into the workings of a professional kitchen. The show has served as a launching pad for some serious culinary talent, with one lucky chef taking home the title of head chef at a major restaurant at the end of the show.

While winning the competition is the fulfillment of a dream for one truly gifted chef, the show is all about bringing out the rising chef in us all. In the pages that follow, the passion and perfection of *Hell's Kitchen* will be brought home to you: You'll learn how to set your kitchen up like a pro, practice mise-en-place and knife skills, and cook over one hundred stupendous recipes from the series, all prepared according to the show's exacting standards. For the first time ever, the *Hell's Kitchen* repertoire—the trial by fire that serves as culinary boot camp to *Hell's Kitchen* contestants—is within reach of your home kitchen! The book concludes with an assortment of menus based on restaurant-worthy dishes contestants have prepared on the show. Now's the time to up your game and cook with the best of them . . . *Hell's Kitchen* is open!

HELL'S KITCHEN: WHERE CHEFS SET FIRE TO THEIR PASSIONS

CHAPTER ONE

IN 2005, A HOT NEW TELEVISION SERIES HIT U.S. AIRWAVES AND QUICKLY BECAME A TOP-RANKED SHOW. BASED IN LOS ANGELES AND HOSTED BY CHEF GORDON RAMSAY, HELL'S KITCHEN IS THE PLACE WHERE ASPIRING CHEFS FROM ALL OVER THE COUNTRY COME TO SET FIRE TO THEIR PASSIONS AND PROVE THEMSELVES AS AMERICA'S NEXT GREAT CHEF.

EACH SEASON, A DOZEN OR SO DRIVEN, HUNGRY HELL'S KITCHEN HOPEFULS ARE SELECTED OUT OF THOUSANDS OF APPLICANTS TO PUT THEIR KITCHEN SKILLS TO THE ULTIMATE TEST. THEY COME FROM ALL WALKS OF LIFE AND EVERY POINT ON THE CULINARY SPECTRUM, FROM THE PRISON CHEF TO THE WAFFLE-HOUSE COOK, LINE COOK, AND ALL THE WAY UP TO EXECUTIVE CHEF. IN TEMPERAMENT THEY RANGE FROM THE WILDLY AMBITIOUS AND CRAZILY COMBATIVE TO SURE AND STEADY AND COOL AND COLLECTED. WHETHER THEY'RE FROM THE WEST COAST OR FROM THE MIDDLE OF THE COUNTRY, WHAT BRINGS THEM TO HELL'S KITCHEN IS VISION AND A BURNING DESIRE FOR SUCCESS. THESE HOPEFULS HOLD ONE THING IN COMMON: THEY THINK THEY HAVE WHAT IT TAKES TO WIN. AND IF THEY DON'T MEASURE UP, THERE'S HELL TO PAY.

Over the past decade, some of this country's most determined and passionately committed chefs have come through *Hell's Kitchen*. The competition extracts the best from the contestants—if they can stand the heat. It's culinary school on steroids, a dueling ground for those with heart, determination, and an obsession with perfection. As the season progresses, the anxiety and excitement builds with hell-raising meltdowns and tempers running wild. The stakes are high, with the winner taking home the opportunity of a lifetime: a head chef position at one of the most acclaimed restaurants in the United States, which comes with a salary of a quarter of a million dollars.

Hell's Kitchen is a phenomenally successful cooking show. But it's more than a show; the set consists of two state-of-the-art kitchens and a restaurant seating one hundred hungry and demanding guests. Though it can come off as a spectator sport, it's the real deal for a diverse bunch of seriously dedicated cooks looking to reach the top of their game and win a prize that can change lives forever.

This hard-hitting, sweat-it-out-in-the-kitchen, real-life competition adds up to a show with staying power, one that has been going strong for more than a decade. And each and every season is better than the last!

BECOMING A CONTESTANT ON THE SHOW

Do you have what it takes to become a culinary great? You'll be separated from your friends and family for weeks on end. You'll be bunked with a group of the fiercest competitors you'll ever know. You'll work long, hard hours, be subjected to punishments from KP duty to cleaning toilets, suffer rejection and humiliation—face tough love to the max, and be pushed to the absolute extreme to reach perfection. If you can handle that, then *Hell's Kitchen* just may be for you.

Since 2005, casting has been open to outspoken and compelling women and men ages twenty-one and up. Prior cooking experience, a fiercely competitive streak, and nerves of steel preferred.

NOW SHOW US WHAT YOU'VE GOT: THE SIGNATURE DISH

The signature dish is our first introduction to the contestants. The chefs each make something that represents what they're all about—the best of their best, whether it's big robust flavor or something a little more delicate, it's all down to that one dish.

You can tell so much about each chef from their signature dish—how adventurous, creative, and skilled they are. Some contestants demonstrate genius from the start; many are horror shows, their first attempts deemed

WINNING JOBS

Winners of *Hell's Kitchen* have been awarded jobs at restaurants including:

Fornelletto at the Borgata in Atlantic City
Araxi Restaurant + Oyster Bar in Whistler, British Columbia
LA Market at JW Marriott in Los Angeles
BLT Steak in New York City
Gordon Ramsay Steak at Paris Las Vegas
Gordon Ramsay Pub & Grill at Caesars Palace Las Vegas
Gordon Ramsay at the London West Hollywood
Gordon Ramsay Pub & Grill at Caesars Atlantic City

THE "BLIND TASTE-TEST": A TRUE TEST OF THE PALATE

In this challenge, each chef is blindfolded and earmuffed and instructed to identify four foods by taste alone. The team with the most correct answers wins. The challenge is important enough to bring back every year, as a great palate is essential to being a great chef. This is a fun one to try at home with friends and family!

It's the rare contestant who gets a perfect score, and as the pressure mounts, the misidentifications range from the bizarre to downright comical—carrot identified as papaya or radish, lobster as mushroom, cauliflower as radish, broccoli as potato, turkey as egg yolk, tuna as pancetta, and prune as licorice.

edible at best and spit out if they don't pass muster. The reviews can be exhilarating or demoralizing, and it's with the signature dish that we get our first impression of the talent of these aspiring chefs.

HELL'S KITCHEN IS OPEN!

With dinner service approaching, the heat is really on, and it's time for the chefs to up their game. In *Hell's Kitchen*, every day is judgment day and any moment could be your last. Cooking on your own can be relaxing and rewarding, but cooking in a brigade with a dozen or more chefs to feed a hundred guests is a completely different ballgame. *Hell's Kitchen* gives us a bird's-eye view into the running of a live, fully equipped, phenomenal restaurant.

Each week the chefs display their skills, how they work as a team, and how they stand up to pressure. The competitors perform fantastic feats of stamina and talent they had no idea they possessed in order to stay in the running. As the season continues, the best chefs are separated from the failures.

RED VS. BLUE: A BATTLE OF THE SEXES

At the start of the competition, each contestant is given a personalized *Hell's Kitchen* chef's jacket—women on the Red Team and men on the Blue Team (though chefs may be reassigned to an opposing team later in the competition). With each team working in their own state-of-the-art kitchen, their first task is nothing less than dinner service in a crowd often peppered with food critics, celebrity chefs, and show business notables.

Chefs on each team are assigned to a station on the line and endeavor to work as a well-oiled machine to crank out award-worthy meals consisting of an appetizer, entrée, side, and dessert, including challenging plates such as risotto, seared scallops, and beef Wellington. Each team is assigned a sous chef to help them achieve exacting standards, and the floor is managed by a maître d' who keeps everything running smoothly.

Hell's Kitchen's standards are uncompromising; the kitchen is shut down rather than being allowed to send out mediocrity. If one plate isn't ready, the whole table will have to wait, and if one dish isn't perfect, the entire order will be sent back and all meals will be prepared from scratch. When you're used to the best, nothing less will do, and the phenomenal successes that eventually come out of *Hell's Kitchen* make it all well worth the effort.

THE COUNTDOWN TO THE PRIZE OF A LIFETIME: OPENING THE DOOR TO YOUR FUTURE

Every challenge in *Hell's Kitchen* is another chance for contestants to prove their worth. But as the competition progresses, the pressure increases, and eventually just five or six hopefuls remain. At this point it's no longer women versus men but every chef for her- or himself.

The fortunate few swap their red or blue chef's jackets for black and cook in a single united team while still competing solely for themselves. The competition continues, with tougher challenges including running the kitchen themselves and examining every dish of a dinner service, keeping a close eye out for mistakes, which are purposely committed by the sous chefs to test the competitors' knowledge and palate.

When just two chefs are left in the competition, the next and final challenge is a face-off in the show's finale, the most important service in the contestants' lives. *Hell's Kitchen* is again divided into two restaurants, with each finalist running their own kitchen. Finalists determine their menu, coming full circle from the signature dish. This time it's a whole dinner of signature dishes with no second chances remaining. The two then lead a team of their former competitors through a full dinner service. After this dinner service, the season's winner is crowned and a life is changed forever.

• • •

This cookbook brings home the recipes we've fallen in love with over the past decade of *Hell's Kitchen* dinner services and varied culinary challenges. Whether you're a *Hell's Kitchen* hopeful, a beginner home cook, or somewhere in between, this book is for you. For starters, you'll get your kitchen ready, outfitting it with all the necessary equipment, then stock your fridge and pantry so you'll be ready to create your private *Hell's Kitchen*, and you'll be poised to turn out one fine restaurant-quality meal after another.

Hell's Kitchen opens with starters, from king crab capellini (page 32) to cioppino (page 36), and just-right risotto (page 58). The main course offers the butcher's best, from veal cheeks (page 162) to tenderloin (page 160) and beef Wellington (page 82), and you'll find some of the finest seafood dishes you'll ever eat. Leave room for your sides, as you'll love how *Hell's Kitchen* elevates potatoes (pages 184 and 187). You'll form a zucchini fry (page 182) habit and go over the moon for truffle mac and cheese (page 191), a *Hell's Kitchen* take on the ultimate comfort food. Desserts to live for—from classic crème brûlée (page 194) to coconut cake (page 205), and a variety of tarts and pies—and unconventional sweets such as white pepper ice cream (page 196) and chocolate empanadas (page 214) are the crowning touches. The book finishes with twenty-five uniquely *Hell's Kitchen* menus, with themes ranging from *Hell's Kitchen* Craps to Black-Tie Charity Night, Modern South, Eclectic Ethnic, and Catch of the Day. It's time to set up your personal *Hell's Kitchen*!

CELEBRITY SIGHTINGS:
VIPS SPOTTED DINING AT HELL'S KITCHEN

Legendary rock musician Steven Tyler of Aerosmith

Academy Award–nominated actor Minnie Driver

Professional boxer Sugar Ray Leonard

Comic book writer Stan Lee

Talk show host Wendy Williams

NBA champion Chris Bosh

Actor Jeremy Sisto of *Suburgatory*

The cast of *Workaholics*

Actor Jaleel White of *Family Matters*

Actress Tatum O'Neal of *Paper Moon*

Actor Fred Willard of *Modern Family*

Musician Taylor Hicks

Musician Lisa Loeb

Actor Eric McCormack of *Will and Grace*

Kevin Frazier, host of *Entertainment Tonight*

Cast members of *Glee*

Entourage star Rex Lee

Actor Greg Grunberg of *Heroes*

Director Paul Feig of *Bridesmaids*

Bob Guiney of *The Bachelorette*

and more . . .

BRINGING HOME HELL'S KITCHEN: WHAT YOU NEED TO KNOW TO COOK LIKE A PRO

CHAPTER TWO

AT THE HEART OF HELL'S KITCHEN IS HIGH-END FINE-DINING CUISINE, COOKED TO PERFECTION BY PASSIONATE, TALENTED CHEFS. WHILE WATCHING THE SHOW, WE GET TO SEE WHAT REALLY GOES INTO PREPARING THE BEST OF THE BEST. BUT YOU DON'T HAVE TO BECOME A RESTAURANT CHEF OR HELL'S KITCHEN CONTESTANT TO BRING THAT JOURNEY HOME. GET INSPIRED FROM THE SHOW, LEARN SOME TRICKS OF THE TRADE, AND PURCHASE A FEW KEY PIECES OF EQUIPMENT AND YOU CAN BRING THE MAGIC OF HELL'S KITCHEN INTO YOUR PERSONAL KITCHEN. LET'S GET STARTED!

PUMP UP YOUR KITCHEN WITH FUNDAMENTAL EQUIPMENT

Watching *Hell's Kitchen* is enough to give any home cook a serious case of kitchen envy. Not one but two state-of-the-art kitchens grace the *Hell's Kitchen* restaurant. No wonder the show has produced some serious talent! But some of the greatest food has come out of the tiniest, well-thought-out kitchens, and the bottom line always comes down to what you put on a plate. Master your technique and the ideal workspace is born from organization, efficiency, and a few choice pieces of equipment. The star of a *Hell's Kitchen*–worthy kitchen is a just-right chef's knife (important enough to merit its own section), along with various tools, utensils, measuring devices, and machines dedicated to slicing, dicing, mincing, and so forth. You don't have to spend a fortune on your kitchen, but you'll find that quality pots, pans, and knives will be well worth the investment.

POTS, PANS, AND SKILLETS

Top-of-the-line heavy-duty pots are built to last for the long haul and can transform your cooking. Go a step beyond stainless steel and consider anodized aluminum: stainless steel with an aluminum or copper core. This material provides even heating and control in cooking, while straight aluminum can warp over high heat and is reactive to acidic foods. Copper is reactive as well, and it requires the same sort of maintenance as a copper bowl (see page 13). Cast iron distributes and retains heat brilliantly and is extremely durable and affordable. On the downside, it's reactive, it requires regular maintenance, and is extremely heavy. Make sure each piece of cookware comes with a lid.

STOCKPOT: Using homemade stock instead of stock from a box elevates your recipes, so a decent-sized stockpot—at least 6-quart capacity—is recommended for your collection of pots and pans. You'll use it for boiling pasta and making soups as well.

SAUCEPAN: The workhorse of the stovetop, required for everything from blanching vegetables to cooking risotto. A 4-quart pan will serve many of your needs. A second, smaller pan—1 to 1½ quarts—is extremely handy to have around. Depending on how busy you get in the kitchen, another pot or two in sizes that fit your needs will help you multitask your way to dinner with ease.

DUTCH OVEN: A heavy metal pot, typically made from cast iron, often passed down from your grandmother. You'll find them coated in porcelain enamel in a range of colors; the coating makes the pot nonreactive and easy to care for. The classic Dutch oven dish is a long braise that goes from the stovetop to the oven; some folks even bake bread in theirs.

CHEF'S TIP: No matter how great the deal may seem, don't buy a full set of pots and pans unless you're sure you'll use every piece.

SKILLET: Also known as a frying pan, this flat-bottomed pan with slanted sides is required for tasks from frying or scrambling eggs to stir-frying and toasting nuts and seeds. A 10- to 12-inch skillet will suit most needs; if omelets are your typical breakfast, an 8-inch skillet will come in handy. Cast iron makes a brilliant skillet, as it's heavy duty and, with proper care, is nonstick. Alternatively, you can purchase a dedicated nonstick pan to use for egg dishes (don't bother with nonstick for the rest of your pans). Do not heat nonstick over high heat.

SAUTÉ PAN: This pan differs from a skillet in that it has straight or slightly curved sides, which provides you with a larger cooking surface and better contains your food as it "jumps" over the heat (the translation of the French word *sauter* is "to jump"). It's used for searing meat and cooking sauces and such. Choose anywhere from 10 to 14 inches depending on the quantity of food you plan to cook in your pan.

ROASTING PAN: Look for a sturdy, heavy roasting pan that performs equally well on the stovetop as in the oven; handles for ease in lifting are a big plus. Choose a size that accommodates the joint of meat you roast most often. Pass on nonstick roasting pans, as you'll miss out on deglazing—scraping up the delicious browned bits that form at the bottom of the pan.

BAKEWARE

Glass, ceramic, and metal are the three most popular picks for bakeware, with metal being the obvious choice for baking sheets. Light-colored metal makes for even browning (darker metal can cause overbrowning), and aluminum is best at conducting heat and reliably produces evenly baked goods. Glass is also a good heat conductor and, unlike aluminum, it's nonreactive. Ceramic's attractiveness lends itself to stove-to-table desserts worthy of showing off. This list will cover your basic baking needs:

9 x 13-inch baking dish

9 x 9-inch baking dish

Round cake pans (8- and 9-inch)

Square cake pan (8- and 9-inch)

9-inch loaf pan

Springform pan (can't make cheesecake without it!)

Muffin pan

Pie plates (8- and 9-inch)

9-inch tart pan plus several mini-tart pans

Ramekins (essential for crème brûlée)

At least 2 baking sheets/cookie sheets

A baking sheet, also known as a half-sheet pan in the restaurant world, is rimmed. Cookie sheets are unrimmed; their advantage lies in their large surface area, perfect for fitting in lots of cookies, but their purposes are limited; without a rim, juices can drip out and errant ingredients will invariably escape. If only one type is in your budget, make it baking sheets (and don't worry, you can bake cookies on them too!).

CUTTING BOARDS

Choose two or three in various sizes. Plastic is dishwasher-safe; wood has a more natural feel to it. Some chefs like to keep a cutting board dedicated to meat or pungent onions and garlic.

CHEF'S TIP: Place a damp kitchen towel or paper towel under your cutting board to keep it from sliding around while you chop.

BOWLS

A set of bowls from tiny to multiple-quart will get you through your mise-en-place (page 23) with finesse and help you through dinner service with ease. Nesting bowls are a great choice, as they don't take up a lot of room and you'll likely use them all. Throw in a number of tiny bowls or ramekins to hold individual ingredients like chopped garlic, diced onions, or minced parsley (silicone pinch bowls are perfect). Lightweight **metal bowls**—choose nothing but stainless steel—work for most purposes, from tempering chocolate to creating a double boiler; **glass** is a nonreactive choice that gives you a clear window into your food, but it's weightier and susceptible to chipping and breaking. **Ceramic bowls** look beautiful on the table but, like glass, have some heft and are prone to breaking. **Plastic bowls** are lightweight and nearly indestructible but can scratch and retain oils. **Silicone bowls** are nonstick, heatproof, and flexible, the best of several worlds. Their drawback is a tendency to hold onto strong odors such as garlic and onion, and their rubbery texture makes them difficult to grab when they're filled with liquid. If you love your soufflés and

CHEF'S TIP: If your mixing bowls don't have a nonskid base, try this trick to steady a bowl: Dampen a dish towel and wring out excess water, then, starting at one corner, roll up the towel to form a ring slightly larger than the base of your bowl; set your bowl inside its towel nest and proceed to mix and whisk securely.

meringues, you might consider investing in a **copper bowl**, as it will enable you to whip voluptuous volume into your egg whites. Note that copper bowls are quite expensive and require that you clean and polish them before and after each use, so make sure you're committed to copper before you make the investment.

CHEF'S TIP: **If you're buying just one bowl type, stainless steel is your best bet.**

MIXING MACHINES

BLENDER: A *Hell's Kitchen* essential, not just for soups and smoothies but for achieving silky-smooth purees, making aioli, and emulsifying dressing. A high-speed blender can get through most anything, but the recipes in this book can be accomplished with just about any blender you probably already have in your kitchen. The recipes in the book can be made with a regular blender.

IMMERSION BLENDER: Also called a stick blender or a wand blender, this device purees right in the pot, avoiding the splashy step of transferring to the blender and cleaning up afterward. It does much of what a regular blender can do, but for soups and sauces that require the smoothest of textures, a regular blender is required.

FOOD PROCESSOR: For chopping, grinding, shredding, dicing, and mixing dough, the food processor is the tool of choice. Most food processors come with dedicated disks for slicing and shredding and a plastic dough blade. A rule of thumb: use a blender for foods that are more liquid than solid and a food processor for foods that are more solid than liquid.

CHEF'S TIP: **Never mash potatoes in a food processor or they will turn to glue; use a food mill, hand masher, ricer, or electric mixer to do the job.**

MIXER: If pastry making or bread baking is your passion, a stand mixer is a worthwhile investment. If your requirements are minimal, a hand mixer will work for most purposes.

TOOLS TO STIR, FLIP, WHISK, AND GRAB

LADLE: For serving soup and transferring stock to containers.

SPOONS: Go for wood or dishwasher-safe bamboo for cooking and a large stainless steel spoon for serving; a slotted spoon is handy for dishing out foods from liquid.

SPATULA (OR TURNER): Look for one made of thin metal with a tapered edge that can easily slip under your food for delicate items like cookies and pancakes; a slotted turner with an upturned edge is ideal for fish. Use a plastic or wooden spatula with a nonstick pan to protect it from scratching.

SILICONE SPATULA: Choose one that's sturdy yet not stiff for your stirring, folding, and scraping needs; silicone is durable and heatproof, so unlike plastic there are no worries of melting and it won't scratch a nonstick surface.

TONGS: Kitchen tongs are an extension of the hand, used for everything from turning meat to scooping out pasta from the pot and removing foods from the fryer. Choose stainless steel tongs with a lock—or they will be unwieldy—and silicone-tipped tongs for use with nonstick cookware.

WHISK: Start with a **sauce whisk**, used for blending and emulsifying sauces. Add a **balloon whisk** if meringues, soufflés, and whipped cream are in your repertoire (its large, round shape facilitates beating air into the ingredients). A **flat whisk** is used in gravy and sauce making; its flat, tapered shape allows it to fit into the corners of a shallow skillet or roasting pan. A **vinaigrette whisk** tackles small jobs like making dressing or scrambled eggs for one or two.

MEASURING DEVICES

MEASURING SPOONS: Do some research and choose a brand recommended for its accuracy, as not all measuring spoons are created equal. Stainless steel is preferred over plastic. Remove the ring they came in and create a dedicated holder on the counter or compartment in a drawer so you don't need to wash them all after using just one.

MEASURING CUPS: Metal for dry ingredients; glass or heavy-duty plastic for liquid ingredients. Choose flat-bottomed metal cups with some heft. A sturdy steel 1-cup measuring cup can double as a butter-warmer. As with measuring spoons, do your research for the most accurate brand and remove the ring they came in and store them nestled in a convenient spot. Better yet, arrange them on a dedicated magnetic knife strip in size order so you can easily find and grab them.

CHEF'S TIP: Buy two sets of measuring spoons and cups to bypass the need for washing between ingredients.

SCALE: Professional kitchens favor weight over volume for greatest precision, and home cooks in this country are increasingly being won over to weighing their ingredients. Choose a digital scale with a large display, both imperial and metric measurements, and a tare function, which allows you to subtract the weight of the container and show only the weight of the food being measured. If the scale comes with a bowl, make sure it's removable.

TOOLS FOR STRAINING

FINE-MESH STRAINER: Strains sauces, captures seeds from berries, drains blanched vegetables, and sifts flour. Both a large one and a small are recommended.

CHINOIS: A conical sieve with a very fine mesh, used to strain soups, sauces, custards, and purees to a state of ultra-smoothness and to get the clearest of stocks. A nice addition to your straining repertoire, but costly and not essential. (Another tool called the China cap is similar in shape to a chinois but made entirely of metal with holes punched in the sides; it gives a less fine strain than a chinois.)

COLANDER: A large-holed strainer for pasta and other draining needs.

SPIDER: A wide, shallow wire-mesh basket with a long handle used for skimming foam from stock and removing large pieces of food from liquid.

ASSORTED TOOLS TO COMPLETE YOUR KITCHEN

TIMER: Make sure it's nice and loud with a display that's easy to read, and preferably with more than one setting so you can manage multiple dishes.

SILICONE LINERS: Nonstick cookie sheet liners; reusable and extremely durable. Also great for rolling out dough.

WIRE RACK: Also called a cooling rack or baking rack; essential for allowing air to circulate freely around the item that's cooling to avoid soggy baked goods. Choose at least a couple in varying sizes.

CHEESE GRATER: A handheld paddle grater or a box grater with four or six sides for various levels of grating, from fine to ultra-coarse to julienne slicer; a pullout bottom for catching ingredients is a plus.

VEGETABLE PEELER: A swivel or straight peeler are a must; you might add a julienne peeler or a serrated peeler for waxy and slippery fruits and vegetables.

MICROPLANE RASP GRATER: A wandlike tool for zesting citrus and grating Parmesan, garlic, and ginger.

PASTRY BRUSH: Also known as a basting brush, used for basting, oiling, and buttering. Pastry brushes are traditionally made with natural bristles. Silicone bristles are a modern, dishwashable choice but are less effective at holding onto the fat.

CITRUS PRESS: A handheld press for lemons and limes. Make sure to choose one big enough to fit either.

FUNNEL: For cleanly transferring olive oil into a pourer and any liquid to a container.

SPICE GRINDER: Choose a dedicated electric grinder. Do not grind spices in the same machine you use for coffee. Tip: grind a little rice in the machine between ingredients to take out the odor.

MORTAR AND PESTLE: For grinding small quantities of spices.

ICE CREAM MAKER: Choose from a removable canister model (the canister must be frozen before each use) or a pricier self-refrigerating model for continuous batches of ice cream.

ROLLING PIN: Choices go beyond wood to metal and silicone, tapered and straight, with handles or without.

METAL SKEWERS: Can't make kebabs without them.

STEAMER BASKET: To fit into a saucepan. Collapsible and expandable are attributes to look for. Typically made of metal, though some are made of silicone.

INSTANT-READ THERMOMETER: Essential when accuracy is needed, as in testing for the doneness of meat, gauging the stage of candy making, and heating oil for frying.

CRÈME BRÛLÉE TORCH: For creating the final caramelized sugar layer, bypassing the need to turn on the broiler.

GARLIC PRESS: A tidy alternative to finely mincing garlic.

SALAD SPINNER: Spinning off excess water keeps leaves from going limp and enables dressing to stick.

CAN OPENER: No need to go electric on this one. A simple hand-operated can opener is all you need to do the job.

CORKSCREW: Either a wing corkscrew with a lever or a sommelier knife, similar in appearance to a pocketknife, is all you'll ever need.

MELON BALLER: For forming beautiful balls of melon or any firm fruit or vegetable to add interest to salads or as a garnish.

PEPPERMILL: The flavor of ground pepper fades fast, so don't be caught without one of these.

DEVELOP FIRST-RATE KNIFE SKILLS

Whether you aspire to become a master chef or simply a solid home cook, learning basic knife skills and practicing them often is a must. Proper knife skills can speed up your work tenfold, transforming prep from a grind to a gratifying experience and contributing to a successful mise-en-place. Purchasing a high-quality chef's knife that fits perfectly into both your budget and the size and shape of your hand is step one. A well-made chef's knife is the backbone of every professional chef and will step up the progress of a novice.

CHOOSING A CHEF'S KNIFE: MAKE IT HIGH CARBON

Nowadays the majority of knives are made from high-carbon steel alloy, a blend of iron, carbon, chromium, and other metals that are rust resistant, easy to sharpen, and hold an edge. Almost every kitchen has at least one. (In the past, carbon steel was the best option; this steel holds an edge but rusts easily. Stainless steel came onto the scene next; it's resistant to rust but

GETTING A HANDLE ON THE BLADE AND THE HANDLE

Metal blades are either forged or stamped. Forged blades are produced from a steel bar that's heated to a high temperature, set into a die, and hammered to form its shape. Forged knives have a bolster (the raised area where the blade meets the handle), which protects your hand and gives your fingers a place to rest while you cut. Stamped blades are stamped out of large, continuous sheets of rolled steel, like a cookie cutter, and do not have a bolster. Top-of-the-line knives are typically forged. They are the toughest and keep their edge well. Stamped blades are more flexible and need more frequent sharpening. While some can rival the price of forged knives, stamped blades generally are a budget-minded choice. If you're looking to invest in just one high-end chef's knife, a forged blade is recommended.

Handles can be made of wood, metal, or composite materials. If you choose a wooden handle, make sure the rivets it's attached with are flush with the handle so as not to irritate your hands while you chop. The best material is one that feels comfortable in your hand.

CONSIDERING SIZE, BUT ALSO BALANCE AND HEFT

Chef's knives typically measure between 6 and 12 inches. Cooks with a larger grip may go for a knife in the 10- to 12-inch range, though the majority of chefs choose a happy medium of 8 inches. A good chef's knife will feel well balanced and have some heft to it, with the weight of the blade balanced by the weight of the handle. Some people find a heavier knife cuts through food with more force, while others feel a lighter knife allows them more room to maneuver. Let "try it before you buy it" be your knife-buying motto and check out several knives of varying weights before you decide. Avoid buying online; instead visit a local kitchenware shop with knowledgeable salespeople who will let you try their knives out, preferably with real produce, as putting a knife to work is the only way to truly get a feel for it. The knife you go home with should feel like a natural extension of your hand.

harder to sharpen.) A good high-carbon knife will last you a lifetime. Other materials include titanium, the hardest metal around (and one of the costliest); ceramic, which is very hard, keeps an edge, and is rust-resistant; and plastic, which does little more than slice lettuce.

REVIEWING THE FULL ARSENAL OF KNIVES

While the chef's knife is indispensible, the full brigade of knives will be found in any good commercial kitchen. Purchase those that meet your needs and add to your collection as you build up your kitchen skills and continue to learn. The two most useful knives for beginners are the paring knife for small jobs and the serrated knife for slicing.

UTILITY KNIFE: A mini, lighter version of a chef's knife, generally 5 to 7 inches, used for light kitchen work.

PARING KNIFE: As its name suggests, this knife is used for paring and trimming vegetables and fruits and ranges from 2 to 4 inches.

BONING KNIFE: About 6 inches long and narrower than a chef's knife so it can work around the bone to remove the meat.

FILLETING KNIFE: Dedicated knife for filleting fish. Similar in appearance to a boning knife but with a more flexible blade for separating the flesh of the fish from the skin.

CLEAVER: Rectangular-bladed hefty knife used to cut through the bone from chunks of meat or whole animals.

SERRATED KNIFE: This saw-toothed knife cuts through foods that are hard on the outside, soft on the inside. A small serrated knife cuts through tomatoes, while a large serrated knife, aka bread knife, slices bread.

ELECTRIC KNIFE SHARPENER OR SHARPENING STONE: If you're going to spend some serious time in the kitchen, you'll need to sharpen your knife often. An electric knife sharpener will get your knife sharp fast but runs the risk of grinding away too much of the blade. A sharpening stone, or whetstone, that you slide the blade back and forth over, gives you the most control. Look up an online video to learn the technique of knife sharpening. It's best understood by seeing it in action.

SHARPENING STEEL: Used to lightly sharpen a knife between full-fledged sharpenings; the knife is drawn at an angle against the rod to sharpen it. Most chefs use their steel daily, and you should too.

MANDOLINE: A cutting utensil that turns out perfectly uniform slices; it makes quick work of dishes that require paper-thin slices such as Dauphinoise Potatoes (page 184). A food holder secures the food and keeps fingers from getting nicked. Wear a dedicated cut-resistant glove for extra protection.

KITCHEN SHEARS: Very strong, detachable scissors with a plastic- or rubber-coated handle designed specifically for kitchen work. Their many purposes range from cutting into chicken and fish bones to snipping chives and opening bags of rice and frozen vegetables. Look for shears that can be sharpened.

HOW TO HANDLE A KNIFE: GOING BEYOND THE HANDLE GRIP

Now that you're set with your knife, learning how to handle it with skill will enable you to use it most effectively. Beginners are most familiar with the handle grip, where the hand rests solely on the handle with fingers tucked behind the bolster. But when you're ready to fine-tune your knife skills, it's time to upgrade to the blade grip, where the thumb and forefinger rest in front of the bolster directly on the blade, with the remaining three fingers loosely wrapped around the handle. Most of the grip comes from the thumb and forefinger. If you find yourself clutching the handle, relax those other three fingers

CHEF'S TIP: Signing up for a knife skills class is one of the best investments you can make in furthering your culinary education.

a bit. This grip adds control and balance as you cut your way through your mise-en-place ingredients. Changing grip can take some getting used to, but in time it will become natural.

Your non-knife hand plays an equally important role in the navigation of your knife. It's your guiding hand, the hand that holds the food securely on the cutting board. For ease of work and safety, use what chefs call the claw grip, tucking your fingers in and gripping the food with your fingernails, with the side of the blade against the first knuckle of the guiding hand. Employ the claw grip with every food that gets set on the chopping block.

Read on for a rundown of the various shapes and sizes we cut our food into, and then it's all about practice, practice, practice. Spend some time with each cut until it becomes natural. You might chop through a five-pound bag of potatoes and turn them to mash, work your way through a bushel of apples and make applesauce, slice through a giant bag of onions for onion soup, or tackle multiple heads of cabbage for coleslaw for your next family picnic. Repetition will be your best learning tool. A better ability to read through a recipe, food that cooks uniformly, and impressive-looking dishes are the rewards for mastering your knife cuts.

CUBE CUTS

CHOPPING is to cut a food into squares about ½ inch in diameter; the squares need not be perfectly uniform in shape and size. Food may be coarsely chopped or chopped medium or fine, a cut often called for when prepping herbs. Chopping allows a food to flavor the dish but still retain its shape and bite.

DICING is to cut food into even squares, a more precise cut than chopping; it's important when even cooking is required. When chefs are barking orders to their crews, they will call out the specific type of dice so no further explanation is required.

LARGE DICE: ¾ inch square

MEDIUM DICE (MACÉDOINE): ½ inch square

SMALL DICE: ¼ inch square

BRUNOISE: ⅛ inch square

FINE BRUNOISE: ¹⁄₁₆ inch square

MINCING is the smallest cut, smaller than dice or chop and a couple of steps above puree—basically as small as you can get the food. It's often indicated for shallots and garlic.

STICK CUTS

BATONNET: Translates to "little stick"; ¼ inch x ¼ inch x 2 to 2½ inches long (the starting point for small dice)

JULIENNE: ⅛ inch x ⅛ inch x 2 to 2½ inches long (the starting point for bruniose)

FINE JULIENNE: 1/16 inch x 1/16 inch x 2 to 2½ inches long (the starting point for fine brunoise)

OTHER CUTS

DIAGONAL: Cut on an angle in varying sizes

OBLIQUE OR ROLL CUT: Cut at an oblique angle, either by rolling the pieces or angling the knife

PAYSANNE: ½ inch x ½ inch by ⅛ inch; a flat, square shape

LOZENGE: ½ inch x ½ inch x ⅛ inch diamond shape

FERMIÈRE: Cut lengthwise and sliced between ⅛ and ½ inch

RONDELLE: Rounds cut between ⅛ and ½ inch

TOURNÉ: An oblong cut that's 2 inches long with 7 faces

CHIFFONADE: TURNING YOUR GREENS INTO RAGLIKE STRIPS

The translation of *chiffonade* is "rag," so to chiffonade is to turn your food—typically herbs such as basil and green vegetables such as collards—into raglike strips. Here's how to do it:

- Strip the stems from your herb or vegetable.
- Stack a few leaves lengthwise facing you.
- Using your fingertips, grab the edge of the stack closest to you and roll up the leaves into a tight bundle.
- Use your chef's knife to cut the bundle crosswise into thin, even strips, then separate the strips and use them in your recipe.

MAKE MISE-EN-PLACE YOUR MANTRA

Time and space are precious commodities. Every chef knows this, and the first thing they're taught in cooking school is mise-en-place, or "put in place": to gather and sort, prep and line up the ingredients and tools required for cooking. Garlic is minced, carrots are chopped, herbs and spices are measured, pots and pans are pulled out and strategically placed. Mise-en-place is a culinary mantra, and chefs have gone so far as to tattoo the term onto their bodies as a permanent reminder.

Mise-en-place makes you a more efficient cook. It allows you to focus on the task at hand without distraction—no last-second searching for ingredients or equipment ("Uh-oh, did I add the salt yet?" "Now where is that garlic press?"). Mise-en-place gets you into the moment. Cooking becomes streamlined, with each element coming together as you build one dish after the next with ease. While the practice of mise-en-place may take more time than the cooking itself—some mise-en-place starts days ahead of service—it actually *saves* you time in the long run, with far fewer failed dishes and overall improved kitchen performance.

One thing you'll notice about the more successful teams in *Hell's Kitchen* is they've got their mise-en-place down. They're working as a well-oiled machine, turning out one successful dish after another. Everything has been planned, prepped, and positioned; they're ready to fire out their apps, their

FOUR STEPS TO MASTERING MISE-EN-PLACE

1. READ THE RECIPE.
Then read it again—and a third time if it's something you've never made before. Go through each and every step in your head and make sure you've got all the required ingredients; now's the time to hop out to the store if needed.

2. PREP THE INGREDIENTS.
Chop, mince, and measure everything from your garlic to the teaspoon of salt that goes in at the end.

3. PUT EACH INGREDIENT IN ITS PLACE.
Have ready a little bowl or ramekin for each ingredient, and position them at your workstation so they flow in a logical direction. And get out your pots and pans and any other equipment, from the cutting board to the chef's knife, mandoline, mixer, or blender.

4. POST YOUR RECIPE IN A CENTRAL PLACE.
On the fridge or a dedicated recipe stand, whatever's most handy. Now get in there and cook like you mean it.

mains, their desserts, and running the pass is no problem. When service is over, they've won the night.

When you master the all-important practice of mise-en-place, you'll be poised to win your own personal culinary challenges, and you'll get to enjoy the fruits of your labor in the form of a fabulous meal shared with friends and family. What could be a better reward?

KEEP YOUR PANTRY PLENTIFUL AND RESTOCK YOUR FRIDGE FREQUENTLY

Shop smart and learn about where your ingredients come from; scour your city for the finest purveyors and buy in bulk to keep your costs down. Seek out specialty shops for hard-to-find ingredients such as exotic spices or truffles, or find them online. Favor farmers' markets for your produce and meat—find one through LocalHarvest.org's comprehensive listing—or better yet, buy direct from the farm. Join a CSA (Community Supported Agriculture), a membership system that offers "shares" of a farm in advance of the season, with the return of a unique box of produce every week so you can create your own *Hell's Kitchen*–style mystery food challenge! Go in with friends or family on a whole hog or cow and you'll save considerably on costs. Buy a second freezer to store your meat. Visit specialty product manufacturers like your favorite chocolate factory, distillery, or cheesemaker. They often give tours and tastings and make for a fun and educational day out.

Keep your pantry plentiful, as it's the backbone of a working chef's kitchen and a ticket to easy weeknight dinners. Buy cases of canned tomatoes, big sacks of flour, and large jugs of olive oil according to available storage space. Don't overdo it on spices; buy just enough to last you six months or so to keep them fresh (buying from the bulk section is a good choice for spices, as it allows you to chose the amount and go home with only what you need). Then make quick weekly or twice-weekly shops around the perimeter of the supermarket or your farmers' market to buy perishable produce, dairy, and meat. Supplement your shopping with sprints to the fishmonger and butcher. The lists that follow cover everything from artichokes to Worcestershire sauce—just about every fundamental ingredient you'll need to work your way through this book.

CHEF'S TIP: Toast spices in a skillet just before using them to boost the flavor of your recipe.

HELL'S KITCHEN PANTRY STAPLES

OIL AND VINEGAR

Extra virgin olive oil

Vegetable oil

Grapeseed oil

Truffle oil

Toasted sesame oil

Vinegar (red wine, white wine, sherry, apple cider, rice)

CANNED, JARRED, AND BOXED GOODS

Chicken stock

Vegetable stock

Anchovy tins

Tomatoes (whole)

Tomato puree

Tomato paste

Artichokes (canned or jarred)

Capers

Horseradish

Sundried tomatoes

Chipotle chilies in adobo sauce

Roasted red peppers

Breadcrumbs: regular and panko

Coconut milk

Clam juice

Mirin

SAUCES AND CONDIMENTS

Hot sauce

Soy sauce

Fish sauce

Oyster sauce

Worcestershire sauce

Ketchup

Mustard

Mayonnaise

Chili oil

BEANS, GRAINS, AND PASTA

Beans (canned)

Rice (including arborio, purple jasmine, and sushi rice) and other grains

Polenta (instant)

Pasta in various shapes and sizes

Soba noodles

NUTS AND SEEDS

Nuts (almonds, Marcona almonds, walnuts, peanuts, pecans, pine nuts, pistachios)

Seeds (black and tan sesame, sunflower, pumpkin)

FRUIT PRODUCTS

Fruit juice

Quince paste

Dried figs

Raisins

Jam

Apple butter

MISCELLANEOUS

Chilies (dried)

Coffee

Tea

Molasses

Dried morel and porcini mushrooms

SEASONINGS

Allspice

Bay leaves

Cardamom

Cayenne

Celery seed/celery salt

Chili powder

Chinese five-spice powder

Cinnamon

Cloves

Coriander

Coriander seeds

Crushed red pepper

Cumin

Curry powder

Fennel seeds

Garlic powder

Ginger

Juniper berries

Mustard seeds

Nutmeg

Onion powder

Oregano

Paprika (sweet, hot, and smoked)

Peppercorns (black and white)

Rosemary

Saffron

Salt (kosher salt, table salt, Maldon sea salt)

Star anise

Thyme leaves

Wasabi powder

BAKING SUPPLIES

All-purpose flour

Cake flour

Granulated sugar

Powdered sugar

Brown sugar

Shredded coconut

Cocoa powder

Malt powder

Graham crackers

Honey

Maple syrup

Corn syrup

Bittersweet chocolate

White chocolate

Gelatin (powdered)

Active dry yeast

Baking powder

Baking soda

Cream of tartar

Cornstarch
Vanilla and other extracts
Vanilla bean

ALCOHOL

Beer
Bourbon
Brandy
Champagne
Grand Marnier or Cointreau
Kahlúa
Pernod
Red and white wine
Rum
Tequila

COLD CASE

Butter
Milk
Half-and-half
Heavy cream
Buttermilk
Eggs
Plain yogurt
Plain Greek yogurt
Crème fraîche
Sour cream
Cream cheese
Bacon
Prosciutto
Pancetta
Parmesan cheese
Pecorino Romano cheese
Mascarpone cheese
Ricotta cheese
Assorted cheeses
Miso
Olives

FREEZER

Corn
Peas
Berries
Edamame

Demi-glace
Puff pastry

This assemblage of herbs, fruits, and vegetables all make appearances in the recipes of this book.

HERBS

Basil
Chervil
Chives
Cilantro
Mint
Parsley
Rosemary
Sage
Tarragon
Thai basil
Thyme

FRUIT

Apples
Asian pears
Avocado
Bananas
Blackberries
Blood oranges
Blueberries
Figs
Grapes
Kiwi
Lemons/Meyer lemons
Limes
Mango
Oranges
Pears
Pineapple
Raspberries
Strawberries

VEGETABLES

Arugula
Asparagus
Baby artichokes
Baby carrots

Baby spinach
Bell peppers
Bok choy
Broccolini
Brussels sprouts
Carrots
Cauliflower
Celery
Chinese long beans
Collard greens
Corn
Delicata squash
Eggplant
Endive
Fennel
Frisée
Garlic
Ginger
Grape tomatoes
Haricots verts
Jalapeño and other chilies
Jicama
Kabocha squash
Kale
Leeks
Lettuce
Mushrooms
Onions (yellow and red)
Parsnips
Pea shoots
Pearl onions
Peas
Potatoes
Radicchio
Radishes
Salsify
Scallions
Shallots
Sunchokes
Sweet potatoes
Zucchini

CHEF'S TIP: Growing herbs in a dedicated garden or sunny windowsill saves money and gives you access to the freshest flavor, as you can use just a snip or two as needed.

CONTINUE YOUR CULINARY EDUCATION

You've seen the shows, chosen a chef's knife, and decked out your kitchen, and more than one hundred of *Hell's Kitchen*'s finest recipes are yours to sink your teeth into. Repeat your mise-en-place mantra with every meal you make, taste your food frequently before you declare it done, and use your intuition and discerning palate to adjust your dishes until they reach perfection.

Challenge yourself with unfamiliar recipes every chance you get. Create your own signature dish if you haven't already; try it out on friends and family and ask them to honestly assess it. Or set up a signature dish party with you as judge. Pick a menu from pages 240 to 253 and invite over a mini brigade of cooking enthusiasts; lead them through a dinner service with you running the pass.

Do a home reenactment of the "Blind Taste-Test," an excellent method of assessing the palate. Start with simple foods like carrots and broccoli, then search out increasingly tough ones from your pantry and fridge. You'll be surprised how difficult this challenge is! Advance to the "Taste It, Make It" challenge: invite a friend who's accomplished in cooking to make something special and challenge yourself to recreate it, or attempt to make a favorite restaurant dish at home. Pick and choose from your favorite *Hell's Kitchen* challenges—make a meal consisting solely of leftovers, cook with friends and invite family to judge each dish without knowing its creator, create a strict budget and restrict your shopping time for a four-course meal to fifteen minutes, or play *Hell's Kitchen* craps with a lettered die that determines which ingredients go into the meal (see page 241 for a sample). Go through the menus at the back of the book and create your own theme-based dinner according to season, occasion, or whim.

And if you get more serious, consider enrolling in cooking school for a formal education and a career in the culinary arts. You might even find yourself applying for a shot at *Hell's Kitchen* if you think you've got the talent, leadership, and creativity that it takes to reach the top. Who knows, you just might be America's next rising star!

THREE

STARTERS SET THE STAGE FOR ANY MEAL, AND GETTING AN APP OUT QUICKLY AND SUCCESSFULLY IS THE KEY TO A TOP-NOTCH DINNER SERVICE. STARTERS ARE TYPICALLY SOME OF HELL'S KITCHEN'S MOST CHALLENGING PLATES, SUCH AS SEARED SCALLOPS, CAPELLINI, AND RISOTTO. AND AS ANY HELL'S KITCHEN AFICIONADO KNOWS, FAILED APPS CAN SHUT DOWN THE KITCHEN, WITH TEMPERS FLARING AND HUNGRY DINERS GETTING UP AND GOING.

IN THIS CHAPTER WE'LL DEMYSTIFY SCALLOPS, SEAR FISH TO PERFECTION, AND LEARN THE BASICS OF A COOKED-JUST-RIGHT RISOTTO. SOMETIMES THE STARTER IS A SALAD, BUT IT'S NEVER JUST A BED OF BORING GREENS. SALAD RECIPES RANGE FROM BUTTER LETTUCE TOPPED WITH BREADED AND FRIED GOAT CHEESE (PAGE 54) TO CAESAR SALAD TOPPED WITH PICKLED ONIONS (PAGE 48) AND A TAKE ON THE

CLASSIC CAPRESE SALAD FEATURING HEIRLOOM TOMATOES (PAGE 42). RECIPES FOR A WIDE RANGE OF SEAFOOD ARE SHARED, FROM THE ICONIC SCALLOPS (PAGE 67) TO THE MUSSELS, COCKLES, SQUID, AND SHRIMP FEATURED IN THE ITALIAN-AMERICAN CLASSIC STEW CIOPPINO (PAGE 36). A NUMBER OF PASTAS ARE COVERED, FROM LOBSTER SPAGHETTI (PAGE 39) TO DUCK RAGÚ RAVIOLI (PAGE 74) AND KING CRAB CAPELLINI (PAGE 32). AND THE CHAPTER WOULDN'T BE COMPLETE WITHOUT A RECIPE FOR THE CLASSIC CRUDO DISH BEEF CARPACCIO (PAGE 53).

BY ADDING INGREDIENTS OR ADJUSTING SERVING SIZES, MANY START-ERS CAN BE MADE INTO MEALS, ESPECIALLY WHEN TIME IS SHORT OR APPETITES ARE LIGHT. STARTERS CAN BE FANCIFUL, STRAIGHT-FORWARD, OR SIMPLE!

STARTERS

KING CRAB CAPELLINI WITH CHILI, LIME, AND GREEN ONION

SERVES 4

The Alaskan king crab, named for its impressive heft and claw span, is thought to be a descendant of the hermit crab. The average weight of a king crab (also known as stone crab) is six to eight pounds, but they can grow up to twenty pounds and their legs can span up to six feet across. There are three main species—red, blue, and golden; the red is most prized for its succulent meat. If king crab isn't available fresh at your fishmonger, frozen is perfectly fine (most king crab is cooked and frozen right on the fishing boat to preserve freshness); just thaw it overnight in the refrigerator. Capellini is one of the thinnest of strand pastas (*capelli d'angelo*, or angel hair, is a yet thinner variation) and therefore very light and splendid set against the sweet, opulent king crab.

½ pound capellini

2 tablespoons extra virgin olive oil

2 small garlic cloves, minced

1 red chili, seeded and minced

2 green onions, white and green parts finely chopped

Kosher salt and freshly ground black pepper

¼ cup dry white wine

Juice of 1 lime, plus more for garnish

½ pound Alaskan king crab meat, picked for shells and chopped

Handful of flat-leaf parsley, roughly chopped

BRING a large pot of salted water to a boil. When it comes to a rolling boil, add the pasta and cook according to package instructions until al dente, about 4 minutes.

HEAT the olive oil in a large sauté pan over medium-low heat. Sauté the garlic, chili, and green onion for 1–2 minutes, then season with salt and pepper.

ADD the wine to the pan, increase the heat to medium, and cook for a minute until the wine is almost evaporated. Add the lime juice and crab meat, stir to combine, and allow to heat through.

DRAIN the pasta, then add it to the pan. Sprinkle with parsley and toss well to combine.

SERVE with a drizzle of lime juice and extra virgin olive oil.

PAN-SEARED GROUPER WITH FENNEL SALAD

SERVES 4

Baquetta grouper, a sweet, mild, white-fleshed fish with brown or red skin, is found from the waters of Baja California up to southern California and is the ideal fish for this dish. If Baquetta is unavailable, another type of grouper, snapper, or halibut may be substituted. Brown butter lends an unexpected toasty flavor and richness to the citrusy dressing. More citrus is found in the fennel salad: Meyer lemons—a sweeter, floral, and less acidic variety of the fruit—and deep crimson blood oranges. If neither is available, the standard varieties can be substituted, though with slightly less dramatic effect. This dish starts off the Catch of the Day menu (page 249).

BROWN BUTTER VINAIGRETTE

1 tablespoon cold butter

1 tablespoon fresh Meyer lemon juice

Juice of ½ blood orange

½ teaspoon minced shallot

½ tablespoon honey

1 tablespoon olive oil

Kosher salt and freshly ground black pepper

FENNEL SALAD

1 large fennel bulb (about 1 pound), fennel fronds reserved for garnish

1 Meyer lemon

1 blood orange

GROUPER

Four 4-ounce Bacqueta or other grouper, snapper, or halibut fillets

2 tablespoons grapeseed oil

Kosher salt and freshly ground black pepper

FOR THE BROWN BUTTER VINAIGRETTE

MELT the butter in a small saucepan over low heat until browned but not burnt, about 5 minutes. Set aside to cool slightly. In a bowl, combine the lemon juice, orange juice, shallot, honey, and olive oil. Whisk in the butter until emulsified. Season with salt and pepper.

FOR THE FENNEL SALAD

USING a mandoline or a sharp knife, thinly slice the fennel.

TO cut the lemon and blood orange into segments, use a small sharp paring knife to cut off both ends, then remove the peel and the pith following the contour of the fruit. Cut out each segment of fruit from between each membrane and remove the seeds.

IN a bowl, combine fennel, orange, and lemon segments and toss with half of the vinaigrette. Set aside while you cook the fish.

FOR THE FISH

HEAT olive oil in a large sauté pan over medium-high heat. When the foam subsides, pat the fish with paper towel so it is completely dry and season with salt and pepper. Cook on each side for 2½–3 minutes or until the fish is slightly pink and translucent in the center.

TO PLATE

DIVIDE the fennel salad among four plates. Top with fish and garnish with fennel fronds.

NUTTY, TOASTY BROWN BUTTER

Brown butter—butter that's cooked until the milk fats separate from the butterfat and start to brown to a hazelnut color (which explains its French name, *beurre noisette*)—is a classic French preparation. The trick to browning butter is to know when it's done, as it can go from browned to burnt in a matter of seconds. Once the butter melts, it foams a bit then subsides, and browned milk-solid specks form at the bottom of the pan. The specks continue to brown when the pan is removed from the heat, so to avoid turning your browned butter to burnt butter, take it off the heat as soon as the specks start to turn color.

CIOPPINO WITH SQUID, TURBOT, SALMON, LIGHT SAFFRON BROTH, MUSSELS AND CLAMS

SERVES 4

Saffron, the most luxurious of spices, is infused in oil to make the most of its exotic golden color and intoxicating flavor. The oil anoints the *Hell's Kitchen* version of cioppino, the brothy Italian-American fish stew that was born in San Francisco more than a century ago. If your budget doesn't allow for the teaspoon of saffron that goes into the oil, skip the flavored oil and stick with the pinch of saffron that goes into the stew.

Cioppino featuring the catch of the day can be found in the eateries dotting San Francisco's Fisherman's Wharf, a culinary destination for seafood aficionados. *Hell's Kitchen's* cioppino, which introduces the Italian Inspired menu (page 249), offers six varieties of seafood. If something other than the six is in season, you're invited to sub that into your stew. Serve with plenty of bread to sop up all the delicious juices.

SAFFRON OIL (OPTIONAL)

1 teaspoon loosely packed saffron threads

½ cup olive oil

CROSTINI

8 slices of baguette cut ¼ inch thick

1 garlic clove, halved

Olive oil

CIOPPINO

2 tablespoons olive oil

1 medium onion (about 1 ¼ cups), coarsely chopped

1 small fennel bulb, trimmed and thinly sliced

2 garlic cloves, minced

1 ¼ teaspoons fresh thyme leaves

1 teaspoon dried oregano

¼–½ teaspoon crushed red pepper flakes

1 bay leaf

Pinch of saffron

1 14-ounce can whole tomatoes with juice, crushed

One 14-ounce can roasted red peppers, diced

½–¾ cup dry white wine

¼ cup Pernod

½ cup bottled clam juice

8 mussels, scrubbed and debearded

12 cockles, scrubbed

Four 2-ounce halibut fillets

Four 2-ounce salmon fillets

8 jumbo shrimp (21-25 count), shelled and deveined

4 ounces squid, cut into rings

Kosher salt and freshly ground black pepper

Chopped fresh parsley, for garnish

FOR THE SAFFRON OIL

IN a spice grinder or with a mortar and pestle, pulverize the saffron threads into a powder. Pour the oil into a small jar and add the saffron powder. Infuse for at least 30 minutes.

FOR THE CROSTINI

PREHEAT the oven to 425°F.

RUB the baguette slices with the halved garlic clove on both sides and brush with olive oil. Arrange on a small baking sheet and bake about 6 minutes, flipping halfway through, until golden brown. Set aside.

FOR THE CIOPPINO

HEAT 2 tablespoons olive oil in a low, wide stockpot over medium heat. Add onions, fennel, and garlic. Cook until onion is translucent, 3 to 4 minutes. Stir in thyme, oregano, red pepper flakes, bay leaf, and saffron. Add

tomatoes and their liquid, roasted peppers, wine, Pernod, clam juice, and 1¼ cups water, and bring to a simmer.

ADD mussels and cockles. Cover the pot and simmer until shells open, 2–3 minutes for the mussels, a minute or two more for the cockles. As they open, transfer the shellfish to a bowl and reserve. Season halibut, salmon, and shrimp with salt and pepper and add to the pot. Cover and simmer for 2 minutes. Add the squid and cook 1 minute more, or until the shrimp is pink and the fish is opaque and beginning to flake. Adjust seasoning.

TO PLATE

DIVIDE the cioppino among four bowls. Drizzle with saffron oil, garnish with parsley, and serve with crostini.

LOBSTER SPAGHETTI

SERVES 4

Lobster is one of the few foods we bring home live from the store to kill and cook ourselves. If you're up for the challenge, it's very easy to do. Just plunge the crustaceans into boiling water and in minutes they'll be out of their misery and onto your plate, nestled into your pasta all buttery, sweet, and tender. For your personal safety, just remember to keep the bands around the claws until after they've been cooked (a luxury not afforded in a Season 3 challenge where contestants were also tasked with creating three lobster dishes in one hour). To declare your lobster done, watch for its color to turn bright red and pull off a small leg; if it comes off easily, it's time to take it out of the pot. That's how Season 8's Nona Sivley worked her lobster into this perfectly executed spaghetti dish for a successful dinner service. For an all-pasta menu, see the Pasta Party (page 252).

Two 1¼-pound live lobsters

12 ounces spaghetti

4 tablespoons extra virgin olive oil, plus more for garnish

3 garlic cloves, finely chopped

1 large shallot, finely chopped

⅛ teaspoon crushed red pepper flakes, or more to taste

½ cup dry white wine

8 ounces tomato sauce, homemade or store-bought

½ cup plus 2 tablespoons vegetable broth

Kosher salt and freshly ground black pepper

2 tablespoons chiffonade fresh basil, plus more for garnish

2 tablespoons chopped fresh parsley, plus more for garnish

½ plum tomato, cut into small dice (optional)

PREPARE a large bowl of ice water. In a large pot of boiling water, cook the lobsters for about 10–12 minutes. Remove the lobsters from the water and transfer to the bowl of ice water to stop the cooking process.

WHEN cooled, remove the meat from the tails, claws, and knuckles. Discard the shells and chop the lobsters into bite-sized pieces.

BRING a large pot of salted water to a boil. Add the spaghetti and cook until al dente, stirring often to prevent the pasta from sticking together.

WHILE the pasta is cooking, heat 3 tablespoons olive oil in a 12-inch sauté pan over moderate heat. Add the garlic, shallot, and crushed red pepper flakes and sauté until soft and lightly brown, about 3 minutes. Add the white wine and reduce to one-third. Stir in the tomato sauce and ½ cup vegetable broth, season to taste with salt and pepper, and simmer for 5 minutes. Add some of the remaining vegetable broth if the sauce is too thick. Then add the lobster to the sauce and heat for 1 minute.

DRAIN the pasta and add it to the sauce. Transfer the pasta to a serving bowl and garnish with fresh basil, chopped parsley, tomato (if using), drizzle with the remaining tablespoon olive oil, and a few turns of black pepper.

GRILLED PEACH SALAD, PEPPERED WHIPPED GOAT CHEESE, BABY ARUGULA, TOASTED ALMONDS, SAUVIGNON BLANC HONEY VINAIGRETTE

SERVES 4

Wait for peach season—spring or summer depending on where you live—for this one, as this special salad demands the perfection of a just-ripe, sweet and juicy peach; out-of-season peaches are reliably tough and mealy. Grilling the peaches further intensifies their sweetness, creating a delightful contrast to the spicy arugula and salty goat cheese. Toasted almonds add a bit of crunch. All of the salad's elements can be prepared in advance and assembled just before serving.

GRILLED PEACHES

2 ripe but firm peaches, each pitted and cut into 16 wedges

Olive oil

WHIPPED GOAT CHEESE

4 ounces goat cheese, at room temperature

3 tablespoons heavy cream, at room temperature

Kosher salt and freshly ground black pepper

TOASTED ALMONDS

½ teaspoon unsalted butter

⅓ cup sliced almonds

SAUVIGNON BLANC HONEY VINAIGRETTE

1 tablespoon minced shallot

1 ½ tablespoons fresh lemon juice

½ teaspoon lemon zest

½ tablespoon sauvignon blanc or white wine vinegar

Kosher salt and freshly ground black pepper

¼ teaspoon honey

2 tablespoons olive oil

2 cups loosely packed baby arugula

FOR THE GRILLED PEACHES

PREHEAT a grill pan over medium-high heat.

PLACE the peaches in a bowl and drizzle with olive oil. Season to taste with salt and pepper and toss to coat. Grill the peaches 1–2 minutes on each side. Set aside.

FOR THE WHIPPED GOAT CHEESE

USING a hand mixer or fork, whip the goat cheese, cream, and salt and pepper to taste in a medium bowl until light, creamy, and fluffy. Set aside.

FOR THE TOASTED ALMONDS

HEAT the butter in a small sauté pan over medium-low heat. Add the almonds in a single layer. Shaking and stirring the pan to help the almonds brown evenly, cook 3–5 minutes until the almonds are golden and aromatic. Transfer to a bowl to cool.

FOR THE SAUVIGNON BLANC HONEY VINAIGRETTE

IN a small bowl, whisk together the shallot, lemon juice, lemon zest, sauvignon blanc, salt, pepper, and honey. Add the olive oil in a slow steady stream, whisking until emulsified.

TO PLATE

DIVIDE the peaches among four plates and drizzle with a bit of vinaigrette. Top with arugula drizzled with more vinaigrette and topped with a dollop of whipped goat cheese. Sprinkle with toasted almonds.

HEIRLOOM TOMATO SALAD WITH BURRATA, PINE NUT GREMOLATA, AND PICKLED RED PEARL ONIONS

SERVES 4

Shop your farmers' market for a variety of heirloom tomatoes—from Yellow Pear to Green Zebra, Cherokee Purple, and Red Brandywine—to add color and flavor to your plate. Gremolata is a classic Italian herb condiment; we've added pine nuts to ours to give it some buttery, crunchy texture. Burrata is a fresh Italian cheese made of mozzarella on the outside and cream on the inside; the cream flows out when sliced, further elevating this *Hell's Kitchen* take on the classic tomato-mozzarella-basil caprese salad. Each salad is topped with pickled red pearl onions for a final sour-tangy burst of flavor.

PINE NUT GREMOLATA

3 tablespoons pine nuts, toasted and chopped

Zest of ½ lemon

3 tablespoons chopped basil

Kosher salt and freshly ground black pepper

½ tablespoon olive oil

PICKLED RED PEARL ONIONS

20 red pearl onions

½ cup champagne vinegar

½ cup red wine vinegar

½ cup water

½ cup sugar

1 tablespoon kosher salt

1 ½ tablespoons mustard seeds

1 teaspoon whole peppercorns

½ teaspoon coriander seeds

1 bay leaf

Pinch red pepper flakes

BALSAMIC VINAIGRETTE

⅛ cup balsamic vinegar

½ shallot, minced

⅓ cup extra virgin olive oil

Kosher salt and freshly ground black pepper

4 heirloom tomatoes (red, green, or yellow), each cut into 4 wedges

2 rounds burrata cheese

FOR PINE NUT GREMOLATA

PLACE the pine nuts, lemon zest, and basil in a small bowl. Add salt and pepper to taste. Stir in olive oil, mixing until all ingredients are well incorporated, and set aside.

FOR THE PICKLED RED PEARL ONIONS

BRING a large saucepan of salted water to a boil. Add the pearl onions and blanch for 1 minute. Run under cold water to cool, then peel the pearl onions and transfer them to a bowl.

COMBINE the vinegars, water, sugar, salt, mustard seeds, peppercorns, coriander seeds, bay leaf, and red pepper flakes in small saucepan and bring to boil. Strain the vinegar mixture over the onions and weigh them down with a small plate; all of the onions should be submerged in the liquid. Set aside to cool.

FOR THE BALSAMIC VINAIGRETTE

PLACE the vinegar and minced shallot in a small bowl. Whisk in the olive oil, taste for seasoning, and set aside. If the vinaigrette is too thick, add a teaspoon of water at a time until it reaches desired consistency.

TO PLATE

PLACE ½ of a burrata round in the center of each plate. Surround with tomato wedges. Drizzle the tomatoes with the gremolata and balsamic vinaigrette. Garnish with 4 pickled red pearl onions.

PAN-SEARED TUNA TATAKI WITH GREEN TEA SOBA NOODLES

SERVES 4

Soba noodles colored and flavored with green tea, known as *cha soba*, make a unique presentation, and the contrasting color of the rare-pink tuna makes this dish a memorable one. As the tuna is just lightly seared and not fully cooked, make sure to purchase tuna labeled "sushi grade" from a trusted fishmonger or the fish section of your grocery store. Green tea soba noodles/*cha soba* can be found at Asian markets; if unavailable, you may substitute regular buckwheat soba noodles or get adventurous and try one of the lesser-known sobas such as *hegi soba*, flavored with seaweed; *mugi soba*, flavored with mugwort; or *jinenjo soba*, flavored with wild yam flour.

SESAME DRESSING

1 ¼ tablespoons soy sauce

¼ tablespoon rice vinegar

1 teaspoon honey

1 teaspoon fresh minced ginger

1 ½ tablespoons vegetable oil

½ tablespoon sesame oil

1 tablespoon sliced scallions, plus more for garnish

GREEN TEA SOBA NOODLES

6 ounces green tea soba noodles or other dried soba noodles (the green tea variety are also called *cha soba* and available at specialty Asian markets)

1 tablespoon mixed toasted white and black sesame seeds

TUNA

1–2 tablespoons grapeseed oil

1 pound sushi grade tuna, cut into four 4-ounce blocks

FOR THE SESAME DRESSING

COMBINE the soy sauce, rice vinegar, honey, and ginger, whisking to combine. Whisk in the vegetable and sesame oils until well emulsified. Fold in the sliced scallions. Separate 1 tablespoon of dressing and set aside to drizzle over tuna.

FOR THE GREEN TEA SOBA NOODLES

COOK noodles in a large saucepan of boiling water according to packet instructions. Drain and rinse under cold running water. Transfer to a bowl and toss with three tablespoons of the sesame dressing and sesame seeds.

FOR THE TUNA

HEAT the oil in a large sauté pan over medium-high heat. Add the tuna and sear it on all sides, about 30 seconds per side. Remove the tuna from the pan and let it rest. Slice the tuna.

TO PLATE

DIVIDE the soba noodles among 4 plates. Top with sliced tuna and drizzle with sesame dressing. Garnish with more sliced scallion.

PAN-FRIED RED SNAPPER WITH ROASTED BEETS AND PINK GRAPEFRUIT DRESSING

SERVES 4

Baby beets are sweeter than mature beets, and when roasted their sweetness is further concentrated. A sweet-sour grapefruit salad complements the humble root, with quickly cooked snapper added to the plate to make this a substantial starter. If golden baby beets are not available, feel free to use all red beets, or experiment with different colored varieties such as white beets and chioggia (candy-striped) beets, which when cut reveal stunning red and white rings inside. You may roast the beets and make the salad dressing a couple of hours in advance, then sear the snapper at the last minute, just before putting the salad together.

PINK GRAPEFRUIT DRESSING

1 tablespoon freshly squeezed pink grapefruit juice

1 small minced shallot

1 teaspoon honey

1 teaspoon sherry vinegar

¼ cup olive oil

Kosher salt and freshly ground black pepper

ROASTED BEETS

2 red baby beets, scrubbed

2 golden baby beets, scrubbed

Olive oil

Kosher salt and freshly ground black pepper

PAN-FRIED RED SNAPPER

2 tablespoons olive oil

2 tablespoons butter

4 red snapper fillets, skin on, lightly scored

Sea salt and black pepper

1 grapefruit, cut into segments

2 radishes, sliced

1 teaspoon chopped basil, plus more for garnish

1 teaspoon chopped cilantro, plus more for garnish

FOR THE PINK GRAPEFRUIT DRESSING

IN a small bowl, combine the grapefruit juice, shallot, honey, and sherry vinegar, whisking well. Whisk in the olive oil in a slow, steady stream until emulsified. Season with salt and pepper.

FOR THE ROASTED BEETS

PREHEAT the oven to 375°F. Peel the beets and place them on two separate pieces of tin foil. Coat them lightly with olive oil and season with salt and pepper. Wrap the beets in the foil and place them on a baking sheet. Roast in the oven until they are cooked through and easily pierced with the tip of a sharp knife, 45–60 minutes.

FOR THE SNAPPER

HEAT olive oil and butter in a large sauté pan over medium-high heat. When the foam subsides, season the red snapper fillets with salt and pepper and cook, skin-side down, about 3 minutes, until they are lightly browned. Then turn the fillets over and sear the other side for another 2 minutes, until just cooked through.

TO PLATE

COMBINE the grapefruit segments and radishes in a bowl. Toss with the pink grapefruit vinaigrette. Fold in the herbs.

ARRANGE the beets on the plate, place the fish, and garnish with the grapefruit segments and radishes.

CAESAR SALAD, ROMAINE HEARTS, PICKLED RED ONION, PARMESAN CROUTONS

SERVES 4

This *Hell's Kitchen* take on the standard Caesar finishes with sweet and spicy pickled onions and homemade croutons; Parmesan is baked right into the croutons for extra deliciousness. To keep the Caesar from going soggy, we use romaine hearts rather than the whole head; they stay crisp and hold their shape when tossed with the creamy dressing.

The dressing uses raw eggs, so make sure the ones you pick are super-fresh, preferably from a local farm. To pare down your Caesar, feel free to omit the pickled onions, use high-quality store-bought croutons, and serve on its own, or toss in some shredded chicken to make the salad into a meal.

PARMESAN CROUTONS

3 slices of day-old baguette, cut into ¾-inch cubes

½ tablespoon extra virgin olive oil

3 tablespoons Parmesan cheese

PICKLED RED PEARL ONIONS

20 red pearl onions

½ cup champagne vinegar

½ cup red wine vinegar

½ cup water

½ cup sugar

1 tablespoon kosher salt

1 ½ tablespoons mustard seeds

1 teaspoon whole peppercorns

½ teaspoon coriander seeds

1 small bay leaf

Pinch red pepper flakes

CAESAR DRESSING

2 tablespoons Dijon mustard

2 tablespoons crème fraîche

Juice of 1 lemon

½ cup Parmesan cheese

2 large egg yolks

2 anchovy fillets

1 small garlic clove

Kosher salt and freshly ground pepper

¼ cup olive oil

FOR THE PARMESAN CROUTONS

PREHEAT the oven to 350°F.

PLACE the bread in a large bowl and toss with the olive oil. Add the Parmesan cheese and toss well to make sure that all of the bread is coated with the oil and the cheese. Spread the bread on a parchment-lined sheet tray in a single layer and bake in the oven until golden brown, about 25–30 minutes.

FOR THE PICKLED RED PEARL ONIONS

BRING a large saucepan of salted water to a boil. Add the pearl onions and blanch for 1 minute. Run under cold water to cool, then peel the pearl onions and transfer them to a bowl.

COMBINE the vinegars, water, sugar, salt, mustard seeds, peppercorns, coriander seeds, bay leaf, and red pepper flakes in small saucepot and bring to boil. Strain the vinegar mixture over the onions and weigh them down with a small plate; all of the onions should be submerged in the liquid. Set aside to cool. Halve the onions.

FOR THE CAESAR DRESSING (YIELDS ABOUT ½ CUP)

WITH an immersion blender, combine the mustard, crème fraîche, lemon juice, Parmesan cheese, egg yolks, anchovies, garlic, and salt and pepper and pulse until the ingredients are incorporated. Scrape down the sides of the bowl with a rubber spatula. While the motor is running, add the oil in a slow and steady stream until the dressing begins to thicken and emulsify. If it is too thick, add a few drops of water. Season with salt and pepper and more Parmesan cheese, anchovies, or lemon according to your taste.

TO PLATE

TOSS the romaine hearts with the dressing and season with salt and pepper. Place in the middle of the plate, overlapping. Garnish with the croutons, pickled red pearl onion halves, and Parmesan cheese.

STEAMED MUSSELS WITH TEQUILA, RED CHILI, GREEN JALAPEÑO, COCONUT MILK, LIME, AND CILANTRO

SERVES 4

When you're looking for a first-class starter but don't have a lot of time to devote to it, mussels make a great choice. They cook in no time flat and take to many types of preparations. Here we're inspired by the quintessential mussel dish, French *moules marnière,* and in a nod to Ja'Nel Witt's celebrity-chef praised opening to the Season 11 finale, give it an Asian twist with the addition of coconut milk, fish sauce, and lime juice. Tequila takes the place of the traditional white wine. Serve with plenty of toasted bread for dunking up the sauces at the bottom of the bowl. See below for tips on choosing and storing mussels.

1 tablespoon vegetable oil

2 large shallots, thinly sliced

5 garlic cloves, thinly sliced

2 red serrano chili peppers, deseeded and sliced

1 small jalapeño, deseeded and minced

¼ cup tequila

3 cups coconut milk (not lite!)

1 teaspoon fish sauce

2 tablespoons fresh lime juice

2 pounds mussels, scrubbed and debearded

3 tablespoons chopped cilantro, divided

Kosher salt and freshly ground pepper

HEAT vegetable oil in a large pot or Dutch oven over medium heat. Add the shallots and garlic and sauté 2–3 minutes. Add the serrano and jalapeño chilies, tequila, coconut milk, fish sauce, and lime juice and simmer 2–3 minutes. Add mussels. Cover and steam until mussels begin to open, about 2 minutes, discarding any mussels that do not open.

USING tongs, transfer mussels to large bowl. Simmer sauce uncovered until slightly reduced, 2–3 more minutes. Add 2 tablespoons cilantro and season with salt and pepper. Pour the sauce over the mussels, garnish with more chopped cilantro, and serve.

CHOOSING AND STORING MUSSELS AND OTHER BIVALVES

When shopping for bivalves—mussels, clams, and oysters—know that they will be live when you buy them. Make sure they are closed or just slightly gaping and use your nose to check for freshness—if they smell like anything other than the sea, shop elsewhere or save your dish for another day. When you get your bivalves home, take them out of the bag if they came in one, put them in a bowl, cover the bowl with a damp paper towel, and let them breathe; they'll keep this way for a day or two until you're ready to cook them.

BEEF CARPACCIO, PICKLED RADISH, FENNEL AND CARROTS, YUZU (OR GRAPEFRUIT) VINAIGRETTE

SERVES 4

This dish appears as the first course in the Meat Lover's menu (page 250). Be particularly choosy with your meat in this recipe, as carpaccio is, plain and simple, raw beef ("cooked carpaccio" is an oxymoron), pounded to tenderness to turn it into a delicacy. Get out your sharpest chef's knife to cut your beef super-thin; freezing the tenderloin briefly beforehand makes slicing easier. (Alternatively, you might ask your butcher to slice your beef for you.) The pickled vegetables served alongside cut the richness of the meat, and yuzu dressing adds a sour note to this *Hell's Kitchen* take on classic Italian carpaccio. Yuzu is a tart citrus fruit common to Japanese cuisine; its flavor is similar to grapefruit with notes of mandarin orange. The fruit is rarely found fresh in this country, so look for yuzu juice in Asian food stores. If unavailable, grapefruit juice may be substituted. Note that the pickled vegetables must be set up a day ahead.

PICKLED RADISH, FENNEL, AND CARROT (Make one day ahead)

6 tablespoons distilled white vinegar

6 tablespoons apple cider vinegar

2½ tablespoons sugar

¼ teaspoon whole mustard seeds

½ teaspoon kosher salt

3 radishes, thinly sliced, on a mandoline if you have one

1 large carrot, thinly sliced, on a mandoline if you have one

½ small fennel bulb, thinly sliced, on a mandoline if you have one, plus fronds for serving

1 small garlic clove, smashed

¼ teaspoon black peppercorns

1 jalapeño pepper, thinly sliced (remove the seeds if you prefer it less spicy)

2 tablespoons minced cilantro

YUZU VINAIGRETTE

2 tablespoons yuzu juice or 1 tablespoon grapefruit juice

½ tablespoon Dijon mustard

1–1½ tablespoons soy sauce

½ teaspoon minced garlic

Zest of half a lemon

¼ cup canola or grapeseed oil

Kosher salt and freshly ground black pepper

BEEF CARPACCIO

10 ounces beef tenderloin from the tip end of the roast

FOR THE PICKLED RADISH, FENNEL, AND CARROT

IN a small saucepan, heat the vinegars, sugar, mustard seeds, and salt, mixing to dissolve. Bring to a simmer, then remove from the heat and cool slightly.

COMBINE the radishes, carrots, fennel, garlic clove, black peppercorns, and jalapeño in a bowl. Pour the vinegar mixture over the vegetables, mixing to combine. Fold in the cilantro. Transfer to a jar fitted with an airtight lid.

FOR THE YUZU VINAIGRETTE

IN a small bowl, whisk together the yuzu juice, mustard, soy sauce, garlic, and lemon zest. Add the oil in a slow, steady stream, whisking to emulsify. Season to taste with salt and pepper.

FOR THE BEEF CARPACCIO

WRAP the tenderloin in plastic wrap and place in the freezer for 2 hours.

UNWRAP the meat and thinly slice into ¼-inch-thick pieces. Lay the meat onto a large sheet of plastic wrap. Top with another sheet of plastic wrap and gently pound the meat with a meat mallet until paper thin.

TO PLATE

DIVIDE the carpaccio among four plates. Top with pickled vegetables, fennel fronds, and drizzle with yuzu vinaigrette.

BUTTER LETTUCE SALAD

SERVES 4

Buttery, soft lettuce leaves concluding in a crunchy stem are the defining feature of butter lettuce, a loose-leaf lettuce in the butterhead family (other family members are Boston lettuce and Bibb lettuce). Though its leaves are tender, butter lettuce holds its own with substantial add-in ingredients, like the goat cheese that's breaded and fried into creamy, crisp deliciousness and set atop the finished salad.

GOAT CHEESE CROQUETTE

½ cup panko bread crumbs

2 tablespoons fresh flat-leaf parsley, finely chopped

2 tablespoons fresh chives, finely chopped

6 ounces goat cheese, well chilled

½ cups all-purpose flour

Kosher salt and freshly ground black pepper

1 large egg

Canola or grapeseed oil

LEMON VINAIGRETTE

2 tablespoons lemon juice

½ teaspoon Dijon mustard

1 ½ teaspoon minced shallot

¼ cup olive oil

Kosher salt and freshly ground black pepper

CANDIED WALNUTS

¼ cup walnut halves/pieces

1 tablespoon white granulated sugar

1 teaspoon unsalted butter

1 small head of butter lettuce, torn into large pieces

1 small granny smith apple, julienned

¼ cup apple butter

FOR THE CANDIED WALNUTS

HEAT a medium nonstick skillet over medium heat. Add walnuts, granulated sugar, and butter, stirring frequently until the butter melts and the nuts are well coated.

TRANSFER to a baking sheet lined with parchment paper and use a fork to separate the nuts right away. Allow the coating to harden, 5–7 minutes.

FOR THE VINAIGRETTE

IN a small bowl, combine the lemon juice, Dijon mustard, and shallot. Slowly whisk in olive oil. Season to taste with salt and pepper. Set aside.

FOR THE GOAT CHEESE CROQUETTE

IN a mini food processor or spice grinder, pulse the breadcrumbs until finely ground. In a medium bowl, combine the breadcrumbs, chopped parsley, and chopped chives.

REMOVE the goat cheese from the refrigerator. With an ice cream scoop or a tablespoon, scoop ¼ cup of goat cheese. Place the flour in a bowl and season with salt and pepper. Place the egg in another bowl and beat lightly. Using a fork, flatten the goat cheese slightly to form a disk and toss it in the flour. Then coat the disk with beaten egg and roll in the breadcrumb mixture until evenly coated. Set the croquette aside on a clean plate and repeat with the remaining goat cheese. When all the croquettes are breaded, cover loosely and refrigerate for 30 minutes.

HEAT about ¼ inch of canola or grapeseed oil in a small skillet over medium-high heat. Gently add the chilled cheese croquettes. Fry until golden brown, ½–1 minute per side. Transfer to paper towels to drain.

TO PLATE

PLACE ¼ of a head of butter lettuce on each plate. Top with a goat cheese croquette and drizzle the lettuce and plate with the vinaigrette. Garnish with apples and walnuts and a dollop of apple butter.

CRAB SHRIMP LETTUCE CUPS WITH BLACK BEAN MANGO SALSA AND CHILI VINAIGRETTE

SERVES 4

The crisp-tender qualities of butter lettuce make it a light little holder that can contain any number of fillings, making it a go-to base for summer apps that call for little or no cooking and a perfect showcase for seafood. Only the shrimp requires you turn on a burner, with just three minutes of stovetop time. See page 54 for a hearty salad recipe featuring these buttery leaves.

CRAB SHRIMP LETTUCE CUPS

3 tablespoons fresh lime juice

2 tablespoons vegetable oil, divided

1 tablespoons soy sauce, divided

1 tablespoon grated fresh ginger

1 garlic clove, minced

16 raw jumbo shrimp, 16-20 count, peeled and deveined

1 cup lump crabmeat, picked over for shells

BLACK BEAN MANGO SALSA

⅓ cup canned black beans, drained and rinsed

¾ cup diced fresh mango

3 tablespoons minced red onion

¼ cup diced yellow pepper

1 tablespoon minced and seeded jalapeño

½ teaspoon minced garlic

1½ tablespoon white wine vinegar

½ teaspoon sugar

Juice of ½ lime

Kosher salt and freshly ground black pepper

2 tablespoons chopped fresh cilantro

CHILI VINAIGRETTE

3 tablespoons fresh lime juice

½ teaspoon sherry vinegar

1 large garlic clove, minced

½ teaspoon ground cayenne

¼ teaspoon ground cumin

½ teaspoon kosher salt

⅓ cup grapeseed oil or canola oil

½ tablespoon parsley

SALAD

1 head butter lettuce

1 ripe avocado, peeled and sliced
Tomatillo salsa, store-bought

Shredded jicama, for garnish

Chopped chives, for garnish

FOR THE SHRIMP

IN a medium bowl, combine lime juice, oil, soy sauce, ginger, and garlic. Add shrimp and let marinate in refrigerator for 30 minutes.

WHILE the shrimp is marinating, make the salsa.

FOR THE BLACK BEAN MANGO SALSA

IN a medium bowl, combine the black beans, mango, red onion, yellow pepper, jalapeño, and garlic. Add the vinegar, sugar, lime juice, and salt and pepper, and mix well. Fold in the cilantro and allow to sit at room temperature so the flavors will develop.

FOR THE CHILI VINAIGRETTE

COMBINE the lime juice, sherry vinegar, garlic, cayenne, cumin, and salt in a bowl. Whisk in the oil until emulsified. Stir in the parsley and set aside.

COOK THE SHRIMP AND CRAB MEAT

HEAT a medium skillet, preferably nonstick, over medium-high heat. Add shrimp and cook 3 minutes total, turning once to cook both sides or until shrimp are pink. Transfer to a bowl and stir in the crabmeat. Add ¾ teaspoon vinaigrette and season to taste. Allow to cool before plating.

TO PLATE

SEPARATE the lettuce into leaves. Spoon about ¼ cup black bean mango relish into the center. Top with sliced avocado, shrimp, and crab. Drizzle with tomatillo salsa and chili vinaigrette and garnish with shredded jicama and chopped chives.

CREAMY ASPARAGUS RISOTTO WITH LEMON AND MASCARPONE

SERVES 4

This is the green-hued arborio rice dish that often catches the camera as it's served as an app to *Hell's Kitchen* diners. And it's one that Kevin Cottle mastered in Season 6's final four competition. It's a spring asparagus, brightened with lemon and enriched with a dollop of mascarpone. Serve your risotto as soon as it's done, as it continues to cook after it's removed from the heat and can start to dry out and become soft.

ASPARAGUS PUREE

1 pound asparagus, bottoms trimmed and discarded

Kosher salt and freshly ground black pepper

RISOTTO

5⅓ cups vegetable stock or chicken stock

1 tablespoon olive oil

⅔ cup white onion, finely diced

1⅓ cups arborio rice or medium-grain white rice

⅓ cup dry white wine

⅓ cup Parmesan cheese, plus more to taste

Juice of ½ lemon

1 tablespoon mascarpone

Kosher salt and freshly ground black pepper

Lemon zest, for garnish

FOR THE ASPARAGUS PUREE

IN a medium skillet, blanch the asparagus, whole, in boiling salted water for 2 minutes or until al dente. Remove the spears with a slotted spoon and shock in ice water. Reserve a half cup of the blanching liquid.

CUT 2 inches from the tops and set aside. Thinly slice the bottoms and put them in the blender on low. Add just enough of the blanching water to loosen and start pureeing. Blend on high until smooth. Season with salt and pepper.

FOR THE RISOTTO

IN a small saucepan, heat the stock and maintain at a slow simmer.

HEAT the olive oil in heavy large saucepan over moderate heat. Add onion and sauté until tender and translucent, about 4–5 minutes. Add the rice and stir 1 minute. Add wine and cook until absorbed, stirring often, 1–2 minutes. Add ½ cup of stock and simmer until the liquid is absorbed, stirring occasionally, 2–3 minutes. Continue in this manner, adding hot stock a half a cup at a time until all of the stock has been added and absorbed and the rice is just tender and mixture is creamy, total cooking time 25 minutes. Stir in the Parmesan cheese, then add the asparagus puree, reserved asparagus tips, lemon juice, and mascarpone, stirring gently to combine and heat through. Season to taste with salt and pepper, garnish with lemon zest, and serve with more Parmesan.

RISOTTO COOKED JUST RIGHT

From oversalted to bland, seasoned with sugar instead of salt, hard, mushy, or cooked in a dirty pan, ruined risottos have run the gamut on *Hell's Kitchen*. But nothing is better than a perfect risotto, cooked until creamy yet still al dente with each grain separate. This Italian rice dish reliably joins beef Wellington (page 82) and seared scallops (page 67) on the *Hell's Kitchen* menu, as it is one of the more difficult recipes to master. For a successful risotto, cook it slowly, ladling broth into the pan only after the previous addition has been absorbed, and taste often to find your way to that sweet spot of perfect doneness.

EGGPLANT INVOLTINI WITH SPICY RED PEPPER EMULSION

SERVES 4

Involtini is a term describing a food—often veal, beef, pork, or chicken—that's thinly sliced, stuffed, and rolled around a cheese filling. Eggplant goes into this involtini for vegetarians, as its "meaty" texture makes it sturdy enough to stand up to the stuffing and rolling it's subjected to. Typical involtini style calls for frying the eggplant before rolling, but here we bake it for a lighter dish that lets the eggplant be the star of the show. A red pepper emulsion—peppers cooked to tenderness and pureed to bring out their essence—stands in for the tomato sauce that eggplant involtini is typically baked in.

SPICY RED PEPPER EMULSION

1 tablespoon olive oil

1 garlic clove, thinly sliced

½ small shallot, thinly sliced

2 large red bell peppers, cored and seeded, cut into ½-inch pieces

½ teaspoon kosher salt, plus more to taste

½ teaspoon sugar

½ cup chicken stock

¼ cup crushed tomatoes, with juices

Crushed red pepper, to taste

Freshly ground black pepper

EGGPLANT INVOLTINI

1 large eggplant, about 1 ½ pounds

Kosher salt and freshly ground pepper

1 cup whole-milk ricotta cheese

¼ pound (about 1 cup) fresh mozzarella cheese, shredded

1 large egg, lightly beaten

½ cup grated Parmigiano-Reggiano cheese

1 tablespoon chopped fresh basil and/or flat-leaf parsley

Olive oil for brushing

SPICY RED PEPPER EMULSION

IN a medium saucepan, combine olive oil and garlic over medium-low heat and sauté until garlic is aromatic, about 1 minute. Add shallot and sauté until translucent. Stir in peppers, salt, and sugar. Cover and cook for 5 minutes. Add chicken stock and crushed tomatoes and simmer, partially covered, until peppers are tender, about 8 minutes. Puree with an immersion blender. Transfer to a bowl and season with crushed red pepper and salt to taste.

FOR THE EGGPLANT INVOLTINI

TRIM the eggplant, then cut lengthwise into eight ¼-inch-thick slices. Layer the slices in a colander set over a plate, sprinkling each layer with salt, and let stand for 30 minutes to drain.

PREHEAT the oven to 450°F.

MEANWHILE, in a bowl, stir together the ricotta, mozzarella, egg, 2 tablespoons Parmigiano-Reggiano, and the basil/parsley, and season with fresh pepper.

WIPE the eggplant and pat dry with paper towels. Brush the slices on both sides with olive oil, then arrange them in a single layer on a rimmed baking sheet lined with parchment paper.

BAKE the slices in the lower third of the oven until lightly browned on the bottom, 8–10 minutes. Turn the slices over and continue to bake until browned on the second side and tender, 8–10 minutes more. Remove the eggplant from the oven. Reduce the temperature to 350°F.

SPOON a thin layer of the red pepper sauce into a 8-inch-square baking dish. Place a spoonful of the cheese mixture near one end of a slice of eggplant and roll up the slice. Place the roll, seam side down, in the dish. Repeat with remaining eggplant. Spoon the remaining sauce over the rolls, then sprinkle evenly with the remaining Parmigiano-Reggiano.

BAKE the rolls until the sauce is bubbling hot and the rolls are heated through, about 25 minutes. Allow to set 5 minutes before serving.

DIVIDE the rolls among the four plates and serve immediately.

GRILLED JUMBO ASPARAGUS SALAD WITH FRIED EGG AND BACON-SHALLOT VINAIGRETTE

SERVES 4

Bacon makes it into just about everything these days, from cookies to ice cream, so why not add its salty, smoky umami essence to salad dressing? The dressing is happily drizzled over thick asparagus spears and topped with bacon's trusted sidekick, the fried egg. If it isn't grilling season or you're an urban dweller, cook the asparagus in a grill pan rather than on the barbecue.

BACON-SHALLOT VINAIGRETTE

4 thick-cut slices bacon, cut into small dice

1 small shallot, minced

¼ cup sherry vinegar

½–1 teaspoon brown sugar

¼ teaspoon Dijon Mustard

Chopped fresh chives

Kosher salt and freshly ground black pepper

FRIED EGGS

4 large fresh eggs

1–2 tablespoons butter

GRILLED ASPARAGUS

28 jumbo asparagus spears, tough ends snapped off or trimmed, stems peeled

Olive oil

Salt and pepper

FOR THE BACON-SHALLOT VINAIGRETTE

HEAT a large frying pan over medium heat. Add the bacon and cook, stirring occasionally, until browned and crispy, about 4 minutes. Remove the bacon to a paper-towel-lined plate and set aside. Discard all but 3 tablespoons of the fat.

PLACE the pan with the remaining bacon fat over medium heat. Add the shallot and cook until fragrant, about 30 seconds. Whisk in the vinegar, brown sugar, and Dijon mustard; remove from heat and season with salt and pepper.

TRANSFER to a small bowl.

ADD the bacon and the chives to the shallot vinegar mixture and stir to combine.

FOR THE FRIED EGGS

PLACE a medium-sized nonstick frying pan over low heat. Add the butter and melt slowly. When all the butter is melted but not foaming, crack the eggs one at a time into a small bowl. Gently slide each egg into the frying pan. Cook about 5 minutes, until the egg white solidifies and the yolk is still runny. Salt just before serving on top of the asparagus spears.

FOR THE GRILLED ASPARAGUS

FILL a medium pot with water, add salt, and bring to a boil over medium-high heat. Place asparagus into water and cook about 5 minutes, or until spears bend without snapping. Drain asparagus and plunge into ice water. Drain.

LIGHT a grill or preheat a grill pan. Brush the asparagus with oil and season with salt and pepper. Grill over high heat, turning until brown, about 5 minutes.

TO PLATE

DIVIDE the asparagus spears among four plates. Drizzle with bacon-shallot vinaigrette and top with a fried egg.

SALAD OF BABY GEM HEARTS, TOASTED WALNUTS, AND RED GRAPES WITH BLUE CHEESE DRESSING

SERVES 4

Baby gem lettuce is similar in appearance to romaine but thinner and smaller, with a compact but loose head. It can be found in both green and red varieties. If unavailable, you may substitute small heads of crisp romaine lettuce or romaine hearts. Baby gems hold up to a creamy dressing, and this one is the very definition of creamy—blue cheese, mayonnaise, and half-and-half, enriched with rich truffle for umami flavor. To elevate your salad, finish with shaved fresh truffle.

TRUFFLE BLUE CHEESE DRESSING

½ cups mayonnaise

1¾ ounces crumbled blue cheese

½ tablespoon white wine vinegar

1¼ tablespoons truffle oil, or more to taste

1½ teaspoons chopped chives

1 tablespoon half-and-half

TOASTED WALNUTS

¾ cup shelled walnut halves

SALAD

¾ pound baby gem lettuce (substitute romaine if you can't find baby gems)

½ cup halved seedless red grapes

Shaved truffle (optional)

FOR THE BLUE CHEESE DRESSING

COMBINE the mayonnaise with the blue cheese and vinegar and mix well. Add the truffle oil and chives. Stir in the half-and-half. Thin to desired consistency with up to 1 tablespoon of water and season to taste.

FOR THE TOASTED WALNUTS

IN a small, dry sauté pan over moderate heat, toast the nuts until fragrant, 5–6 minutes.

TO PLATE

DIVIDE the lettuce among four plates. Drizzle with dressing and garnish with walnuts, grapes, and shaved truffle, if using.

SALAD OF SCALLOPS WITH TRUFFLE VINAIGRETTE

SERVES 4

Can you cook scallops to *Hell's Kitchen*'s stringent standards? Without the distraction of the cameras and lights that cause many a *Hell's Kitchen* hopeful to burn or under-cook their scallops, cooking this shellfish at home is really quite easy. The key is to have all your ingredients at the ready, because once things hit the pan it all moves very fast. You'll want to get the pan very hot, and a chef's tip is to place the scallops in a circle around the perimeter of the pan; when their undersides start to brown, use tongs to turn the scallops in the order you added them to the pan, then brown them on the second side until just cooked through and perfectly tender inside. Season 7's Jay Santos did the show proud with his take on this *Hell's Kitchen* classic in that season's finale. Read more about truffles and truffle oil on page 68. And to go all out, serve this dish as part of the Festival of Truffles menu (page 249).

POTATOES

4 small Yukon Gold potatoes, peeled

Kosher salt

1 tablespoon olive oil

1 tablespoon unsalted butter

TRUFFLE VINAIGRETTE

2 egg yolks

2 tablespoons grapeseed oil

1 tablespoon truffle oil

1 teaspoon white wine vinegar

1 teaspoon finely chopped fresh truffle (optional)

Kosher salt and freshly ground black pepper

SCALLOPS

12 large fresh scallops, side muscles removed and discarded

2 teaspoons curry powder plus 2 teaspoons of kosher salt

1 tablespoon olive oil

SALAD

5 cups petite Asian greens like mizuna, tatsoi, mustard greens, and shiso

2 tablespoons truffle vinaigrette

Meyer lemon wedges

FOR THE POTATOES

PLACE the potatoes in a large pot and cover with 2 inches of water. Stir the salt into the pot and bring to a boil over high heat. Reduce to a simmer and cook the potatoes until tender and easily pierced with the point of a paring knife, about 20 minutes. Slice evenly. Set aside.

FOR THE TRUFFLE VINAIGRETTE

WITH a whisk, beat egg yolks until thick and pale, then add the grapeseed oil in a slow and steady stream, whisking until the mixture is creamy. Now, slowly add in the truffle oil and vinegar. If too thick, adjust the texture with a little water. Transfer the vinaigrette to a bowl and stir in the chopped truffles (if using). Season to taste with salt and pepper

FRY THE POTATOES AND SAUTÉ THE SCALLOPS

HEAT 1 tablespoon of olive oil and the butter in a sauté pan over medium-high heat. Add the potato slices in a single layer and fry until they are browned on both sides. Remove them from the pan and transfer to a plate and keep warm.

PAT the scallops dry with a paper towel, then season them with the curry powder salt. Add another tablespoon of olive oil to the hot pan. Add the scallops and sear over high heat for 2 minutes or so on each side until nicely caramelized. Season to taste with salt and pepper.

FOR THE SALAD

TOSS the salad leaves with the 2 tablespoons of truffle vinaigrette and season to taste with salt and pepper. Put small mounds in the center of four dinner plates.

TO PLATE

ARRANGE the potatoes, scallops, and truffles alternately around the salad along with a wedge of Meyer lemon. Serve immediately.

TRUFFLES AND TRUFFLE OIL: A CLASSIC HELL'S KITCHEN FINISH

Truffles are in the fungus family but are tubers rather than mushrooms because they grow underground; they range from the size of a marble to that of a fist. There are more than seventy species of truffle, with the most prized being the black and white varieties. Their earthy, seductive, umami-rich flavor, unlike any other food on earth, makes them a cherished ingredient and among the most expensive foods in the world. French gastronome Jean Anthelme Brillat-Savarin called them the "diamonds of the kitchen." Among the most sought-after truffles are the French black Périgord truffle and the white truffle of Alba from Piedmont, Italy. The white has a very short season, from fall to early winter. Black truffles are available in both summer and winter and typically are less expensive than the white. Truffles grow near trees, and specially trained pigs or dogs are employed to sniff them out from under the ground.

Truffles are typically grated or scraped on top of a dish (there's even a dedicated truffle slicer that can be used for the job), and a small amount is all you need to elevate a dish. Truffles can transform a salad (page 65), take seared scallops to new heights (page 67), and further elevate steak (page 94 and 153). They are a natural with potatoes (page 96), pair perfectly with pasta (page 122 and 148) and creamy sauces, and a little truffle atop an omelet is an upscale way to start your day. Making a compound butter by blending a little grated truffle into softened butter extends the essence of the truffle. Store fresh truffles for up to a couple of days in a jar of rice or a container filled with eggs to infuse them with the flavor and aroma of the truffles.

Truffle oil, used in recipes throughout this book as a final flourish, is a way of adding truffle flavor to your dishes that's much lighter on the budget. Check your labels carefully, as many brands are made with artificial truffle flavoring; real truffle oil is olive oil infused with real truffles. Both truffles and truffle oil can be found in gourmet food stores. Online sources for truffles include Dartagnan.com, iGourmet.com, and Eataly.com.

SEARED FOIE GRAS ON BRIOCHE FRENCH TOAST WITH CARAMELIZED APPLES AND FIGS

SERVES 4

Foie gras, made from duck or goose liver, is a French delicacy and the ultimate in opulence. The name translates to "fat liver," and it is incredibly rich. It's often made into pâté, but here we serve it in slices set atop the best French toast you'll ever eat, with caramelized apples and figs to further gild the lily. Holli Ugalde served a version of this dish as starter to her Season 7 competition-winning dinner. Serve it as part of the Classic French menu (page 244) or the Elegant Dinner Party menu (page 252). Foie gras is available at specialty grocers and some butcher shops; it may require a special order.

CARAMELIZED APPLES AND FIGS

3 tablespoons unsalted butter

2 tablespoons dark brown sugar

1 large Granny Smith apple, peeled and sliced into 12 slices

12 firm ripe black mission figs, halved lengthwise

Kosher salt and freshly ground black pepper

2 tablespoons heavy cream

FRENCH TOAST

2 slices day-old brioche bread, ½ inch thick

2 large eggs

1 vanilla bean, seed scraped, or ½ teaspoon vanilla extract

¼ teaspoon ground ginger

2 tablespoons heavy cream

Grapeseed or other neutral oil

FOIE GRAS

½ pound Grade-A duck or goose foie gras, veins and impurities removed, cut with a heated knife into four ½-inch-thick slices, refrigerated until ready to use

Kosher salt and freshly ground black pepper

Fresh mint leaves, for garnish

FOR THE CARAMELIZED APPLES AND FIGS

MELT the butter in a medium sauté pan over medium heat. As it begins to foam, add the sugar, mixing until it dissolves. Add the apples in a single layer. Sauté until brown and tender, about 8 minutes. Add the figs and cook cut side down 2–3 minutes, or until they begin to brown. Season with salt and pepper and transfer the apples and figs to a plate to keep warm. Add the cream to the pan and mix until the sugar and butter are completely combined and a rich caramel color. Set aside and keep warm.

FOR THE FRENCH TOAST

PREHEAT the oven to 200°F and line a baking sheet with parchment paper.

CUT the slices of bread in half.

IN a shallow bowl, whisk together the eggs, vanilla, ginger, and cream. Heat the grapeseed oil in a nonstick sauté pan over medium heat. Dip the brioche in the egg mixture, then add it to the pan and cook 2 minutes on the first side, then flip and cook 1 more minute. Transfer the French toast to the lined baking sheet and place in the oven to keep warm.

FOR THE FOIE GRAS

SEASON the foie gras on both sides with salt and pepper. Heat a sauté pan until very hot. Add the foie gras and sear 30–45 seconds on each side until golden.

TO PLATE

PLACE one slice of French toast on each plate. Top with one slice foie gras and serve with caramelized apples and figs. Drizzle the foie gras with the sauce and spoon more around the plate. Garnish with mint.

SEARED AHI TUNA LOIN WITH HARICOTS VERTS, HARD-BOILED QUAIL EGGS, AND BLACK OLIVE DRESSING

SERVES 4

Ahi tuna, also known as yellowfin tuna, is mild in flavor and firm in texture. It's a standard sushi-menu offering, and it is often served lightly cooked as well. Here it's bathed in an herb, soy, and vinegar marinade before it hits the pan to give it a very brief sear. Quail eggs are miniature brown-and-black-spotted eggs; they are a bit richer in taste than chicken eggs and cook more quickly. Haricots verts are a longer, thinner, and more tender version of green beans. If they are unavailable, American green beans can be substituted. Salty, umami-tasting black olive dressing plays off the bitter frisée salad.

SEARED AHI TUNA LOIN

¼ cup balsamic vinegar

¼ cup soy sauce

2 tablespoons toasted sesame oil

1 cup olive oil

1 tablespoon sugar

1 pound sushi-grade tuna loin

2 tablespoons chopped fresh basil

2 tablespoons chopped fresh chervil or flat-leaf parsley

2 tablespoons chopped fresh thyme

2 tablespoons chopped fresh cilantro

2 tablespoons grapeseed or other high-heat oil

BLACK-OLIVE VINAIGRETTE

1 teaspoon minced shallot

1 tablespoons white wine vinegar

Freshly ground black pepper

4 pitted Niçoise or Kalamata black olives, finely chopped

⅛ cup olive oil

HARD-BOILED QUAIL EGGS

4 quail eggs or fresh medium eggs

HARICOTS VERTS

¼ pound haricots verts

Kosher salt

SALAD

1 small head frisée

FOR THE TUNA

IN a flat, shallow dish, combine the balsamic vinegar, soy sauce, sesame oil, olive oil, and sugar. Add the tuna, turning to coat. Cover and refrigerate for 2 hours, turning the tuna occasionally.

REMOVE the tuna from the marinade and pat lightly.

COAT the tuna loin with the herbs; roll tight in plastic and refrigerate.

FOR THE BLACK OLIVE VINAIGRETTE

IN a small bowl, whisk the shallot and white wine vinegar and season with pepper. Then add the olives and whisk in the olive oil.

FOR THE QUAIL EGGS

FILL a small saucepan two-thirds full with water and bring to a boil. Prepare a small bowl of ice water. With a slotted spoon, add the quail eggs and gently stir. Boil for 3–4 minutes. Remove the eggs with a slotted spoon and immediately plunge them into the ice water to stop the cooking. When they eggs are cool enough to handle, carefully peel them and set aside.

FOR THE HARICOTS VERTS

HAVE a large bowl of ice water ready. Bring a pot of salted water to a boil. Add the haricots verts and cook 2–3 minutes until crisp-tender. Drain, then plunge the beans into ice water to stop cooking. Drain again and pat dry.

COOK THE TUNA

HEAT olive oil in a large sauté pan over high heat until the oil is hot but not smoking. Add the tuna and sear for 30 seconds on each side. Transfer to a plate to rest.

TO PLATE

PLACE a small amount of frisée in the middle of the plate. Slice the tuna loin with a very sharp knife into 8 thin slices and place 2 slices on each plate on top of the frisée. Drizzle the frisée and tuna with black olive vinaigrette. Slice the quail eggs in half and use as garnish. Serve with haricots verts.

SHALLOT AND CARAMELIZED ONION TARTE TATIN

SERVES 6

Tarte Tatin, an upside-down tart that's inverted when served, is most famously made with apples (and see page 225 for a pineapple version). It also takes to savory preparations, like this version made with caramelized onions and shallots. Using store-bought puff pastry makes this recipe a cinch, easier than rolling out pastry for a standard right-side-up tart. Choose a puff pastry made with butter rather than vegetable oil for the most flavorful and flaky tarte Tatin.

SHALLOT AND CARAMELIZED ONION TARTE TATIN

3 tablespoons olive oil, divided

1 garlic clove, finely chopped

2 tablespoons unsalted butter, divided

¾ pound red onions, cut into ¼-inch slices

2 tablespoons sugar, divided

2 tablespoons balsamic vinegar

3 sprigs fresh thyme

1 pound small shallots, the smallest you can find

1½ tablespoons red wine vinegar

1 sheet puff pastry, defrosted but kept cold

FRISÉE SALAD

¼ pound frisée

2 tablespoons fresh tarragon leaves

2 teaspoons fresh chervil

3 red pearl onions, pickled (optional, recipe on page 42)

¼ cup olive oil

Kosher salt and freshly ground black pepper to taste

Four 1½-inch slices goat cheese, preferably Crottin de Chavignol (available from Vermont Creamery), at room temperature

FOR THE TARTE TATIN

TO make onion jam for the tarte Tatin, heat a large saucepan over medium-low heat. Add 1 tablespoon olive oil and garlic and stir occasionally until starting to color, 2 minutes. Add 1 tablespoon butter and onions, and stir frequently for 6–7 minutes until the onions are translucent. Add 1 tablespoon sugar and continue to cook, stirring occasionally, until onions begin to break down, about 10 minutes. Stir in the balsamic vinegar, add thyme sprigs, and adjust heat to maintain a moderate simmer. Stir frequently until the onions are jammy, 30–35 minutes. Remove the thyme sprigs, season to taste, and set aside to cool.

PEEL and trim the roots of the shallots without cutting off the core; you want the shallots to stay together. If the shallot has two lobes, separate the lobes. If you have some larger shallots, cut them in half lengthwise.

HEAT a large sauté pan over medium heat; add the remaining olive oil, then the shallots. Stir occasionally, being careful to keep the shallots intact. Cook until golden, 4–5 minutes. Add the other tablespoon of sugar and cook for 3 minutes, then add the remaining butter. Cook, stirring occasionally, until the shallots are a deep caramel color, about 5 minutes. Add red wine vinegar, season to taste, and cook until shallots are soft, about 5 more minutes. Allow to cool.

PREHEAT the oven to 400°F.

TRIM the pastry into a 9-inch round. Keep refrigerated until ready for use. Cut a 9-inch circle of parchment paper and lay it in the bottom of a 9-inch cake pan.

STARTING in the middle of the pan, arrange the shallots in a circular pattern, snugly together in one layer, leaving about ½ inch between the shallots and the edge of the pan. Then spread the onion jam over the shallots. Lay the puff pastry on top of the shallots and onions and tuck the dough snugly around the shallots. Bake the tart in the center of the oven for 30 minutes until golden brown and crisp. Allow to cool for 5 minutes. Loosen the edges with a small knife and then carefully invert the tart onto a plate. Top with goat cheese.

FOR THE FRISÉE SALAD

IN a small salad bowl, toss the greens, herbs, and onions with olive oil, salt, and pepper.

TO PLATE

SLICE the tart, top with sliced goat cheese, and serve with frisée salad.

DUCK RAGÙ RAVIOLI AND PUMPKIN-SEED PUREE WITH BROWN BUTTER

SERVES 4

Ragù, an Italian meat-based sauce, is turned inside out by stuffing it into pasta to make this savory ravioli. Chicken confit—chicken cooked low and slow in its own fat until meltingly tender—goes into the ragù for a hearty starter to your meal. If you're not yet ready to tackle pasta-making, you may use wonton wrappers to make your ravioli; they won't be authentic Italian, but they will still be delicious.

The ravioli can be made in advance and frozen: Working in batches, place the ravioli on a baking sheet as they are formed and freeze just until solid, transferring them into a freezer container or bag as each batch is done (if you were to place them directly into the bag before freezing, they would stick). Make extra to stock your freezer with ravioli so you can put together a first-class meal at a moment's notice.

PASTA FOR RAVIOLI (This makes about ¾ pound of dough)

2 cups all-purpose flour

Pinch of kosher salt

3 large eggs

½ teaspoon olive oil

OR

32 Nasoya wonton wrappers

Cornmeal, for dusting

RAGÙ

1 D'Artagnan duck confit leg (1 cup pulled duck confit), skin and bone removed and chopped

2 tablespoons chopped chives

Zest and juice from 1 lemon

¼ cup crème fraîche

2 teaspoons shallots, minced

FOR THE RAVIOLI

IF using wonton wrappers, proceed to making the ragù.

TO make the pasta dough, combine the flour and salt in the bowl of a food processor fitted with a blade attachment. Pulse a few times to combine. Add the eggs and olive oil, and pulse 30–60 seconds, or until the dough comes together in a ball. If it doesn't come together after a minute and looks like small pebbles, add a teaspoon of water and pulse again. Repeat until the dough comes together. If the dough is sticky, add a tablespoon of flour and process again. Repeat until the dough comes together.

TURN the dough out onto a clean surface. Knead until it comes together to form a smooth ball. Dust the dough with a little flour and place it in a small mixing bowl. Cover with plastic wrap and rest at room temperature for at least 30 minutes.

DIVIDE the dough into 4 pieces. Cover the dough with plastic wrap and work with one piece at a time.

SET pasta machine to widest setting. Flatten 1 dough piece into a 3-inch-wide rectangle. Run through machine 3 times, dusting lightly with flour if sticking. Continue to run piece through machine, adjusting to next-narrower setting after every 3 passes, until dough is about 26 inches long. Cut crosswise into 3 equal pieces. Run each piece through machine, adjusting to next-narrower setting until strip is a scant 1/16 inch thick and 14 to 16 inches long. Return machine to original setting for each piece. Arrange strips in single layer on sheets of parchment and dust with cornmeal.

FOR THE RAGÙ

WHILE the dough is resting, combine all the ingredients in a food processor and pulse until well combined and mixture resembles a coarse pâté. Set aside.

PUMPKIN-SEED PUREE

½ cup toasted pumpkin seeds

1 tablespoon olive oil

2 tablespoons chopped onion

1 small garlic clove, crushed

½ slice white bread, torn into small pieces

¼ cup chicken broth

2 tablespoons heavy cream

2 tablespoons dry sherry

Kosher salt and freshly ground black pepper

Paprika, for garnish

1 egg

BROWN BUTTER

6 tablespoons unsalted butter, cut into cubes

2 teaspoons sherry vinegar

Chopped chives

Toasted pumpkin seeds, for garnish

PUMPKIN-SEED PUREE

GRIND the pumpkin seeds in a spice grinder to a powder. Set aside.

HEAT the olive oil in a medium sauté pan over medium heat. Add the onions, garlic, and bread. Sauté until the onions are translucent. Add the pumpkin-seed powder and cook 1 minute. Transfer the mixture to a small food processor and add 1–2 tablespoons of broth until mixture comes together in a smooth puree. Transfer the puree back to the sauté pan, add the broth, cream, and sherry over medium-low heat, and heat through.

TO ASSEMBLE RAVIOLI

MAKE an egg wash by combining 1 egg and 1 teaspoon of water.

FOR HOMEMADE PASTA DOUGH

DUST your work surface with flour and lay out the dough. Brush the surface with the egg wash, then place tablespoons of the duck ragù filling on half of the sheet, about 2 inches apart. Fold the other half over the filling like a blanket. With a small cup (like an espresso cup) or with your fingers, press out air pockets around each mound of filling. Use a sharp knife to cut each into squares and crimp the edges with the tines of a fork to seal.

LINE a sheet pan with parchment paper and dust with cornmeal. Transfer the ravioli to the sheet pan and dust the ravioli with cornmeal to prevent them from sticking.

FOR WONTON WRAPPERS

LAY out 8 wrappers on a flat work surface. Paint each lightly with egg wash. Place 1 tablespoon of filling in the center of each and lay another wrapper on top to cover filling. Seal tightly by pressing firmly around the filling, working your way to the outer edges, making sure that no air bubbles remain.

RAVIOLI can be left square, trimmed if desired, or cut into rounds using a medium cookie cutter.

PLACE the ravioli on a parchment-lined sheet pan while you repeat the process with remaining wrappers and filling.

TO cook the ravioli, bring a large pot of salted water to a boil. Lower the heat to a strong simmer and add the ravioli one at a time, gently stirring so they don't stick to each other. Cook 3–4 minutes until the pasta is al dente.

WHILE the ravioli cooks, make the brown butter.

FOR THE BROWN BUTTER

MELT the butter in a small skillet over moderately low heat. Simmer butter until golden brown with a nutty aroma, about 5 minutes. Remove from the heat and swirl in the sherry vinegar. Season with salt and pepper

TO PLATE

LIFT the ravioli from the pot with a strainer or slotted spoon and divide among 4 individual bowls.

DRIZZLE with brown butter and garnish with chopped chives. Serve with a dollop of pumpkin-seed puree and garnish puree with toasted pumpkin seeds and a dusting of paprika.

A TRIO OF OYSTERS:
TEMPURA-FRIED OYSTERS WITH CITRUS AIOLI,
FRESHLY SHUCKED OYSTERS WITH
BLOODY MARY GRANITA,
BAKED OYSTERS ROCKEFELLER

SERVES 4

Raw, baked, and fried, this threesome of oysters is a decidedly upscale start to a meal. To open an oyster, you'll need a short, thin-edged knife (purchase a dedicated oyster knife if you find yourself serving oysters often) that's strong enough to pry open the shells; a flat screwdriver will do in a pinch. Hold an oyster with a kitchen towel and insert the knife between the two shells to find the hinge; pop open the oyster by twisting the knife blade, then carefully slide the knife between the shells to separate them and remove the top shell, keeping as much of the liquid from the oysters as possible. For tips on choosing and storing oysters, see page 50.

BLOODY MARY GRANITA

½ cup V8 juice

¼ teaspoon Worcestershire sauce

¼ teaspoon horseradish

¼ teaspoon hot sauce

¾ tablespoon finely chopped fresh parsley

Freshly ground pepper

¼ teaspoon celery salt

Juice of half a lemon

¾ teaspoon olive juice from a jar of pimento stuffed green olives (optional)

¼ teaspoon sweet paprika

CITRUS AIOLI

1 garlic clove, pressed

⅛ teaspoon kosher salt, plus more to taste

¼ cup mayonnaise

1 tablespoon olive oil

¾ teaspoon lemon juice

¾ teaspoon lime juice

FOR THE BLOODY MARY GRANITA

IN a large bowl, whisk the V8 juice, Worcestershire sauce, horseradish, hot sauce, parsley, a few grinds of pepper, celery salt, lemon juice, and olive juice, if using. Pour into a 8-inch metal pie plate. Freeze for at least 1 hour.

FOR THE CITRUS AIOLI

ON a cutting board, mash the garlic with the salt to form a paste. Transfer to small bowl and whisk in the mayonnaise, olive oil, lemon juice, and lime juice. Season to taste and set aside.

FOR THE OYSTERS ROCKEFELLER

HAVE a bowl of ice water ready. Bring 2 quarts of salted water to a boil. Add spinach and blanch for 3 minutes. Drain in a colander, then plunge the spinach in the ice water to stop cooking. Squeeze the spinach to get the remaining water out, then finely chop and set aside.

WHILE the spinach is blanching, cook the bacon in a medium sauté pan until crispy. Drain on a paper-towel-lined plate, then crumble and set aside.

PREHEAT the broiler.

IN a medium sauté pan, melt 2 tablespoons of butter over medium. Add shallots and garlic and cook until softened, about 2 minutes. Add the white wine and reduce to almost dry. Stir in Parmesan and season with salt and pepper. Remove the pan from the heat.

ADD the chopped spinach to the pan and mix to combine.

ARRANGE the reserved oyster shells on the baking sheet. Put 1 oyster in each shell and top with 2–3 tablespoons of the sauce, spreading the sauce evenly out to the edge of the shell to completely cover the oyster. Sprinkle

OYSTERS ROCKEFELLER

2 cups baby spinach, tightly packed

2 slices bacon

2 tablespoons unsalted butter

2 tablespoons shallots, minced

1 large garlic clove, minced

¼ cup white wine

2 tablespoons Parmesan cheese

Kosher salt and freshly ground black pepper

2 tablespoons Italian flavored breadcrumbs, store-bought

A drizzle of Pernod

FRIED OYSTERS

Vegetable oil, for frying

2 tablespoons cornstarch

2 tablespoons all-purpose flour

Pinch salt

Pinch baking powder

¼ cup Newcastle Brown Ale or any pale ale, very cold

24 Blue Point oysters, bottom deep, shells reserved

1 small scallion, white and green parts thinly sliced on the diagonal, for garnish

with bread crumbs, bacon, more Parmesan, and a drizzle of Pernod. Broil for about 10 minutes.

FOR THE FRIED OYSTERS

POUR 1 ½–2 inches of oil in a small sauce pot and heat to 350°F.

MEANWHILE, mix dry ingredients together in a mixing bowl. Add ale to dry ingredients until you reach desired consistency, mixing gently with a fork. The batter should be somewhat lumpy. Set up a bowl of ice and nestle the bowl of batter in the ice.

WHEN the oil is to temperature, dredge oysters in the batter. Carefully add the oysters to the hot oil and cook, turning occasionally until golden on all sides, 1–2 minutes. Remove the oysters with a slotted spoon and drain on a paper-towel-lined plate. Season with salt.

TO PLATE FRESH OYSTERS

TOP two fresh oysters with the Bloody Mary granita and garnish with celery salt and celery leaves.

TO PLATE BAKED OYSTERS ROCKEFELLER

SERVE two oysters Rockefeller per person.

TO PLATE FRIED OYSTERS

PLACE each oyster in an empty oyster shell, two per plate. Serve with a dollop of aioli and garnish with scallions.

SUNCHOKE RISOTTO WITH CRISPY SQUID AND CHILI OIL

SERVES 4

Sunchokes, also known as Jerusalem artichokes, are a knobby-looking tuber with a sweet, nutty flavor, similar in appearance to ginger. They're crunchy when raw, and when cooked their flesh becomes creamy. Here they're cooked then blended into a puree that heightens the creaminess of a classic risotto. The dish is finished with crispy squid and a drizzle of spicy chili oil.

SUNCHOKE PUREE

1 pound sunchokes

⅔ cup cream

⅔ cup milk

2½ tablespoons butter

Kosher salt and freshly ground black pepper

RISOTTO

1 tablespoon olive oil

⅔ cup white onion, finely diced

1⅓ cups arborio rice or medium-grain white rice

⅓ cup dry white wine

5⅓ cups warm vegetable stock or chicken stock

⅓ cup Parmesan cheese plus more to taste

CRISPY SQUID

¼ cup Wondra flour

¼ cup cornstarch

Kosher salt and freshly ground black pepper

High-heat oil for frying

12 clean squid tentacles

Chili oil, store-bought

Flat-leaf parsley

FOR THE SUNCHOKE PUREE

PEEL and thinly slice the sunchokes. Place the sunchokes in a medium saucepan and cover with milk, cream, and butter. Bring to a boil over medium-high heat, then reduce to a simmer and cook over medium heat until tender, about 20 minutes.

STRAIN the sunchokes and reserve the liquid.

TRANSFER the sunchokes to a blender and, with the motor running, gradually add the reserved liquid until the mixture forms a smooth puree. Season to taste with salt and pepper and set aside.

RISOTTO

HEAT the olive oil in heavy large saucepan over moderate heat. Add onion and sauté until tender and translucent, about 4–5 minutes. Add the rice and stir 1 minute. Add wine and cook until absorbed, stirring often, 1–2 minutes. Add ½ cup of stock and simmer until the liquid is absorbed, stirring occasionally, 2–3 minutes. Continue in this manner, adding warm stock a half a cup at a time until all of it has been added and absorbed, and the rice is just tender and mixture is creamy, total cooking time 25 minutes. Stir in the Parmesan, then add the reserved sunchoke puree, stirring gently to combine and heat through. Season to taste with salt and pepper and serve with more Parmesan.

FOR THE CRISPY SQUID

WHILE the risotto is cooking, pour 1 ½–2 inches oil in a deep frying pan over medium-high heat. Combine the flour with the cornstarch and season with salt and pepper. Add half of the squid tentacles to the flour then shake the pieces in a fine mesh strainer to remove the excess. When the oil is hot, about 375°F, add them to the oil and fry until golden, about 1–2 minutes. Use a slotted spoon to transfer the squid to a paper-towel-lined plate to drain. Season to taste with salt. Repeat with the remaining tentacles.

TO PLATE

DIVIDE the risotto among 4 plates. Drizzle with chili oil, top with crispy squid, and garnish with parsley.

SQUAB SALAD WITH BLOOD ORANGE, PEA SHOOTS, AND CITRUS VINAIGRETTE

SERVES 4

Make the most of pea shoot season—a short window in early spring—with this citrusy salad served with squab. Pea shoots come from the pea plant, with delicate leaves and tendrils their defining feature. Look for them at farmers' markets as well as Asian grocers, as they are common in Chinese cuisine. You'll see them on Chinese restaurant menus under the name *dou miao* or *dau miu*.

Squab, aka pigeon, expands your poultry repertoire beyond the typical turkey and chicken. It has moist, lean, dark flesh with a mild flavor; most of the meat is found in the breast.

TOASTED PISTACHIOS

¼ cup shelled raw pistachios (or buy them roasted and skip the instructions for toasting them)

CITRUS VINAIGRETTE

2 tablespoons freshly squeezed blood orange juice

½ teaspoon freshly squeezed lemon juice

1 teaspoon minced shallot

2 tablespoons olive oil

Kosher salt and freshly ground black pepper

SQUAB BREAST

4–6 squab breast halves, deboned, skin on (have the butcher do this for you)

Kosher salt and freshly ground black pepper

2 tablespoons grapeseed or other neutral oil

2 tablespoons unsalted butter

2 sprigs thyme

2 smashed garlic cloves

PEA SHOOT SALAD

16 ounces pea shoots

8 ounces shredded radicchio

8 blood orange segments

FOR THE TOASTED PISTACHIOS

HEAT a small skillet over medium heat. Add the pistachios and cook, shaking the pan frequently to ensure even browning, about 10 minutes. Transfer the pistachios to a small bowl and allow to cool.

FOR THE CITRUS VINAIGRETTE

WHISK together the blood orange juice, lemon juice, and shallot in a small bowl. Whisk in the olive oil, season with salt and pepper, and set aside.

FOR THE SQUAB BREAST

SEASON the squab breasts with salt and pepper. Heat oil in a medium sauté pan over high heat. Add the squab skin side down and sauté until golden brown, 2–3 minutes. Add butter, thyme, and garlic cloves to the pan. Flip and spoon the melted butter over the breasts to baste. Cook 2–3 more minutes, or until the internal temperature is 145°F. Remove the squab from the pan and allow to rest for 5 minutes.

WHILE the squab rests, make the salad.

FOR THE PEA SHOOT SALAD

MIX the pea shoots, radicchio, and blood orange segments with the citrus vinaigrette. Season to taste with salt and pepper.

TO PLATE

SLICE the squab on the bias and fan out on each plate. Serve with salad on the side.

CHAPTER FOUR

THE MAIN COURSE IS THE STAR OF THE SHOW, WHERE HELL'S KITCHEN HOPEFULS HAVE A CHANCE TO SHOW OFF THEIR SIGNATURE DISHES AND WORK AS A TEAM TO PRODUCE A RESTAURANT-QUALITY MEAL. THE RECIPES THAT FOLLOW ARE HELL'S KITCHEN CLASSICS, DISHES THAT HAVE WOWED DINERS THROUGHOUT THE SEASONS.

THE CHAPTER STARTS WITH A CLASSIC WELLINGTON (PAGE 82), THE MOST LOVED AND FEARED DISH ON HELL'S KITCHEN. YOU'LL TACKLE CHICKEN, COOKING IT UNDER A BRICK (PAGE 91) AND ROASTING IT TO JUICY TENDERNESS (PAGE 110 AND 119). STEAK IS AN IMPORTANT PART OF THE HELL'S KITCHEN REPERTOIRE, AS IT'S RELIABLY ONE OF THE MOST IN-DEMAND ENTRÉES OF A GIVEN SEASON; YOU'LL TACKLE THE MOST TENDER OF CUTS, THE TENDERLOIN (PAGE 160), THEN ENJOY THE SUPREME NEW YORK STRIP IN A HELL'S KITCHEN TAKE ON STEAK FRITES (PAGE 153), AS WELL AS LEARN HOW TO BRAISE SHORT RIBS (PAGE 137), MAKE A FAT, JUICY BURGER (PAGE 134) YOU CAN BE PROUD

OF, AND "CHICKEN-FRY" YOUR STEAK (PAGE 94). FROM CHOPS TO TENDERLOIN AND BELLY, PORK MAKES A NUMBER OF APPEARANCES, AS DO VEAL, DUCK, AND LAMB. SEAFOOD IS BIG ON THE MENU TOO, FROM THE FAMILIAR HALIBUT, SALMON, AND SHRIMP TO THE MORE EXOTIC JOHN DORY AND BRANZINO, WITH COOKING METHODS RANGING FROM MARINATING AND SEARING TO GRILLING AND BAKING. AND YOU'LL MAKE THE CLASSIC ITALIAN FRUTTI DI MARE (PAGE 129), A PASTA DISH THAT FEATURES MUSSELS, CLAMS, AND SHRIMP.

WHILE MANY OF THESE ENTRÉES HAVE MULTIPLE COMPONENTS, DON'T BE DAUNTED. YOU'LL FIND SUGGESTIONS TO PARE DOWN MORE COMPLEX RECIPES AND TIPS ON HOW TO MULTITASK LIKE THE MOST SKILLED OF HELL'S KITCHEN CONTESTANTS. BY NOW WE HOPE YOU'VE GOTTEN INTO A MISE-EN-PLACE MIND-SET (SEE PAGE 23), PREPPING YOUR INGREDIENTS IN ADVANCE, POSITIONING THEM TO BE READY FOR ACTION, AND NAVIGATING THE KITCHEN LIKE A MASTER.

BEEF WELLINGTON, BLACKBERRY SAUCE, WHIPPED POTATOES, GLAZED BABY CARROTS

SERVES 4

For a successful Wellington, first you'll sear the beef on all four sides to build an initial layer of flavor. Then you'll brush the hot-out-of-the-pan beef with mustard, roll the beef in a layer of prosciutto and a concentrated mushroom filling known as duxelles, and wrap the whole thing in puff pastry (at this point you can refrigerate the Wellington overnight if you're planning your meal ahead). Then it's into the oven at a low temperature and cooked to medium rare.

When you've declared your Wellington done, let it rest for about ten minutes to relax and reabsorb its juices for a filet that's succulent, tender, and worthy of *Hell's Kitchen*. Whipped or mashed potatoes are a must to accompany your Wellington, and a drizzle of blackberry sauce serves as a sweet-tart finale. You'll find this special dish in the *Hell's Kitchen* Classic menu (page 244) and the Surf and Turf menu (page 249).

MUSHROOM DUXELLES

1 pound cremini mushrooms, coarsely chopped

½ teaspoon kosher salt

¼ teaspoon freshly ground black pepper

2 tablespoons minced chives

BUILDING THE WELLINGTON

2 pounds filet mignon

Kosher salt and freshly ground black pepper to taste

2 tablespoons canola or grapeseed oil

¼ cup whole-grain Dijon mustard

½ pound prosciutto di Parma

1 egg yolk

1 tablespoon whole milk

1 sheet puff pastry, thawed

BLACKBERRY SAUCE

8 ounces blackberries

¾ cup red wine

¾ cup brown chicken stock (see page 87)

1 heaping tablespoon honey

2 tablespoons seedless blackberry jam

2 tablespoons unsalted butter

Kosher salt and freshly ground black pepper

FOR THE MUSHROOM DUXELLES

ADD mushrooms, salt, and pepper to a food processor and process until they are finely minced, forming a rough paste.

IN a medium sauté pan over medium heat, add mushroom paste. Spread the mixture evenly over the surface and cook on a medium heat until the moisture in the paste is mostly evaporated, 15–20 minutes, and the mixture has the consistency of a spreadable pâté. Remove from heat, stir in the chives, and let cool.

TO BUILD THE WELLINGTON

SEAR the Filet.

PAT filet mignon dry with paper towels and season generously with salt and pepper. Heat a skillet over medium-high heat and add oil. When the oil is hot but not smoking, add the filet mignon and brown from 1–2 minutes on all sides. Remove from heat and place on a cutting board. Brush Dijon mustard onto the filet and allow to cool.

ROLL THE BEEF WELLINGTON

PLACE a sided baking sheet in the oven and preheat the oven to 425°F.

ON a cutting board, lay out a long piece of plastic wrap. In the middle of the wrap, lay out the prosciutto shingle-style to form a rectangle large enough to encompass the whole filet. Spread mushroom duxelles in a thin layer over the prosciutto. Place the filet on top of the mushrooms. Use the plastic wrap to help in rolling the beef up tightly in the duxelles-covered prosciutto, tucking in the ends so the beef is completely encompassed. Refrigerate for 20 minutes.

IN a bowl, mix together egg yolk and milk.

WHIPPED POTATOES

1¾ pounds Yukon Gold potatoes, peeled and cut into 1-inch cubes

½ teaspoon kosher salt

3 tablespoons unsalted butter, softened

1 cup cream

Freshly ground black pepper

CARROTS

24 baby carrots

2 tablespoons unsalted butter

1 tablespoon chopped fresh flat-leaf parsley

ON a floured surface, gently roll out puff pastry until it is ¼ inch thick, no thinner. Depending on size of the pastry sheet, two overlapping sheets can be used to ensure the filet will be completely covered and sealed. Set the beef in the center of the pastry and generously brush the pastry with the egg wash. Bring pastry up and around the beef and seal tightly. Pinch the ends closed and trim off any excess puff pastry. Refrigerate for 5–10 minutes to let it firm up again.

REMOVE Wellington from the refrigerator. Place the Wellington seam side down on the preheated baking sheet. Brush the top of the puff pastry with the remaining egg wash and score it with a sharp paring knife. Sprinkle with sea salt and place pan in the oven.

BAKE for approximately 35 minutes or until the internal temperature of the steak reaches 120°F for medium rare.

REMOVE from the oven and let rest for at least 10 minutes before slicing.

FOR THE BLACKBERRY SAUCE

PLACE the blackberries, red wine, and stock in a heavy-based saucepan and bring to a boil. Cook for about 5 minutes until the blackberries have softened.

PUSH the mixture through a fine mesh strainer and discard the seeds and pulp. Return the sauce to the saucepan over medium-high heat, add the

(continued)

honey and jam, and bring to a boil, cooking until the mixture reduces by half and thickens to a smooth sauce. Remove from the heat and swirl in the butter. Season to taste and set aside to keep warm.

FOR THE MASHED POTATOES

PUT the potatoes in a large saucepan and cover with cold water by two inches. Add ½ teaspoon salt and bring to a boil. Lower the heat to simmer, cover the pot partially, and cook until the potatoes are very tender when tested with the tip of a sharp paring knife, 20–25 minutes.

DRAIN the potatoes, reserving some of the cooking water.

COMBINE the cream and butter in a small saucepan over medium heat and bring to a simmer.

PUT the potatoes through a potato ricer or food mill and return them to the pot over low heat. Add the hot cream-and-butter mixture and mix with a wooden spoon. If the potatoes are too thick, add a small amount of the reserved cooking water until they are the consistency you like. Season to taste with salt and pepper and set aside to keep warm.

FOR THE CARROTS

BRING a quart of salted water to a boil. Have a bowl of ice water ready.

ADD the carrots and cook about 4 minutes until they are crisp-tender. Use a slotted spoon to transfer the carrots to the bowl of ice water to stop the cooking, then drain. In a large sauté pan, melt the butter over medium heat. Add the carrots and toss to coat; cook until heated through. Stir in the parsley and season to taste with salt and pepper.

TO PLATE

MOUND the mashed potatoes in the center of each plate. Top with sliced beef and drizzle with blackberry sauce.

WHAT'S WITH WELLINGTON?

Beef Wellington is a dish *Hell's Kitchen* aficionados are well acquainted with, as it makes its way onto the menu almost every episode. This seared filet of steak wrapped in buttery puff pastry is a British culinary tour de force, and one of *Hell's Kitchen's* absolute favorites. It's also one of the more challenging dishes contestants are tasked with making, a true test of a chef's mettle. Many less than perfect Wellingtons—undercooked, overcooked, falling apart—have been sent back.

Practice makes a perfect Wellington, and the most crucial component is timing. The *Hell's Kitchen* recipe instructs you on how to make your Wellington in the comfort of your own home, bypassing the pressure tests and fear of elimination, with your guests and your own discerning palate as the judges of your success.

OVEN-ROASTED PORK CHOPS WITH APPLE BUTTER, CIDER-BRAISED KALE, AND PORK JUS

SERVES 4

In recent years, kale has become a superstar vegetable. When you pair it with bacon, it only gets better. To avoid overcooked, dry pork chops, we marinate ours in a flavorful brine with juniper berries and black peppercorns (note that you'll need to plan ahead, up to overnight, for the brining). The pork chops are cooked *au jus*, or in their own juices, as we cooked the Lemon and Thyme Roasted Chicken Breast on page 110. Taking off from a pork-chops-and-applesauce theme, we finish the dish with a dollop of apple butter for concentrated apple flavor.

PORK CHOP WITH PORK JUS

¼ cup kosher salt

¼ cup packed dark brown sugar

½ cup boiling water

3 cups cold water

2 teaspoons juniper berries

1 teaspoon whole black peppercorns

½ head garlic, halved crosswise

4 sprigs thyme

4 bone-in, center-cut pork chops, ¾ inch thick

3 tablespoons unsalted butter, divided

1 medium onion, chopped

½ cup white verjus or dry white wine

1 cup brown chicken stock, store-bought or homemade

BRAISED KALE

2 slices smoked bacon, diced

1 large shallot, thinly sliced

1 pound lacinato kale, thick stems removed, roughly chopped

⅓ cup apple cider or apple juice

1 tablespoon apple cider vinegar

Kosher salt and freshly ground black pepper

1 cup store-bought apple butter

FOR THE PORK CHOP BRINE

IN a large bowl, combine the salt and sugar. Add the boiling water, stirring until dissolved. Then add the cold water and 1 cup ice cubes to cool down the mixture. Add the juniper berries, black peppercorns, garlic, and thyme.

PLACE the pork chops in a zipper-lock bag. Pour the brine over the pork chops and seal the bag. Place the bag in a bowl and refrigerate for at least 4 hours or overnight.

FOR BRAISED KALE

HEAT a large saucepot or Dutch oven over moderate heat. Add the bacon and cook 15 minutes or until crisp. Remove the bacon from the pan with a slotted spoon and drain on a paper-towel-lined plate.

DRAIN all but 1 teaspoon of fat from the pan.

ADD shallot and sauté 3–4 minutes or until tender, stirring occasionally. Add kale and cook 5 minutes or until wilted, stirring frequently. Add apple cider and vinegar; cover the pan and cook 7–8 minutes, stirring occasionally. Season to taste with salt and pepper. Crumble the bacon and stir it into the kale.

FOR THE PORK CHOPS AND JUS

PREHEAT the oven to 450°F. Place a rack in the lower third of the oven.

REMOVE the chops, discard the brine, pat the chops dry, and season both sides with salt and pepper.

HEAT 2 tablespoons butter in a large, heavy skillet, preferably cast-iron, over moderately high heat until foam subsides. Add the pork chops and brown, turning once, about 4 minutes on one side, 3 minutes on the other. Transfer the chops to a large, shallow baking pan that can hold the pork in one layer.

PLACE the pork chops in lower third of oven and roast until the internal temperature reaches 150°F, 12–15 minutes.

WHILE the pork chops roast, make the jus. In the same skillet, add the onion and remaining tablespoon butter to skillet and cook over moderate heat,

(continued)

turning occasionally, until golden brown and tender, about 6 minutes. Add verjus and scrape up the brown bits from the bottom of the pan. Boil and reduce until the wine is reduced by half. Add the stock and cook until the sauce is thickened and reduced by about half. Strain through a fine mesh strainer, pressing down on the onions with the back of a spoon to get out all of the jus. Adjust the seasoning and keep warm.

TRANSFER the pork chops to a plate or cutting board, tent them with foil, and allow them to rest before serving.

TO PLATE

MOUND the braised kale in the center of each plate. Top with pork chop and a dollop of apple butter. Drizzle with jus and serve with Dauphinoise Potatoes (see page 184).

BROWN CHICKEN STOCK

YIELDS 6 CUPS

The secret to a fabulous soup or stew is a long-cooked, heavily seasoned stock. Cartilage-rich chicken wings give wonderful body to this stock, and browning the wings before adding them to the stockpot gives an extra layer of flavor. Caramelizing vegetables and then deglazing the pot with an extra-generous glug of wine further elevates the stock and any dish you add it to.

Extra stock can be cooled, divided into zipper-lock freezer bags, and frozen for later use. Or freeze your stock in ice cube trays; remove the frozen stock cubes, store them in a freezer bag, and pop them into recipes that call for just a small amount of stock.

5 pounds chicken wings

3 medium onions, chopped

3 carrots, chopped

3 celery stalks with leaves, chopped

2 cups dry white wine

4–6 sprigs fresh thyme

10 black peppercorns

2–3 bay leaves

PREHEAT the oven to 450°F.

IN a large roasting pan or rondo, roast the chicken wings for 45–60 minutes or until golden brown.

TRANSFER the wings to a large 6-quart stockpot, leaving all of the fat in the pan. Place the roasting pan over medium-high heat on the stovetop. Add the onions, carrots, and celery and cook them for 20–25 minutes or until they are caramelized.

WHEN the vegetables are ready, add the wine, scrape up the brown bits, and reduce until almost dry, 20–25 minutes.

ADD the vegetables to the stockpot with the thyme, peppercorns, and bay leaves. Add 4 quarts of water, enough to cover everything completely. Partially cover the pot and bring to a low simmer. Cook for 3 hours.

STRAIN the stock into large bowl, allow to cool, and refrigerate overnight. Remove the fat and store for further use.

PECAN-CRUSTED MAHI MAHI WITH EDAMAME SUCCOTASH AND MAPLE BUTTER

SERVES 4

We put a twist on succotash by swapping in edamame—fresh young soybeans—for the traditional lima beans, with vibrant-tasting results. Fresh edamame can be found at the occasional farmers' market; if you see it, grab a bunch and pop the beans out of their pods and into your succotash. Pecans make a crunchy coating for the fish, and maple syrup–infused butter adds a deep, rich finish to the dish. Mahi mahi, also known as dolphinfish (no relation to the mammal) or dorado, is a flavorful, firm-fleshed fish. If unavailable, you can substitute monkfish, swordfish, tuna, or catfish.

EDAMAME SUCCOTASH

1 slice thick-cut bacon, cut into small dice

1 cup yellow onion, cut into small dice

1 tablespoon olive oil

½ tablespoon unsalted butter

8 ounces frozen sweet corn

6 ounces frozen shelled edamame

½ cup diced red bell pepper

¼ cup low sodium chicken broth, store-bought or homemade

1 tablespoon red wine vinegar

½ cup diced grape tomatoes

½ teaspoon sugar

Kosher salt and freshly ground black pepper

1 tablespoon chopped chives, plus more for garnish

2 tablespoons torn basil

PECAN-CRUSTED MAHI MAHI

¾ cup pecans, crushed

1½ tablespoons all-purpose flour

1 large egg

Kosher salt and freshly ground black pepper

1 teaspoon olive oil

Four 6-ounce mahi mahi fillets

MAPLE BUTTER

2 tablespoons maple syrup

½ stick unsalted butter

Kosher salt and freshly ground black pepper

Fresh chives, chopped on the bias, for garnish

FOR THE EDAMAME SUCCOTASH

IN a medium-to-large skillet fitted with a lid, cook the bacon over moderate heat until it's crisp. Use a slotted spoon to transfer the bacon to a small bowl and reserve.

ADD the onion to the skillet and sauté until soft, about 5 minutes. Increase the heat to medium. Add the oil, butter, and corn and cook another 5 minutes until the corn begins to brown. Add the edamame and red pepper; sauté 3–4 minutes. Stir in the broth and vinegar and, with a wooden spoon, scrape up the brown bits from the bottom of the pan. Add the tomatoes, sugar, and reserved bacon. Season with salt and pepper and stir well to combine. Cover the pan and remove from the heat. Five minutes before serving, place pan with succotash over medium heat until warmed through. Stir in the chives and basil.

FOR THE MAHI MAHI

PREHEAT the oven 400°F.

WITH a large sharp knife, chop the pecans until they resemble a coarse meal. Mix the pecans with flour in a shallow pan.

WHISK the egg with the oil and season with salt and pepper.

PAT the fillets dry with a paper towel and season with salt and pepper. Lightly brush each fillet with the egg mixture and then dip each filet into the pecan mixture, pressing well to coat both sides.

LINE a baking sheet with parchment paper brushed with a little oil. Place the fillets on the sheet and bake for 12 to 14 minutes, depending on the thickness of your fish, or until the fish flakes easily with a fork.

FOR THE MAPLE BUTTER

WHILE the fish is cooking, bring the maple syrup to a simmer in a small saucepan over medium heat. Swirl in the butter and season with salt and pepper.

TO PLATE

MOUND the edamame succotash in the center of each plate. Top with a fish fillet and drizzle with maple butter. Garnish with chives.

BRICK CHICKEN WITH HERB GREMOLATA

SERVES 4

Brick chicken, or "chicken under a brick," is your ticket to chicken that's crisp on the outside, tender on the inside, and cooked in half the time as it takes to roast it in the oven. To brick chicken, you'll first employ a technique called spatchcocking, which is simply removing the chicken's backbone. Then the chicken goes into a hot pan skin side down and is topped with a heavy weight—if you don't have a brick or two handy, a second heavy skillet will work just as well. The weight enables the skin to crisp, with the fats and juices that are rendered cooking the flesh into succulent and juicy deliciousness.

Gremolata is a classic herb condiment using lemon peel, garlic, and mixed herbs. It is traditionally served with veal, as in the classic Italian dish ossobuco. You might also try it with a simple seafood dish to add a note of brightness to the plate.

GREMOLATA

1 tablespoon finely minced lemon peel

¼ cup finely minced parsley

1 tablespoon fresh tarragon

2 teaspoons finely minced garlic

BRICK CHICKEN

1 whole 3- to 4-pound chicken, backbone removed, trimmed of excess fat, rinsed, and dried

Kosher salt and freshly ground black pepper to taste

2 tablespoons extra virgin olive oil, divided

1 lemon, cut into quarters

FOR THE GREMOLATA

MIX ingredients in a small bowl and set aside.

FOR THE BRICK CHICKEN

PREHEAT the oven to 500°F.

MIX 1 tablespoon olive oil and salt and pepper together in a small bowl. Place the chicken on a cutting board, skin side down. Using your hands, press down firmly on the breastbone to flatten the breast. Brush the chicken on both sides with the olive oil mixture.

HEAT an ovenproof skillet (preferably nonstick if you have one) large enough to hold the flattened chicken over medium-high heat for about 3 minutes. Put remaining olive oil in the pan and wait about 30 seconds for it to heat up.

PLACE the chicken in the skillet, skin side down; weight it with another skillet or with one or two bricks wrapped in aluminum foil. The idea is to flatten the chicken by applying weight evenly over its surface.

COOK over medium-high heat for 5 minutes, then transfer to the oven. Roast for 15 minutes more. Take the pan out of the oven and remove the weights; turn the chicken over and roast 10–15 minutes more, or until the juices run clear or an instant-read thermometer inserted into the thickest part of the thigh registers 165°F.

TO PLATE

SERVE the chicken topped with herb gremolata and lemon wedges on the side (or cut the chicken into parts and serve with herb gremolata and lemon wedges).

BAKED COD WITH GREEN-OLIVE CRUST, MARINATED BELL PEPPERS, CAPER-AND-RAISIN PUREE

SERVES 4

This dish makes a show-stopping presentation, but if you manage your time—preparing the caper-and-raisin puree and olive crust while the bell peppers are marinating and the oven is preheating, or prepping all the components a day ahead—it can be put together in under an hour, perfect for a weeknight dinner with a heavy dose of the "wow" factor.

GREEN-OLIVE CRUST

5 ounces (1 cup) green olives, pitted

5 ounces day-old brioche, torn into chunks

1¾ ounces (1½ tablespoons) butter, softened

Parsley

MARINATED BELL PEPPERS

1 tablespoon olive oil

1 yellow pepper, seeded and cut into ¼-inch strips

1 red pepper, seeded and cut into ¼-inch strips

1 tablespoon chopped fresh thyme leaves

2 garlic cloves, crushed

CLASSIC VINAIGRETTE

¼ cup white wine vinegar

¾ cup extra virgin olive oil

Kosher salt and freshly ground pepper

CAPER-AND-RAISIN PUREE

2½ tablespoons capers, rinsed

2½ tablespoons golden raisins

2 tablespoons unsalted butter

Kosher salt and freshly ground pepper

BROILED COD

Four 6-ounce cod fillets

1 tablespoon olive oil

Kosher salt and freshly ground pepper

FOR THE GREEN-OLIVE CRUST

COMBINE the olives, brioche, butter, and parsley in a food processor, pulsing until just combined, taking care not to turn it into a paste. Refrigerate until needed.

FOR THE MARINATED BELL PEPPERS

HEAT oil in a large nonstick skillet over moderate heat. Add bell peppers, thyme, and garlic cloves and season with salt and pepper. Cook, stirring occasionally, until peppers are just tender, about 10 minutes. Transfer to a bowl.

IN a separate bowl, whisk together the white wine vinegar, olive oil, and salt and pepper. Pour the vinaigrette over the pepper to cover. Set aside to marinate.

FOR THE CAPER-AND-RAISIN PUREE

COMBINE the capers, raisins, butter, and 4 tablespoons of water in a small saucepan. Bring to a very low simmer and cook for 10 minutes, making sure the liquid is not evaporating. Remove from heat, cool slightly, and puree with an immersion blender.

FOR THE BROILED COD

PREHEAT the oven to 400° for 15 minutes.

BRUSH both sides of the fillets with olive oil and season to taste with salt and pepper. Arrange the fillets on a parchment-lined baking sheet. Top the fillets with the olive mixture, pressing gently. Bake for 12–15 minutes, until the fillets are just tender and opaque inside.

TO PLATE

MOUND the marinated peppers in the center of each plate. Top with cod fillet garnished with the caper relish.

CHICKEN-FRIED RIB-EYE WITH YUKON GOLD MASHED POTATOES AND WHITE TRUFFLE CREAM GRAVY

SERVES 4

Folks from certain parts of the country will be surprised to learn that there's no chicken to be found in chicken-fried steak. Also known as country-fried steak, this breaded and fried steak (named for the leftover fat from frying chicken) is the ultimate in Southern comfort food. In keeping with the *Hell's Kitchen* tradition of combining comfort food with fine dining, this down-home classic has been decked out: We finish the dish with a luxurious truffle oil–anointed gravy and serve it with a side of indulgently creamy Yukon Gold mashed potatoes. Try this dish as part of the Modern South (page 244) menu.

YUKON MASHED POTATOES

1 ¾ pounds Yukon Gold potatoes, peeled and cut into 1-inch cubes

Kosher salt and freshly ground black pepper

1 cup cream

3 tablespoons unsalted butter, softened

CHICKEN-FRIED STEAK AND GRAVY

2 cups all-purpose flour, divided

Kosher salt and freshly ground black pepper

2 large eggs, lightly beaten

Vegetable oil

4 thinly sliced (⅓-inch thick) boneless rib-eye steaks, trimmed of fat

1 teaspoon garlic powder

3 cups whole milk

¼–½ teaspoon white truffle oil

Chopped fresh flat-leaf parsley, for garnish

FOR THE MASHED POTATOES

PUT the potatoes in a large saucepan and cover with cold water by two inches. Add ½ teaspoon of salt and bring to a boil. Lower the heat to simmer, cover the pot partially, and cook until the potatoes are very tender when tested with the tip of a sharp paring knife, 25–30 minutes.

DRAIN the potatoes, reserving some of the cooking water.

COMBINE the cream and butter in a small saucepan over medium heat and bring to a simmer.

PUT the potatoes through a potato ricer or food mill and return them to the pot over low heat. Add the hot cream-and-butter mixture and mix with a wooden spoon. If the potatoes are too thick, add a small amount of the reserved cooking water until they are the consistency you like, or use a hand mixer for a smoother texture. Season to taste with salt and pepper and set aside to keep warm.

FOR THE CHICKEN-FRIED STEAK AND GRAVY

SET up two shallow bowls, one with 1 ¾ cups flour seasoned with salt and pepper, one with the eggs. In a large, deep cast-iron skillet, pour in enough oil to coat the bottom of the pan and begin to come about a quarter inch up the sides. Test that the oil is hot enough by putting the handle end of a wooden spoon into the oil. If the oil bubbles vigorously around the handle, it's ready. Season the steak with salt, pepper, and garlic powder. Dredge in flour, shaking off the excess, then put the steak into the egg and back into flour. Once the oil is hot, carefully add two of the steaks to the pan and fry until brown and crispy, 4 minutes on one side, 3 minutes on the other. Use tongs to transfer the streaks to a paper-towel-lined cookie sheet to drain. Repeat with the remaining two steaks.

POUR off all but 4 tablespoons of the frying oil and return the pot to the stove over low heat. Whisk in the remaining ¼ cup flour to the pan. Use a wooden spoon to continue stirring continuously until the mixture becomes a golden color. Slowly whisk in the milk, then season to taste with salt and pepper. Add the truffle oil and serve over the steak.

TO PLATE

PLACE the mashed potatoes in the center of each plate. Rest the steak over some of the potatoes and top with gravy. Garnish with chopped parsley.

FILET OF BEEF AU GRATIN, TRUFFLE POMMES ANNA, BRAISED SALSIFY, AND PEARL ONIONS

SERVES 4

Pommes Anna, "Anna's potatoes," is a French gratin dish dating back to the time of Napoleon III. These potatoes are very thinly sliced and arranged in circular layers in a heavily buttered skillet, with additional butter drizzled between the layers. Here we swap in some luxurious truffle oil, and to put your pommes over the top, you're invited to shave a bit of fresh truffle into the dish.

Tender filet of beef also gets served au gratin, baked in a sauce of egg yolk–enriched cream and Parmesan that includes a medley of mushrooms. Salsify, a winter root that looks like a stick and is related to parsnip, has a flavor reminiscent of oysters, a taste that plays off the earthiness of the mushrooms. To lighten up or simplify this dish, skip the salsify and swap in a mixed green salad.

POMMES ANNA

2½ pounds new potatoes, peeled and sliced very thin, preferably on a mandoline

2 tablespoons unsalted butter, melted

Kosher salt and white pepper

1¼ teaspoons truffle oil

Shaved truffle, optional

BRAISED PEARL ONIONS AND SALSIFY

Juice of 1 lemon

4 salsify, about 8 inches (2 ounces) each

2 tablespoons olive oil

1 tablespoon unsalted butter

1 pound frozen white pearl onions, defrosted, drained, and patted dry

Kosher salt and freshly ground black pepper

½ cup beef or chicken stock, store-bought or homemade

1 bay leaf

1 sprig thyme

2 sprigs flat-leaf parsley, plus more for garnish

FOR THE POMMES ANNA

PREHEAT the oven to 425°F with the rack in the middle of the oven.

POUR the melted butter into a 10-inch cast-iron skillet, swirling it around so it covers the bottom and comes about a quarter inch up the sides of the pan. Beginning in the center, arrange the potatoes in a circular pattern in the pan, overlapping. Sprinkle with salt and pepper and drizzle with ¼ teaspoon truffle oil and shaved truffle (if using). Repeat layers 3–4 times, ending with truffle oil. Press the potatoes firmly to pack. Cook over medium-high heat for 3 minutes without stirring.

COVER the pan with foil and bake in the oven 30 minutes. Then uncover and bake 20–25 minutes more, until the potatoes are golden brown and tender when pierced with a sharp paring knife. Loosen the edges of potatoes with a spatula or knife. Place a plate upside down on top of pan; invert potatoes onto plate.

FOR THE BRAISED PEARL ONIONS AND SALSIFY

WHILE the potatoes are in the oven, braise the onions and salsify.

PREPARE a bowl of cold water and lemon juice, also called acidulated water. Trim both ends of the salsify root. Peel the salsify with a vegetable peeler and cut in to 2-inch pieces. Drop the salsify into the bowl of acidulated water so it doesn't turn brown.

REMOVE salsify from the water and pat dry. Heat 1 tablespoon of olive oil in a large sauté pan over medium heat. Add the salsify and cook, stirring occasionally, until it begins to turn golden, 4–5 minutes. Season to taste with salt and pepper. Remove from the pan and set aside.

WIPE out the pan, return it to the stove over medium-high heat, and add the remaining tablespoon of olive oil and the butter. Add the pearl onions

FILET OF BEEF AU GRATIN

¼ cup olive oil, divided

1 shallot, finely chopped

1 garlic clove, crushed

3½ ounces mixed mushrooms (shiitake, oyster), roughly chopped

3½ ounces crimini mushrooms, roughly chopped

¼ cup heavy cream

1 large egg yolk, lightly beaten

2 tablespoons fresh minced chives

3 tablespoons freshly grated Parmesan cheese, divided

Kosher salt and freshly ground black pepper

4 filet steaks, about 6½ ounces each and 1½ inches thick

and sauté until the onions begin to brown evenly on all sides, 8–10 minutes. Add the salsify, stock, bay leaf, thyme, and parsley, cover the pan, and cook 25 minutes until the onions are tender and most of the stock has evaporated. Remove the thyme and parsley, season to taste with salt and pepper, and keep warm.

FOR THE FILET AU BEEF AU GRATIN

INCREASE the oven to 450°F and move the rack to the center of the oven.

IN a large sauté pan, heat 2 tablespoons of olive oil over moderate heat. Add the shallot and garlic and sauté until translucent and tender, about 3 minutes. Add the mushrooms, stir so they are well coated, increase the heat to medium-high, and leave in a single layer, undisturbed, for 5 minutes until the mushrooms are browned. Stir and continue cooking for another 2–3 minutes until the mushrooms are browned all over and there is no liquid in the pan. Remove the garlic clove and transfer the mushrooms to a bowl to cool.

USING a whisk, whip the cream until soft peaks form.

FOLD in the mushrooms along with the egg yolk, chives, and a tablespoon of the grated Parmesan, then season with salt and pepper. Set aside.

SEASON the steaks with salt and pepper.

HEAT a large cast-iron or nonstick frying pan until hot—but not smoking—and add the steaks. Cook about 3–4 minutes total time, turning them to brown all over. Remove from the pan.

PUT the steaks in a shallow baking tray. Pile the mushroom mixture on top of the steaks and dust with the remaining Parmesan. Cook in the oven, uncovered, for 7–9 minutes until the steak is rare (internal temperature 120°F) and the topping is golden.

TO PLATE

DIVIDE the steaks among 4 plates. Serve with a slice of Pommes Anna and the braised vegetables. Garnish with a sprig of parsley.

HERB-CRUSTED RACK OF LAMB, WARM SUNDRIED TOMATO TAPENADE, BRUSSELS SPROUTS, CONFIT POTATOES

SERVES 4

To "confit" is to cook a food slowly over low heat in oil or fat. Most of us are familiar with duck confit, but potatoes can be cooked in this manner as well, with succulent results. Duck fat is generally available at butcher shops, or use the fat saved from cooking duck (see page 103 or 105); it freezes well. Brussels sprouts are roasted until crisp on the outside and tender on the inside, making this a vegetable everyone can love. The lamb, heavily seasoned with herbs and Parmesan, makes a phenomenal presentation. Bring out your finest tableware, carve it up, and get ready to celebrate!

CONFIT POTATOES

1 pound fingerling potatoes

1 garlic clove, minced

1 shallot, roughly chopped

6 sprigs fresh thyme

Olive oil or duck fat, to cover

Kosher salt and freshly ground black pepper

ROASTED BRUSSELS SPROUTS

1 pound Brussels sprouts, outer leaves discarded and ends trimmed but kept whole

2 tablespoons extra virgin olive oil

Kosher salt and freshly ground black pepper

SUNDRIED TOMATO KALAMATA OLIVE TAPENDADE

2–3 anchovy fillets, finely chopped

1 large garlic clove, minced

½ teaspoon fresh finely chopped rosemary

2 teaspoons extra virgin olive oil

8 sundried tomatoes, chopped

8 pitted Kalamata olives, rough chopped

FOR THE CONFIT POTATOES

PLACE the potatoes, garlic, shallot, and thyme in a medium saucepan. Cover the potatoes with olive oil (or duck fat if using) and bring to a slow simmer over medium heat. Cook the potatoes until just tender, 30–35 minutes. Allow the potatoes to cool in the oil, then drain and place in a bowl. Slice each in half, lengthwise.

FOR THE ROASTED BRUSSELS SPROUTS

WHILE the potatoes are cooking, preheat the oven to 425°F.

DISCARD the outer leaves of the Brussels sprouts and trim the ends, but keep the sprouts whole. Slice in half. Toss them in a bowl with olive oil and season to taste with salt and pepper. Pour the Brussels sprouts onto a rimmed baking sheet lined with parchment paper. Roast 30 minutes or until the sprouts are crispy on the outside and fork tender on the inside, tossing occasionally to ensure even cooking.

KEEP the oven at 425°F for the lamb.

FOR THE SUNDRIED TOMATO KALAMATA OLIVE TAPENADE

USING a mortar and pestle, mash the anchovy, garlic, and rosemary together with oil to form a paste.

TRANSFER this mixture to a small saucepan and add the tomatoes and olives. Add enough olive oil to cover, and over low heat warm the mixture. Be sure it doesn't simmer. Once hot, remove from the heat and set aside to cool.

FOR THE LAMB

GENEROUSLY season the lamb with salt and pepper.

IN a large skillet, heat 2 tablespoons olive oil. Add one of the lamb racks and sear all sides until brown. Remove the lamb from the pan and transfer it to a shallow baking dish, large enough to hold both racks. Add second rack and repeat. When both racks of lamb are browned, place the pan in the oven and roast 10 minutes.

MEANWHILE, make the crust. Place the breadcrumbs, Parmesan, parsley, thyme, cilantro, rosemary, and the remaining 2 teaspoons olive oil in a food

LAMB

2 racks of lamb, 1¼–1½ pounds each

Kosher salt and freshly ground black pepper

2 tablespoons plus 2 teaspoons olive oil

4 slices stale bread made into breadcrumbs, or 1 cup panko breadcrumbs

½ cup grated Parmesan cheese

Leaves from 1 sprig parsley

Leaves from 1 sprig thyme

Leaves from 1 sprig cilantro

Leaves from 1 sprig rosemary

processor. Pulse several times until well combined. Transfer the mixture to a bowl and shallow dish and set aside.

REMOVE the lamb from the oven and brush it generously with mustard.

PAT the crust mixture all over the lamb, coating it completely and evenly.

RETURN pan to the oven and continue roasting for 15–20 minutes more or until an internal temperature of 125°F (medium rare) is reached. Remove pan from the oven and allow to rest for 15 minutes before serving.

TO PLATE

DIVIDE the potatoes and Brussels sprouts in the center of the plate.

SLICE the rack of lamb and serve three chops per plate on top of the potatoes and Brussels sprouts. Garnish with tapenade.

GRILLED LAMB CHOPS WITH SAUTÉED LINGUINE AND TOMATO BROTH

SERVES 4

To "french" a rack of lamb means to remove the meat, fat, and membranes that connect the individual rib bones from the rack to expose the bones. It makes for a high-end restaurant presentation, and if you haven't yet made it through cooking school, all you have to do is ask the butcher to french your lamb for you.

The key to tender lamb is to avoid overcooking it; remove it from the grill as soon as it hits 120°F, as it will continue to cook a bit as it rests. Rosemary and garlic bring out the most in the lamb, and a Mediterranean mix of vegetables and linguine serves as a bed for your luscious lamb chops, with tomato broth poured just before serving to complete the dish.

LAMB CHOPS

8 rib lamb chops (3 ounces each), frenched

Kosher salt and freshly ground black pepper

2 sprigs rosemary, minced

1 large garlic clove, minced

½ cup of extra virgin olive oil

LINGUINE

½ pound linguini

TOMATO BROTH

2 tablespoons olive oil

1 shallot, minced

1 garlic clove, minced

½ cup white wine

1 cup canned roasted diced tomatoes, with juice

¾ cup chicken stock

2 sprigs rosemary leaves (1 tablespoon), minced

Kosher salt and freshly ground black pepper

VEGETABLES

2 tablespoons unsalted butter

1 garlic clove, minced

Pinch dried oregano

1 tablespoon pine nuts

4 asparagus spears, trimmed and cut into thirds

1 small red pepper, finely diced

¼ cup (about 8) sundried tomatoes, packed in oil, sliced

¼ cup canned artichoke, cut into quarters

5 Kalamata olives, pitted and halved

½ cup dry white wine

Kosher salt and freshly ground black pepper

2 tablespoons feta cheese, crumbled

FOR THE LAMB MARINADE

IN small bowl combine salt, pepper, garlic, rosemary, and olive oil. Put the lamb chops in a shallow dish and pour the olive oil mixture cover the lamb chops. Cover and allow to marinate while you prepare the rest of the components of the dish.

FOR THE PASTA

BRING a large pot of salted water to a boil. Add the linguine and cook according the package directions for al dente. Drain and set aside.

FOR THE TOMATO BROTH

IN a medium skillet, heat olive oil over moderate heat. Add the shallots and garlic and sauté until tender, about 3 minutes. Add white wine, tomatoes, and stock. Season to taste with salt, pepper, and rosemary. Adjust heat and simmer gently for 10 minutes. Strain through a fine mesh strainer and reserve.

FOR THE VEGETABLES

MELT the butter in a large skillet over medium heat. Add the garlic and cook 1 minute. Add oregano and pine nuts and cook until they begin to turn golden brown, 2–3 minutes. Add peppers, asparagus, sundried tomatoes, artichokes, and olives and cook 5 minutes until the peppers and artichokes

(continued)

begin to get tender. Add wine and cook for 2 minutes, then add the linguine and season to taste with salt and pepper.

FOR THE LAMB CHOPS

WHILE the vegetables are cooking, preheat the grill or a grill pan over medium-high heat. Remove the lamb chops from the marinade and season with salt and pepper. Place on the grill, 4–5 minutes on each side until the internal temperature is 120°F for medium rare.

TO PLATE

PLATE the pasta and sautéed vegetables in center of each bowl and top with two lamb chops crossed in front. Ladle tomato broth into bowl and lightly atop lamb. Top with feta cheese.

DUCK BREAST WITH FIVE-SPICE BRAISED ENDIVE AND PARSNIP PUREE

SERVES 4

Duck and orange are well-suited partners, most notably in the classic roasted duck *à l'orange*. Here we cook the duck on the stovetop (see page 105 for tips on cooking your duck to perfection), bathed in a generous amount of the orange-flavored cognac Grand Marnier. Earthy, creamy mashed parsnips are served on the side, accompanied by braised endive seasoned with aromatic five-spice powder. The powder—used primarily in Chinese cuisine—is a mix of star anise, cloves, Chinese cinnamon, Sichuan pepper, and fennel seeds.

PARSNIP PUREE

4 tablespoons butter

1 ¼ pounds parsnips (about 4 medium parsnips), peeled and cut into ½-inch pieces

½ cup heavy cream

Kosher salt and freshly ground black pepper

BRAISED ENDIVE

3–4 tablespoons butter

½ teaspoon powdered sugar

¼ teaspoon Chinese five-spice powder

2 large endives, trimmed and cut in half lengthwise

½ cup Grand Marnier or Cointreau

¾ cup orange juice, strained of any pulp

DUCK BREAST

4 duck breasts, about 8 ounces each, skins on

Kosher salt and freshly ground black pepper

1 tablespoon unsalted butter

1 tablespoon olive oil

1 shallot, minced

2 garlic cloves, minced

2 cups Grand Marnier

3 cups chicken stock, store-bought or homemade

1 star anise

1 sprig thyme

FOR THE PARSNIP PUREE

MELT the butter in a small saucepan over a moderate heat. Add the parsnips and cream and cook, covered, until completely soft and falling apart, about 25–30 minutes. Season to taste with salt and pepper. Transfer the parsnips and the liquid to a blender and puree until smooth. Keep warm.

FOR THE ENDIVE

MELT the butter in a large sauté pan over medium. Combine the powdered sugar and five-spice powder and dust the cut sides of the endive with the mixture. Add to the pan, cut side down, and sauté gently for about 2 minutes or until the endive starts to turn golden brown and caramelize. Flip it over and add the Grand Marnier, cooking for a minute or two to burn off the alcohol. Then add the orange juice, cover the pan, and allow to braise for 4 minutes until the endive is just tender with a slight crunch in the middle. Season with salt and pepper. Transfer the endive to a plate and keep warm.

FOR THE DUCK BREAST

USING a small sharp knife, score the duck skin in crosshatch pattern (do not pierce meat).

SEASON the duck breasts with salt and pepper and place them skin side down in a large sauté pan over medium-high heat. Add duck, skin side down, and cook until skin is browned and crisp and most of the fat is rendered, 10 minutes. Turn duck breasts over, reduce heat to medium, and cook until browned and cooked to desired doneness, about 4 minutes longer for rare and 6–7 minutes longer for medium rare. Transfer to a plate and tent with foil to keep warm and let rest 10 minutes while you make the sauce.

WIPE out the sauté pan and return it to the stove. Add the butter and oil over moderate heat. Add the shallots and garlic and cook until the shallots are tender translucent, about 3 minutes. Add the Grand Marnier, scraping up any loose bits from the pan, and cook for 2 minutes to burn off alcohol. Add the chicken stock, star anise, and thyme sprig and raise heat to medium. Simmer until the sauce is reduced and thick enough to coat the back of a spoon. Season to taste with salt and pepper.

TO PLATE

MOUND the puree in the center of each plate. Top with the sliced duck and drizzle with pan sauce. Serve with braised endive.

DUCK BREAST WITH WALNUT-GRAPE COMPOTE

SERVES 4

Duck must be cooked to a perfect rare to medium rare to truly shine—a minute or two more and it goes from succulent to dry. To successfully prepare your duck, score the skin in a crosshatch fashion, season it, and cook it skin side down without moving it until most of the fat is rendered, then flip it and cook it briefly to desired doneness, keeping your eyes on the pan all the time. We take a shortcut using instant polenta, as it cooks in just five minutes but gives all the flavor of long-cooked polenta (chef's secret!), and sweeten the dish with a walnut-grape compote that's bursting with herby flavor.

WALNUT-GRAPE COMPOTE

1 tablespoon olive oil

3 large shallots, peeled and minced

Kosher salt and freshly ground black pepper

2 large garlic cloves, minced

2 cups chicken stock (you can also use duck or veal stock if you have some)

1 cup dry red wine

6 ounces (1¼ cups) red seedless grapes, halved

2 teaspoons chopped fresh thyme

2 teaspoons chopped fresh rosemary

4 ounces (1 cup) chopped and toasted walnut halves

DUCK BREAST

Four 8-ounce boneless duck breasts, skin on

Kosher salt and freshly cracked black pepper

POLENTA

1 garlic clove, peeled

2 cups chicken stock

1 cup half-and-half

2 teaspoons chopped fresh thyme

2 teaspoons chopped fresh rosemary

1 cup instant polenta

¼ cup mascarpone cheese

¼ cup Parmesan cheese

3 tablespoons unsalted butter

Kosher salt and freshly ground black pepper

FOR THE WALNUT-GRAPE COMPOTE

HEAT olive oil in a medium sauté pan over medium-low heat. Add the shallots, season with salt and pepper, and cook until tender, 3 minutes. Add the minced garlic and cook one minute. Increase the heat to medium, add the stock and wine, and simmer until the sauce coats the back of a spoon and is reduced by almost two-thirds. Lower the heat, stir in the grapes, thyme, and rosemary, and cook until heated through. Season to taste with salt and pepper. Remove from the heat and stir in ½ cup of the chopped walnuts. Set aside.

FOR THE DUCK BREAST

WHILE the compote is reducing, prepare the duck. Using a small, sharp knife, score the duck skin in crosshatch pattern (do not pierce meat). Season the duck breasts with salt and pepper and place, skin side down, in a large sauté pan over medium-high heat. Add duck, skin side down, and cook until skin is browned and crisp and most of the fat is rendered, 10 minutes. Turn duck breasts over, reduce heat to medium, and cook to desired doneness, about 4 minutes longer for rare and 6–7 minutes longer for medium-rare. Transfer to a plate, tent with foil, and let rest 10 minutes.

FOR THE POLENTA

WHILE the duck is resting, make the polenta. In a medium saucepan, combine the garlic clove, chicken stock, and the half-and-half over medium heat. Bring to a simmer. Remove the garlic clove, season to taste with salt and pepper, and add the thyme and rosemary. Add the polenta in a slow, steady stream, whisking constantly. Reduce heat to medium-low and continue stirring with a wooden spoon until smooth and thickened, about 4–5 minutes. Remove from the heat and stir in the mascarpone, Parmesan, and butter. Taste for seasoning and serve.

TO PLATE

MOUND the polenta in the middle of each plate. Slice and fan the duck over the polenta and drizzle with compote and pan juices. Garnish with the remaining ½ cup of walnuts for crunch.

HERB OIL–POACHED HALIBUT WITH POTATO-FENNEL PUREE, ROASTED TOMATOES, AND LEMON-FENNEL SAUCE

SERVES 4

Poaching fish in oil ensures the most tender results, with the herbs infusing their flavor as it cooks. Fennel is a classic flavoring for fish. Here we include both a fennel-infused potato puree and a lemon-fennel sauce spiked with the anise-flavored liqueur Pernod. Although this dish includes four distinct elements, it's completely doable if you manage your time well: while the tomatoes are in the oven, work on the potato-fennel puree and sauce and, toward the end, poach the fish. There's a lot going on, but if you've mastered your mise-en-place (see page 23), you'll pull this one off with ease. You'll find this dish in the Light Summer Supper menu (page 246).

ROASTED TOMATOES

4 plum tomatoes, cut in half lengthwise, seeds and juice removed

Kosher salt and freshly ground black pepper

2 tablespoons olive oil

4 sprigs thyme

2 sprigs rosemary

2 garlic cloves, crushed

POTATO-FENNEL PUREE

1 tablespoon olive oil

1 small fennel bulb, trimmed, sliced, core removed

½ shallot, rough chopped

5 fennel seeds

2 tablespoons plus ½ cup heavy cream

¾ pound Yukon Gold potatoes, peeled, cut into 1-inch cubes

1½ tablespoons unsalted butter

Kosher salt and freshly ground black pepper

HERB OIL–POACHED HALIBUT

3-4 cups extra virgin olive oil

4 garlic cloves, crushed

1 sprig sage

4 sprigs rosemary

4 sprigs thyme

Four 7-ounce halibut fillets

Kosher salt and freshly ground b lack pepper

FOR THE ROASTED TOMATOES

PREHEAT the oven to 425°F.

ARRANGE tomato halves, cut side up, on rimmed baking sheet lined with parchment paper. Season with salt and pepper, then drizzle with oil, 4 thyme sprigs, 2 rosemary sprigs, and 2 garlic cloves. Roast tomatoes until caramelized and tender, about 25–30 minutes. Set aside to cool. Cool completely on sheet.

FOR THE POTATO-FENNEL PUREE

MEANWHILE, in a large sauté pan fitted with a lid, heat 1 tablespoon olive oil over medium heat. Add the fennel and sauté until tender, about 15 minutes. Add the shallot and cook 1–2 minutes until the shallot is tender. Remove one-third of the mixture from the pan and set aside. Add fennel seeds, 2 tablespoons cream, and 3 tablespoons water to the pan and bring to a simmer. Cover the pan and simmer over low heat until the fennel is tender when pierced with a sharp knife, 25–30 minutes. Puree in a blender or with an emersion blender, then return to the pot.

WHILE the fennel is cooking, put the potatoes in a medium saucepan and cover with cold water by two inches. Add a ½ teaspoon salt and bring to a boil. Lower the heat to simmer, cover the pot partially, and cook until the potatoes are very tender when tested with the tip of a sharp paring knife, 20–25 minutes. Drain the potatoes, reserving some of the cooking water.

COMBINE the remaining ½ cup cream and butter in a small saucepan over medium heat and bring to a simmer.

PUT the potatoes through a potato ricer or food mill and return them to the pot. Add the hot cream-and-butter mixture, stirring with a wooden spoon until well combined. Puree in a blender, then add the potatoes to the pot with the pureed fennel. Stir just until combined. Place pot over low heat and season to taste with salt and pepper. Adjust the consistency if necessary with a tablespoon or two of the reserved water. Keep warm.

LEMON-FENNEL SAUCE

1 tablespoon Pernod

1 lemon, zested and juiced

½ cup homemade or store-bought chicken stock

1 tablespoon butter

Salt and pepper to taste

Kosher salt and freshly ground black pepper

1 sprig parsley, chopped, for garnish

FOR THE HERB OIL–POACHED FISH

COMBINE 3-4 cups olive oil, 4 garlic cloves, sage, rosemary, and thyme in a saucepan fitted with a lid and large enough to hold all 4 fish fillets in a single layer. Heat the oil over moderate heat for 10 minutes. Season halibut with salt and pepper and add to the oil. Place a circle of parchment paper over the fish and cover with the lid. Cook fish for 5 minutes and remove the pan from heat. Leave fish in the hot oil, covered, for 5 minutes more or until just cooked through.

FOR THE LEMON-FENNEL SAUCE

WHILE the fish is poaching, combine the reserved one-third fennel mixture in a saucepan with Pernod, lemon juice, and zest and cook over medium heat until the liquid is reduced by half. Then add chicken stock and bring to a simmer. Puree in a blender, then strain the sauce through a fine mesh strainer into a clean saucepan over lowest heat. Swirl in the butter and season to taste with salt and pepper. Keep warm.

TO PLATE

SPOON potato-fennel puree on bottom of each bowl. Top with roasted tomatoes and one poached halibut fillet. Spoon lemon-fennel sauce over the fish and around bowl. Garnish with chopped parsley.

JOHN DORY WITH NEW POTATOES, CARROT PUREE, ARTICHOKES, AND FENNEL VELOUTÉ

SERVES 4

John Dory is a firm, flaky, white-fleshed fish prized for its mild, sweet flavor. It's more likely to found on a UK menu than in the United States, so if you're unable to find it, tilapia can be substituted. *Velouté* is one of the five "mother" sauces of French cuisine (the other four are tomato, hollandaise, béchamel, and espagnole). This stock-based velvety sauce is thickened with a roux or heavy cream, and ours is flavored with fennel. As you get more proficient in the kitchen, you'll find yourself working through all of the elements of this dinner together, stirring and adding ingredients with ease and expertly making use of all four of your stovetop's burners at once. That's how Season 7 contestant Holli Ugalde worked her John Dory to perfection in a top-four dinner service competition. Her fish got her to the top three, and ultimately she was crowned the winner of the show.

POTATOES

12 baby new potatoes

2 tablespoons olive oil

2 tablespoons butter

CARROT PUREE

2 tablespoons olive oil

3 tablespoons butter

1–2 tablespoons sugar

10 carrots, sliced into ½-inch pieces

1–2 star anise

Kosher salt and freshly ground black pepper

FENNEL VELOUTÉ

1 tablespoon olive oil

1 small fennel bulb, roughly chopped

¼ cup dry white wine

⅛ cup dry vermouth

1 cup fish stock or vegetable stock

⅛ cup heavy cream

Kosher salt and freshly ground black pepper

FOR THE POTATOES

BRING a medium pot of salted water to a boil. Add the potatoes and boil 20 minutes or until just tender. Drain, and when the potatoes are cool enough to handle, remove the skin and slice the potatoes into ½-inch rounds. Set aside.

FOR THE CARROT PUREE

IN medium saucepan, heat the oil, butter, and sugar in a pan over medium heat. Add the carrots and star anise and cook until the carrots are lightly caramelized, about 15 minutes. Pour in 1 cup of water, just enough to cover the carrots. Cook for 25 minutes or until the carrots start to break down when gently pressed. Remove the star anise and strain the carrots. Reserve the cooking liquid. Puree the carrots in a blender, adding some of the cooking water if too thick. Season to taste and keep warm.

FOR THE FENNEL VELOUTÉ

IN a medium saucepan, heat the olive oil over medium-low heat. Add the fennel with a pinch of salt and cook until translucent and tender, about 10 minutes. Add the wine and dry vermouth. Bring to a boil and reduce until almost dry and the liquid is syrupy. Add the fish (or vegetable) stock and reduce by half, then add the cream. Return to a boil and reduce until thickened. Strain through a fine mesh strainer and season to taste. Set aside and keep warm.

HEAT the oil and butter in a large sauté pan. Add the potato slices to the pan and cook for 5 minutes until golden and crisp. Season to taste.

JOHN DORY

Four 6-ounce John Dory or tilapia fillets, skin removed

1 tablespoon olive oil

1 tablespoon butter

Kosher salt and freshly ground black pepper

Fresh dill, chopped, for garnish

Grilled or marinated baby artichokes, store-bought

FOR THE FISH

IN a large sauté pan, heat the oil and butter over medium-high heat. Season the fish with salt and pepper. Add the fillets in a single layer and sauté about 2 minutes. Reduce heat to moderate and cook 1 minute more. Turn fillet and cook 2–3 minutes or until fish flakes.

TO PLATE

MOUND the carrot puree into the center of each plate. Top with fish fillet. Garnish each plate with 2 artichokes and sautéed new potatoes. Drizzle the velouté around each plate and garnish with dill.

LEMON AND THYME ROASTED CHICKEN BREAST, SWEET CORN POLENTA, SAUTÉED SPINACH, AND CHICKEN JUS

SERVES 4

Au jus, or "in its own juice," is a simple yet sophisticated way of creating a sauce using the natural juices released from a food while cooking. The chicken jus starts with the drippings from bone-in roasted chicken breast (always choose skin-on, bone-in for most flavor). The fat is drained from the pan; the pan is placed on the stovetop and is deglazed with wine, scraping up all the tasty browned bits from the bottom of the pan. The liquid is then reduced, butter is whisked in, and the resulting sauce is poured over the finished dish—slices of tender lemony-thyme chicken set atop creamy polenta and served with a side of sautéed spinach.

LEMON AND THYME ROASTED CHICKEN BREAST

4 tablespoons softened butter

2 tablespoons chopped thyme leaves

2 teaspoons lemon zest

Kosher salt and freshly ground black pepper

2 whole bone-in, skin-on chicken breasts, about 3 pounds total

¼ cup chicken stock

½ tablespoon unsalted butter

SWEET CORN POLENTA
(makes 3 cups)

2 cups milk

1 cup cream

2 sprigs thyme

1 garlic clove, smashed

1 cup instant polenta

1–2 tablespoons unsalted butter, softened

2–3 tablespoons grated Parmesan cheese

SPINACH

2 tablespoons olive oil

1 shallot, minced

1 pound baby spinach

Kosher salt and freshly ground black pepper

Chopped chives, for garnish

FOR THE LEMON AND THYME CHICKEN BREAST

PREHEAT the oven to 450°F.

IN a small bowl, use a wooden spoon to combine the softened butter, minced thyme, lemon zest, salt, and pepper.

PAT the chicken skin dry, then carefully use your finger to loosen the skin on the breasts. Spread 2 tablespoons of the lemon-thyme butter between the skin and the flesh. Then spread the remaining butter on the surface of the chicken and season generously with salt and pepper.

PLACE the chicken on a rack in a stove-safe roasting pan and roast in the oven 35–40 minutes or until the internal temperature is 165°F. Transfer to a cutting board and allow the chicken to rest 5 minutes.

PLACE the roasting pan on the stove over medium-high heat. Add the stock and wine to deglaze and, with a wooden spoon, scrape up the brown bits on the bottom of the pan. Boil until reduced by half. Strain the jus through a fine mesh strainer into a small saucepan. Season to taste with salt and pepper and whisk in the butter. Keep warm.

FOR THE POLENTA

WHILE the chicken is roasting, make the polenta. Combine the milk, cream, thyme, and garlic in a medium saucepot. Heat over medium-high until the mixture just boils. Remove the thyme and garlic, lower the heat to medium, and add the polenta to the milk and cream in a slow, steady stream, whisking constantly. Now with a wooden spoon, continue mixing for about 5 minutes or until the mixture thickens. Remove from the heat. Stir in the butter and Parmesan, season to taste with salt and pepper, and keep warm.

FOR THE SPINACH

IN a large sauté pan, heat the olive oil over medium heat. Add the shallot and cook until tender, about 3 minutes. Add the spinach and cook, tossing to coat, until the spinach is wilted. Season to taste with salt and pepper.

TO PLATE

MOUND the polenta in center of each plate. Cut the chicken breast off the bone and slice. Fan the sliced chicken over the polenta. Drizzle with jus and garnish with chopped chives.

MISO-SAKE MARINATED CHILEAN SEA BASS WITH SEAWEED SOBA SALAD

SERVES 4

Miso, mirin, and sake make a classic Asian marinade for bass, the medley of flavors blanketing and penetrating the flesh for a roasted fish dish that's sweet, tender, and simple enough that you'll likely find yourself adding this one both to your dinner rotation and special-occasion celebrations. Soba is a Japanese-style buckwheat noodle; it can be found in Asian food markets and natural food stores, as can wakame seaweed, mirin, and Asian pears where they're in season.

SEA BASS

½ cup light miso

¼ cup mirin

¼ cup sake

½ tablespoon finely chopped ginger

¼ cup canola oil

¼ cup sugar

Four 7-ounce pieces skinless Chilean sea bass

Freshly ground black pepper

WAKAME SEAWEED SOBA SALAD

½ pound dried soba noodles

½ cup dried wakame seaweed

½ cup peeled, seeded, finely-diced cucumber

1 tablespoon rice wine vinegar

2 teaspoons sesame oil

¼ cup plus ¼ cup scallions, chopped (green only)

½ teaspoon sugar

Kosher salt and freshly ground black pepper

⅛ cup fresh cilantro, chopped

⅛ cup soy sauce

1 tablespoon minced ginger

⅛ cup rice wine vinegar

1 teaspoon toasted sesame oil

1 small Asian pear, cut into small dice, for garnish

Sliced scallions (optional), for garnish

Chopped cilantro (optional), for garnish

FOR THE BASS

IN a nonreactive bowl, whisk miso, mirin, sake, ginger, oil, and sugar to combine. Add the bass, tossing gently to coat and marinate for 20 minutes.

WHILE the bass is marinating, bring a large pot of salted water to a boil for the soba noodles.

FOR THE SEAWEED SOBA SALAD

HAVE a bowl of ice water ready. Add the soba noodles to the boiling water and cook until al dente, about 6 minutes. Drain and transfer the noodles to the ice bath. Drain the noodles and transfer them to a bowl.

WHILE the noodles cook, in a medium bowl combine the wakame seaweed with enough warm water to cover by 2 inches. Soak for 10 minutes, then drain and squeeze out any excess water. Add the seaweed to the bowl, along with the cucumber, vinegar, oil, ¼ cup scallions, and sugar. Season to taste with salt and pepper.

TO the bowl of noodles add cilantro, the remaining ¼ cup of scallions, soy sauce, chopped ginger, rice wine vinegar, and wakame salad to the noodles. Toss and season with salt and pepper to taste.

FOR THE FISH

PREHEAT the oven to 450°F. Place fish in a shallow baking dish and season with pepper. Bake the fish until just opaque in the center, 9–10 minutes. Preheat broiler. Place fish on the rack closest to the broiler. Broil fish until well browned on top and opaque in center, watching closely to avoid burning, 1–2 minutes.

TO PLATE

SPOON the soba noodles into the center of the plate. Top with the bass. Garnish with Asian pear and, if using, sliced scallions and cilantro.

PAN-SEARED SEA BASS, POTATO-LEEK PUREE, SAUTÉED HARICOTS VERTS, CAPER-RED ONION-TOMATO RELISH

SERVES 4

Haricots verts are the French version of green beans—they are longer, thinner, and more tender than the standard American variety. If haricots verts are unavailable, American green beans are perfectly acceptable. The relish, featuring Spanish Marcona almonds—a rounded, more delicate version of the nut—can be made ahead and refrigerated; bring to room temperature before serving. To save a little time, trim the ends from the haricots verts up to a few hours in advance, then the potato-leek puree, haricots verts, and fish can be put together in under an hour, yielding a spectacular presentation with minimal prepping. Marcona almonds can be found in specialty grocers and various online sources including Nuts.com.

CAPER-RED ONION-TOMATO RELISH

1 cup grape tomatoes, halved

2 tablespoons olive oil, divided

Kosher salt and freshly ground black pepper

¼ cup diced pickled red onions, diced, or ¼ cup red onion

¼ cup capers, rinsed

1 tablespoon parsley, minced

Juice of ½ lemon

¼ cup Marcona almonds or toasted almonds, chopped

POTATO-LEEK PUREE

8 ounces Yukon Gold potatoes, peeled and cut into 1-inch cubes

½ teaspoon kosher salt

4 tablespoons unsalted butter, room temperature

1 small leek, white parts only, cleaned and sliced thin (½ cup)

½ cup cream

Freshly ground black pepper

FOR THE CAPER-RED ONION-TOMATO RELISH

PREHEAT the oven to 400°F. Line a sided baking pan with parchment paper. Place tomatoes in the pan and toss with 1½ tablespoons of olive oil, salt, and pepper. Roast for 20–25 minutes, tossing occasionally, until the tomatoes are shriveled.

TRANSFER the tomatoes to a medium bowl and combine with the red onion, capers, parsley, and lemon juice. Add the remaining ½ tablespoon of olive oil. Fold in the Marcona almonds and adjust the seasoning.

FOR THE POTATO-LEEK PUREE

PUT the potatoes in a large saucepan and cover with cold water by two inches. Add a half teaspoon salt and bring to a boil. Lower the heat to simmer, cover the pot partially, and cook until the potatoes are very tender when tested with the tip of a sharp paring knife, 20–25 minutes.

WHILE the potatoes cook, melt 2 tablespoons of butter in a large sauté pan over medium-low heat. Add the leeks and season with salt and pepper. Cook until the leeks are very tender but not brown, about 10–12 minutes.

DRAIN the potatoes, reserving some of the cooking water.

COMBINE the cream and remaining 3 tablespoons butter in a small saucepan over moderate heat and bring to a simmer.

PUT the potatoes through a potato ricer or food mill and return them to the pot over low heat. Add the hot cream-and-butter mixture and mix with a wooden spoon. If the potatoes are very thick, add a small amount of the reserved cooking water. Using an immersion blender, puree potatoes until they are smooth and silky. Fold in the leeks, season to taste with salt and pepper, and puree with an emersion blender or in a blender. Set aside and keep warm.

FOR THE HARICOTS VERTS

IN the large sauté pan over high heat, add enough water just to coat the bottom of the pan. Bring to a boil, then add the beans; lower the heat to a

SAUTÉED HARICOTS VERTS

½ pound haricots verts, stem ends removed

Kosher salt and freshly ground black pepper

1 tablespoon unsalted butter

Pan Seared Sea Bass

½ tablespoon olive oil

½ tablespoon unsalted butter

Four 5-ounce sea bass fillets, skin on

simmer and cover the pan. Cook 1 minute. Add the butter, season to taste with salt and pepper, and cook just until the water is evaporated. Transfer the beans to a plate and drizzle with butter.

FOR THE FISH

HEAT olive oil and butter in a large sauté pan over medium-high heat. When the foam subsides, season the sea bass fillets and cook skin side down, about 3–4 minutes until they are lightly browned. Reduce heat, turn the fillets over, and sear the other side for another 2–3 minutes, depending on the thickness of the fish, until just cooked through.

TO PLATE

MOUND the potato-leek puree in the center of each plate. Top with sea bass fillet and a spoonful of the relish. Serve with haricots verts.

PAN-SEARED TUNA WITH BOK CHOY AND WASABI MASHED POTATOES WITH A SOY GINGER VINAIGRETTE

SERVES 4

Yukon Gold potatoes have a moist, sweet flesh that works with virtually any cooking method. They make a brilliant mash, with wasabi adding a sharp hint of sushi-style heat. In keeping with the Asian theme, tuna is coated with a mix of soy sauce and additional wasabi, then rolled into a mix of black and tan sesame seeds. The tuna is lightly seared and therefore raw inside, so make sure to purchase tuna labeled "sushi grade" from a trusted fishmonger or the fish section of your grocery store.

SOY GINGER VINAIGRETTE

½ tablespoon of ginger

2 tablespoons soy sauce

1 tablespoon rice vinegar

2 tablespoons orange juice

1 teaspoon Dijon mustard

¼ cup olive oil

WASABI MASHED POTATOES

1¾ pounds Yukon Gold potatoes, peeled and cut into 1-inch cubes

½ teaspoon Kosher salt

1 cup cream

3 tablespoons unsalted butter, softened

1 teaspoon wasabi powder

Freshly ground black pepper

BOK CHOY

½ pound baby bok choy, cleaned, ends trimmed

1 tablespoon unsalted butter

Kosher salt and freshly ground black pepper

TUNA

½ cup soy sauce

½ teaspoon wasabi powder

Two 8-ounce sushi-grade tuna fillets

¼ cup black sesame seeds

¼ cup white sesame seeds

2 tablespoons grapeseed oil

FOR THE SOY GINGER VINAIGRETTE

MINCE the ginger add to the soy sauce, vinegar, and orange juice. Put the mustard in a bowl, whisk in the orange juice mixture and balsamic vinegar, and slowly stir in the olive oil.

FOR THE WASABI MASHED POTATOES

PUT the potatoes in a large saucepan and cover with cold water by two inches. Add ½ teaspoon salt and bring to a boil. Lower the heat to simmer, cover the pot partially, and cook until the potatoes are very tender when tested with the tip of a sharp paring knife, 20–25 minutes. Drain the potatoes, reserving some of the cooking water.

COMBINE the cream and butter in a small saucepan over medium heat and bring to a simmer.

PUT the potatoes through a potato ricer or food mill and return them to the pot over low heat. Add the hot cream-and-butter mixture. Fold in wasabi powder, season to taste with salt and pepper, and adjust the consistency if the potatoes are too stiff by adding a bit of the reserved cooking water. Whip with the immersion blender and set aside to keep warm.

FOR THE BOK CHOY

HEAT a medium sauté pan over medium heat. Add the butter and melt. Add the bok choy and toss to coat. Add 1 tablespoon water, cover the pan, and cook 2 minutes. Uncover and cook until the liquid has evaporated, about 3 more minutes. Season to taste with salt and pepper and keep warm.

FOR THE TUNA

IN a small bowl, whisk together wasabi powder and soy sauce. Place the tuna in the wasabi soy mixture and toss to coat. Mix the sesame seeds on a plate. Lay the tuna on the sesame seeds and turn to coat.

HEAT oil in a large sauté pan over medium-high heat. When the oil is hot but not smoking, add the tuna and sear 30–40 seconds on all sides, depending on the thickness of the fish.

TO PLATE

MOUND the potatoes in the center of the plate and top with bok choy. Slice and fan tuna on top. Drizzle with soy vinaigrette.

ROASTED CHICKEN BREASTS AND KABOCHA SQUASH WITH MAPLE JUS

SERVES 4

Kabocha squash is an Asian winter squash with a bumpy, dark green skin that when cut open reveals a bright orange flesh. It's a squash worth seeking out come fall at your farmers' market. Though butternut squash is the more commonly used variety, kabocha beats butternut hands down in terms in sweetness, moistness, and meatiness. Those qualities are intensified when the squash is roasted, making it a substantial starch component for this classic roasted chicken dish or any meat dish that's typically accompanied by potatoes.

ROASTED KABOCHA SQUASH

1 small kabocha squash (about 2 pounds)

1 teaspoon cumin seeds

2–3 tablespoons olive oil

Kosher salt and freshly ground black pepper

ROASTED CHICKEN BREASTS

¼ cup olive oil

1 garlic clove, minced

Juice of 1 lemon

Kosher salt and freshly ground black pepper

2 whole bone-in, skin-on chicken breasts

1–2 tablespoons chopped fresh rosemary

1–2 tablespoons chopped fresh thyme

½ cup chicken stock, store-bought or homemade

1 tablespoon maple syrup

½ tablespoon unsalted butter

FOR THE ROASTED KABOCHA

ADJUST two racks in your oven, one in the upper third, one in the bottom, and preheat the oven to 450°F.

IN a small dry sauté pan, toast the cumin seeds over medium heat until fragrant, about 1 minute. Transfer the seeds to a spice grinder or mortar and pestle and crush. Transfer to a small bowl, add the olive oil, and mix to combine. Cut the kabocha squash in half and scoop out the seeds with a spoon. Cut each half into 12 slices. Lay the squash on a parchment-lined rimmed baking sheet and season with salt and pepper. Drizzle with the cumin oil, tossing to coat.

PLACE the pan on the upper rack and roast the squash, 20–25 minutes. Turn slices over and continue roasting 10–15 minutes more until the squash is soft. Remove from the oven and keep warm.

FOR THE CHICKEN

WHILE the squash is roasting, prep the chicken. In a small bowl, whisk together olive oil, garlic, and lemon juice. Season to taste with salt and pepper.

GENEROUSLY season the chicken with salt and pepper. Lay the chicken into a 13 x 9-inch baking dish in one layer. Pour the olive oil mixture over the chicken and turn to coat. Sprinkle with rosemary and thyme.

THEN transfer the pan to the oven to the lower rack, below the squash. Roast until the internal temperature is 165°F in the thickest part of the breast, about 35–40 minutes. Transfer to a cutting board and allow the chicken to rest 5 minutes.

DEGLAZE the pan to make a jus. Place the pan on the stove over medium-high heat. Add the stock and, with a wooden spoon, scrape up the brown bits on the bottom of the pan. Boil until reduced by half. Add the maple syrup, cook 1 more minute, then strain the jus through a fine mesh strainer into a small saucepan. Season to taste with salt and pepper and whisk in the butter. Keep warm.

(continued)

TO PLATE

LAY 6 slices of roasted squash on in the center of each plate. Cut the breasts off the bone and slice. Fan the chicken over the squash. Whisk the maple jus again to emulsify and drizzle over the chicken and around the plate.

SERVE with Creamed Spinach (page 181).

ROULADE OF VEAL ON CARAMELIZED ONIONS

SERVES 4

Roulade may look like an elaborate preparation, but it sounds harder than it is. It's little more than layering ingredients and rolling them up. To successfully roll up your veal, make sure to evenly distribute the filling ingredients on top and roll from the short end away from you, squeezing tightly as you go, until the prosciutto is completely wrapped around the veal.

CARAMELIZED ONIONS

1 tablespoon unsalted butter

1 tablespoon olive oil

2 large Spanish onions, thinly sliced

Kosher salt and freshly ground black pepper

½ teaspoon sugar, as needed

ROULADE OF VEAL

½ cup panko bread crumbs

2 tablespoons chopped flat-leaf parsley, plus more for garnish

⅓ cup grated Parmesan cheese

1 teaspoon granulated garlic

1 teaspoon onion powder

4 pieces veal scallopini, about 4 ounces each

4 slices prosciutto

¾ cups grated mozzarella cheese

1 tablespoon unsalted butter

1 tablespoon olive oil

⅓ cup all-purpose flour

½ cup veal demi-glace

½ teaspoon Dijon mustard

¼ cup heavy cream

Freshly ground black pepper

Chopped parsley, for garnish

FOR THE CARAMELIZED ONIONS

HEAT the butter and olive oil a large skillet, fitted with a lid, over medium heat. Add the onions, toss to coat, cover the pan, and cook 10 minutes until the onions give off some of their liquid and begin to be translucent. Then uncover, season to taste with salt and pepper, and sprinkle with ½ teaspoon of sugar. Reduce the heat to medium-low and sauté, stirring frequently until tender and caramelized, 20–25 minutes more.

FOR THE VEAL ROULADE

PREHEAT the oven to 350°F. In mixing bowl, combine panko, Parmesan, parsley, garlic, and onion powder. Set aside.

LAY the veal flat and season with pepper. Place one piece of prosciutto in the center of the veal. Top with 3 tablespoons mozzarella and 3 tablespoons of the breadcrumb mixture. Fold in the long sides of the veal, then roll starting at the short end and secure with two toothpicks. Repeat with the remaining veal. Season the outside of the veal roll with salt and pepper.

MELT butter and olive oil in a large ovenproof sauté pan over medium-high heat. Spread the flour onto a plate and season with salt and pepper. Dredge the veal roulades in the flour, shaking off the excess. When the butter and oil is hot but not smoking, add the veal and brown on all sides, about 4 minutes total. Transfer to the oven and cook 7–8 minutes. Remove the roulade from the pan and tent to keep warm.

RETURN the pan to the stove over medium heat. Add the demi-glace and heat for 1 minute, scraping up the brown bits on the bottom of the pan. Add the Dijon and heavy cream and stir to combine. Simmer until the sauce begins to thicken and coat the back of a spoon, about 1–2 minutes. Strain through a fine mesh strainer and season to taste.

TO PLATE

SPOON the caramelized onions in the center of each plate. Slice the veal and serve on top of the onions. Drizzle with the sauce and garnish with chopped parsley. Serve with Rainbow-Colored Carrots with Parsley Butter (page 171).

SHEEP'S MILK RICOTTA GNUDI

SERVES 4

Gnudi (pronounced "nude-y"), so called because it's based on just ricotta and Parmesan—the filling without the pasta—is gnocchi's lighter cousin. Draining the ricotta before mixing the dough ensures a moist but not wet gnudi. You'll need to reserve an hour or two for the gnudi to set in the refrigerator, where the semolina will coat the ricotta to add texture to the finished dish. This elegantly simple dish gets a memorable finish: butter-bathed morels and English peas, with a drizzle of truffle oil added at the end. With vegetable stock used for the morels and peas, this is a meal that vegetarians at the table will welcome.

RICOTTA GNUDI

1½ cups sheep's milk ricotta cheese, drained

2 large eggs

1 cup grated Parmesan cheese

½ teaspoon kosher salt

Freshly ground black pepper

Pinch cayenne

½ cup all-purpose flour

Semolina flour, for dusting

MORELS AND PEAS

6 tablespoons unsalted butter

8 fresh sage leaves

3 shallots, finely diced

2 large dried morels, soaked and drained

½ cup vegetable or chicken stock

¼ cup heavy cream

⅔ cup fresh or frozen English peas

Kosher salt and freshly ground black pepper

Truffle oil, for garnish

Shaved Parmesan cheese, for garnish

FOR THE GNUDI

IN a large mixing bowl, combine the ricotta cheese, eggs, Parmesan cheese, salt, pepper, and cayenne and whisk until well combined. With a spatula, fold in the flour, taking care not to overwork the dough. Cover and chill for 1–2 hours.

REMOVE the dough from the refrigerator. Dust a rimmed baking sheet generously with semolina flour. Using 2 tablespoons of equal size, shape the gnudi dough into football shapes or quenelles; place them on the baking sheet.

BRING a large pot of salted water to a boil while you make the sauce.

FOR THE BROWN BUTTER WITH MORELS, PEAS, AND SAGE

IN a large skillet, melt 4 tablespoons butter over medium heat. Add the sage leaves and cook until crisp, about 2 minutes. Remove with a slotted spoon. Add the shallots to the pan and sauté until translucent, about 2–3 minutes. Chop the morels, add them to the pan, and cook 2 more minutes.

ADD ½ cup vegetable or chicken stock and reduce until by half. Add the heavy cream to pan and cook, stirring, until the sauce thickens. Keep warm while you cook the gnudi.

COOK THE GNUDI

GRADUALLY add the gnudi to the pot, making sure the water stays at a gentle boil. Within 1–2 minutes, the gnudi will rise to the surface. Continue cooking until they are cooked through and tender, 5–6 minutes. Gently remove them with a slotted spoon to a paper-towel-lined plate and reserve ½ cup of the cooking liquid.

JUST before serving, stir the peas into the mushroom mixture over medium heat and season with salt and pepper. Add the gnudi to the sauce and gently toss to coat. If the sauce is too thick, add just enough of the cooking liquid to loosen and smooth it out. Simmer gently for 1–2 minutes.

TO PLATE

DIVIDE the gnudi between 4 dinner bowls. Top with the morel-peas sauce. Garnish with the sage leaves, drizzle with truffle oil, and top with shaved Parmesan cheese.

GRILLED SALMON WITH WHITE BEAN, CHORIZO, AND LOBSTER RAGÙ

SERVES 4

This grilled salmon dish is built on rich and creamy lobster bisque, further enriched by luxurious lobster tail. The flavor base starts with pancetta. The fat is rendered, and a mirepoix—the classic mixture of carrot, celery, and onion—is cooked into the fat, then wine is cooked down into the base to add another layer of flavor.

Tarragon is the featured herb in the dish. This lesser-known herb with a distinct anise flavor plays a large part in French cooking—along with parsley, chives, and chervil, it is one of the four *fines herbes* of French cooking, and it is often used in béarnaise sauce.

LOBSTER RAGÙ

1 tablespoon olive oil

2 ounces dried chorizo sausage, cut into small dice

¼ cup finely diced celery

¼ cup finely diced carrot

½ cup onion, minced

2 garlic cloves, minced

1 sprig tarragon

½ cup canned crushed tomatoes

½ cup cream sherry

Two 15-ounce cans cannellini beans, rinsed and drained

2 cups vegetable broth

2 tablespoons heavy cream

3½–4 ounces cooked lobster meat from tails and knuckles

Kosher salt and freshly ground black pepper

GRILLED SALMON

Kosher salt and freshly ground black pepper

Four 6-ounce salmon fillets, skin on

2 tablespoons olive oil

Chiffonade basil, for garnish

Chopped parsley, for garnish

FOR THE RAGÙ

IN a large sauce pan or Dutch oven, heat olive oil over medium-high heat. Add the chorizo and sauté until browned. Remove from the pan with a slotted spoon and set aside on a paper-towel-lined plate. Pour off all but 1 tablespoon of the fat or add remaining tablespoon olive oil. Reduce heat to medium and carrot, celery, and onion. Sauté until the vegetables are tender, about 3–4 minutes. Add the garlic and the tarragon and cook for 1 minute more. Stir in the crushed tomatoes and cook for 4–5 minutes. Add the sherry and reduce until almost dry. Add white beans and the broth, season with salt and pepper, and simmer 10 minutes. Return the chorizo to the pan and reduce heat to low while you grill the salmon.

FOR THE GRILLED SALMON

SEASON the salmon fillet with salt and pepper.

HEAT 2 tablespoons of olive oil in a large sauté pan over medium-high high heat. Place the fish skin side down in the pan and cook until seared on one side, about 4 minutes. Turn the fish over, reduce the heat, and cook for 3 minutes more until the salmon is almost cooked but still a bit pink inside.

FINISH the ragù. Add the cream and lobster meat and allow to heat through, 1–2 minutes.

TO PLATE

TO serve, pour the ragù into individual shallow serving bowls. Place the salmon fillet on top and drizzle with olive oil. Garnish with basil and parsley.

KISS IT AND FLIP IT

The "kiss it and flip it" technique is a reliable indicator of doneness for cooking fish. First the fish is placed in the pan skin side down. Resist the urge to touch it until it's time to turn it to ensure a good sear. Then flip it and "kiss" it, which means to cook it on the second side briefly, just until it's done to your liking. The flesh should still be a little less than cooked through when it comes out of the pan, as it will continue to cook.

LEMON TAGLIATELLE WITH TOASTED PINE NUTS AND ARUGULA

SERVES 4

Tagliatelle is a ribbony noodle closely related to fettuccine but slightly wider. It's often available fresh in Italian or specialty shops and is worth seeking out for an authentic pasta-eating experience. Adding the trio of lemon, basil, and cheese, plus buttery pine nuts for a little crunch, is a way of turning an ordinary pot of pasta into something extraordinary. Rather than serve the pasta with a typical arugula side salad, the arugula is cooked into the pasta, for a little heat and a touch of bitter flavor to round out this special vegetarian dish.

12 ounces tagliatelle

¼ cup pine nuts

4 tablespoons unsalted butter

Juice of 1 lemon

Finely grated zest of 1 lemon

2 tablespoons coarsely chopped fresh basil, plus more for garnish

1 cup freshly grated Parmesan cheese, plus more for garnish

½ pound (about 4 cups) baby arugula

Kosher salt and freshly ground pepper

BRING a large pot of salted water to a boil. Cook the tagliatelle according to the package directions until al dente. Drain the pasta, reserving ½ cup of the cooking water.

WHILE the pasta cooks, toast the pine nuts. In a small dry skillet over medium, toast the pine nuts until they are lightly browned and fragrant, watching carefully so that they don't burn. Transfer to a bowl and reserve.

RETURN the drained pasta to the pot. Add butter, lemon juice and zest, basil, Parmesan cheese, and the reserved cooking water. Cook over moderate heat, tossing just until creamy. Add the arugula and toss to combine, cooking until just wilted. Season to taste with salt and pepper.

DIVIDE the pasta between four bowls. Garnish with more chopped basil and reserved pine nuts and serve with more Parmesan cheese.

FRUTTI DI MARE

SERVES 4

Frutti di mare—or "fruit of the sea"—is a classic Italian mixed seafood dish found all along the coast of Italy. It's heavily flavored with wine and tomatoes and tossed with linguine to sop up all the delicious juices. This frutti di mare uses clams, mussels, and shrimp, though many versions include scallops and squid as well.

It couldn't be easier to cook your clams and mussels: sauté some garlic, add the clams and mussels to the pan with some wine to steam them in, cover, and cook until they open, discarding any stubborn ones that stay shut. Keep a watch on the shrimp after you add them; they're done when they just turn pink. See page 50 for tips on choosing and storing mussels and clams.

¼ cup all-purpose flour

12 littleneck clams, scrubbed

32 fresh mussels, scrubbed and debearded

¾ pound linguine

2 tablespoons extra virgin olive oil

3 garlic cloves, thinly sliced

One 28-ounce can whole plum tomatoes, chopped with the juice reserved

1 cup dry white wine

Pinch crushed red pepper

16 large shrimp, peeled and deveined

Kosher salt and freshly ground black pepper

Fresh basil

FILL a large bowl with cold water. Add all-purpose flour and stir. Add the clams and mussels and let soak in the refrigerator 1 hour. Drain and set aside.

MEANWHILE, cook the pasta. Bring a large pot of salted water to a boil. Add the pasta and cook according the package directions for al dente. Drain and set aside.

WHILE the pasta is cooking, heat the olive oil in a large saucepan fitted with a lid over medium-high heat. Add the garlic and sauté for 1 minute until fragrant. Add the tomatoes, white wine, and crushed red pepper and simmer for 3 minutes. Add the clams and cook, covered, about 4 minutes, shaking the pan occasionally. Then add the mussels and shrimp and season with salt and pepper. Cook 3 minutes or until the shrimp are pink. Discard any mussels or clams that haven't opened. Stir in fresh basil.

DIVIDE the pasta between four bowls. Top with seafood and garnish with a drizzle of olive oil and more basil.

ELSIE'S TURKEY TACOS

SERVES 4

Though Season 1 contestant and mother of six, Elsie Ramos, was not crowned the *Hell's Kitchen* winner, she created some impressive recipes, among them her turkey tacos. Made with a mix of dark and white meat, the tacos feature a homemade version of the Latin seasoning mix *sazón*—a mix of cumin, coriander, and other spices. Making your own *sazón* guarantees freshness and avoids the MSG and artificial ingredients often found in packaged brands. These tacos can be easily put together any night of the week, perfect for busy moms, dads, and anybody needing a quick-prep meal.

2 tablespoons vegetable oil, divided

1½ pounds ground dark and white meat turkey

¾ tablespoon sazón (see below)

1 medium onion, finely chopped, plus more for garnish

½ cup tomato sauce, store-bought or homemade

2 tablespoons chicken stock

Kosher salt and freshly ground black pepper

12 corn tortillas

1 medium tomato, finely chopped

½ head iceberg lettuce, shredded

½ cup finely chopped fresh cilantro leaves

8 ounces shredded queso fresco

Tabasco sauce (optional)

SAZÓN
(make 6 tablespoons)

1 tablespoon ground coriander

1 tablespoon ground cumin

1 tablespoon turmeric

1 tablespoon garlic powder

1 tablespoon kosher salt

2 teaspoons oregano

1 teaspoon ground black pepper

FOR THE SAZÓN

MIX all of the ingredients together in a small bowl.

FOR THE TACOS

HEAT 1 tablespoon vegetable oil In a large skillet over medium heat. Add the turkey and sazón and season with salt and pepper. Cook, stirring occasionally, until the turkey is no longer pink, about 5 minutes. Add the remaining tablespoon oil, then the onion, and sauté until translucent, about 3 minutes. Add the tomato sauce and chicken stock. Simmer 5 minutes. Transfer the meat mixture to a bowl and keep warm.

HAVE a clean dishtowel ready—you will transfer the warmed tortillas from the pan onto the towel. Heat a large skillet, preferably nonstick, over high heat. Dip one tortilla in a bowl of water, then add to the skillet and cook, 30 seconds on each side. Transfer to the dish towel and repeat with the remaining tortillas. Wrap the tortillas in the towel and let them steam for 5 minutes.

TRANSFER to a plate and keep warm while you repeat with the remaining tortillas.

TO PLATE

SERVE family style so everyone can make their own tacos: a bowl of the turkey, the tortillas on a plate wrapped in the towel, and tomato, lettuce, cilantro, queso fresco, and Tabasco (optional) on the side.

ORECCHIETTE WITH BROCCOLI AND ITALIAN SAUSAGE

SERVES 6

This dish demonstrates that you can put a restaurant-quality meal on the table in less than the time it takes to watch an episode of *Hell's Kitchen*! What will make this dish stand out is using superstar ingredients—the very best sausage from your butcher, cheese imported from Italy if you can find it, and fresh or imported orecchiette ("little ear" pasta) cooked just to al dente, with a little pasta cooking water added back to the finished dish to enrich the sauce and keep the pasta moist.

1 pound broccoli crowns

Kosher salt

1 tablespoon extra virgin olive oil

½ pound bulk hot or sweet Italian sauce with fennel

¼ teaspoon crushed red pepper flakes

2 garlic cloves, thinly sliced

12 ounces dried orecchiette

⅓ cup freshly grated Parmesan or Pecorino Romano cheese, plus more to serve

PREPARE a large bowl of ice water.

SEPARATE the broccoli florets from the stems. Cut the large florets in half and leave the remainder whole.

BRING a large pot of salted water to a boil over high heat. Add the stems and cook for 3–4 minutes; add the florets and cook for another 3 minutes until both the stems and the florets are just tender. Use a slotted spoon to transfer the broccoli to the ice bath. Drain the broccoli and chop it coarsely.

FILL the pot again with salted water and bring to a boil.

MEANWHILE, heat the olive oil in a 12-inch sauté pan or large skillet over medium heat. Add the sausage and cook, breaking it up with a wooden spoon, until it's no longer pink. (Drain excess fat if there is more than 2 tablespoons.) Add the red pepper flakes and garlic and sauté briefly until fragrant, about 1 minute. Add the broccoli and season well with salt. Stir to coat the broccoli with the seasonings. Keep warm over low heat.

COOK the pasta in the boiling water until it's just barely al dente. Reserve ¾ cup of the cooking liquid, then drain the pasta and return it to the pot.

ADD the broccoli mixture to the pasta over moderate heat, stirring constantly, until the pasta is al dente, adding reserved pasta water as needed to keep the pasta moist.

REMOVE the pan from the heat and stir in half of the cheese, tossing to combine. Divide the pasta among 6 bowls. Serve with more grated cheese.

EIGHT-OUNCE BEEF BURGER WITH CARAMELIZED ONION AND BACON JAM, SHARP CHEDDAR, AND SPECIAL SAUCE ON A BRIOCHE BUN WITH SWEET POTATO FRIES

SERVES 4

The difference between a greasy-joint burger and a chef-quality burger is all in the beef. Pick the very best your budget will allow—top choices are chuck and sirloin in a ratio of 80 percent lean to 20 percent fat. And if you can get your meat freshly ground from your butcher, you'll further improve your burger.

When it's time to put together your burgers, gently form the meat into patties, handling the meat as little as possible (overworking the meat will result in a tough burger). A final chef's tip is to make an indentation in the middle of each patty so your burgers are evenly flat (as the patties hit the screaming hot skillet they tend to puff up in the middle).

CARAMELIZED ONION AND BACON JAM

⅓ pound bacon (about 6 slices), finely diced

2 cups Spanish onion, finely diced

1½ tablespoons dark brown sugar

¼ teaspoon cumin

½ teaspoon mustard seed

¼ cup brewed coffee

2 tablespoons balsamic vinegar

SWEET POTATO FRIES

4 medium sweet potatoes

½ teaspoon cornstarch

2 tablespoons olive oil

Salt and pepper

1 teaspoon garlic

1 teaspoon paprika

Pinch cayenne pepper

FOR THE CARAMELIZED ONION AND BACON JAM (MAKES ¾ CUP)

COOK the bacon in a large sauté pan over medium heat, stirring occasionally until the fat is rendered and the bacon is brown and crisp, about 15 minutes. Use a slotted spoon to transfer to a paper-towel-lined plate to drain. Set aside.

DRAIN off all but 1 tablespoon of fat. Add the onions and cook over medium heat until softened and slightly translucent, about 5 minutes. Reduce the heat to low and add the brown sugar, cumin, mustard seed, reserved bacon, and coffee to the pan. Add vinegar and cook, partially covered, over moderate heat for 35–40 minutes or until the mixture becomes jamlike in consistency. Add 1–2 tablespoons of water if the mixture is too dry as it cooks. Season to taste with salt and pepper

TRANSFER to a bowl to cool.

WHILE the jam is cooking, make the sweet potato fries.

FOR THE SWEET POTATO FRIES

PREHEAT the oven to 425°F.

PEEL the sweet potatoes and cut them into fry-shaped pieces.

TRANSFER to a bowl. Sprinkle with cornstarch and drizzle with olive oil. Toss to coat. Season with salt, pepper, garlic, paprika, and cayenne and toss again.

POUR the fries onto a large enough baking sheet to hold them in an uncrowded single layer. Bake for 15 minutes, then flip the fries and continue baking for 10–15 more minutes or until they are crispy, browned, and tender.

(continued)

SPECIAL SAUCE

¼ cup mayonnaise

2 tablespoons ketchup

2 tablespoons sweet relish or minced kosher dill pickle (maybe a little pickle juice)

1 tablespoon Dijon mustard

Pinch garlic powder

Pinch paprika

A few grinds of freshly ground black pepper

Pinch cayenne pepper

BEEF BURGER

2 pounds ground beef chuck or ground sirloin

1½ teaspoons salt

1 teaspoon Dijon mustard

½ small onion, minced

Two dashes Worcestershire sauce

8 slices sharp aged cheddar cheese

4 brioche rolls

FOR THE SPECIAL SAUCE

COMBINE the mayonnaise, ketchup, sweet relish, mustard, garlic powder, paprika, pepper, and cayenne in a small bowl. Mix well to combine.

FOR THE BEEF BURGER

WHILE the fries are in the oven, form the burgers. In a large bowl, use your hands to gently combine the beef with salt, mustard, onion, and Worcestershire sauce. Divide the meat into fourths and shape into patties, being careful to handle the meat as little as possible. Make a depression in the center of each patty with the back of a measuring spoon to help the burger hold its shape.

HEAT a cast-iron skillet over medium-high heat until it smokes slightly, about 2 minutes. Cook the patties, flipping them once, until they're browned and cooked through, 2 minutes a side for rare, 3 minutes a side for medium rare.

PLACE a slice of cheese atop each patty and keep the skillet covered until the cheese has melted, about 1 minute.

TO PLATE

PLACE the burger on one side of the bun. Top with special sauce and caramelized onion and bacon jam. Serve with sweet potato fries.

WHITE-WINE-BRAISED SHORT RIBS

SERVES 4

Short ribs are a restaurant-quality dish that's easy to make at home; what's needed most is time, as the short ribs must cook low and slow—for at least two hours—to get them falling-off-the-bone tender. Bone-on meat is the way to go for a fully developed stew, as the bones enrich the stock with beefy flavor. This is high-end comfort food and a very satisfying winter meal.

4 bone-in beef short ribs, about 3 pounds total

Kosher salt and freshly ground black pepper

2 tablespoons olive oil

1 medium yellow onion, coarsely chopped

2 celery ribs, coarsely chopped

1 carrot, peeled and coarsely chopped

2 large garlic cloves, smashed

2 tablespoons chopped fresh thyme

2 tablespoons tomato paste

1 ½ cups dry white wine

1 cup low sodium chicken or beef stock, store-bought or homemade

PREHEAT the oven to 325°F.

GENEROUSLY season the short ribs with salt and pepper.

HEAT the olive oil in a Dutch oven over high heat until very hot. Add the short ribs, reduce the heat to medium-low, and brown the meat on all sides. Remove the meat from the pan and set aside. Drain all but 2 tablespoons of fat from the pan and add the onion, celery, and carrot; sauté for 5 minutes or until the onion is translucent and the vegetables begin to soften. Season with salt and pepper, then add the garlic and thyme, cooking another minute. Stir in the tomato paste and cook 5 minutes. Add the wine, scraping up the brown bits from the bottom of the pan. Boil until the liquid is reduced by ⅓. Add the short ribs back to the pan and pour the stock over the meat. Bring to a boil, then cover the pan and transfer to the oven. Cook 2–2 ½ hours or until the meat is very tender.

REMOVE the meat from the pot and set aside. Allow the braising liquid and vegetables to sit for a few minutes so the fat rises to the top. Skim the fat and discard. Using an immersion blender, puree the vegetables and the sauce and season if necessary. Return the short ribs and the sauce to the pot and keep warm.

TO serve, spoon the sauce into the center of each plate. Top with short ribs and serve with Rainbow-Colored Carrots with Parsley Butter (page 171).

BRANZINO, ROASTED FENNEL, CARAMELIZED LEMON, OLIVES

SERVES 4

Branzino, also known as Mediterranean sea bass or European sea bass, is a moist, white-fleshed fish most famously used in Mediterranean cuisine. If unavailable, red snapper, flounder, or tilapia may be substituted. The fish gets a decidedly Mediterranean treatment, with the roasted fennel and caramelized lemon playing off each other in a uniquely sweet-tart way. When lemons are caramelized, their natural sugars are drawn out while the fruit retains its signature sour flavor; caramelized lemons give added interest to any number of recipes, from chicken to pasta, turning a simple weeknight dish into something quite spectacular.

ROASTED FENNEL

2 fennel bulbs, stalks removed, bulbs cut in half lengthwise then into wedges, fronds reserved

2 tablespoons olive oil

2 teaspoons balsamic vinegar

¼ cup grated fresh Parmesan cheese

Kosher salt and freshly ground black pepper

CARAMELIZED LEMONS

1 tablespoon olive oil

1 tablespoon butter

1 lemons, sliced into 12 ⅛-inch-thick rounds, seeds removed

½ tablespoon sugar

Kosher salt

PAN-SEARED BRANZINO

Four 4-ounce branzino fillets with skin (you can also use red snapper, flounder, or tilapia for this dish)

Kosher salt and freshly ground black pepper

Olive oil

½ cup Sauvignon Blanc or other dry white wine

3 tablespoons fresh lemon juice, or more to taste

1 tablespoon unsalted butter

2 scallions, finely sliced on the bias

1 tablespoon capers, drained and rinsed

1 ripe plum tomato, seeded and cut into ¼-inch dice

3–4 small green or black (Gaeta) pitted olives

FOR THE ROASTED FENNEL

PREHEAT the oven to 400°F. Place the fennel wedges in a bowl and toss them with olive oil and balsamic vinegar. Line a roasting pan or baking dish with parchment paper brushed with olive oil. Arrange the fennel wedges on the pan in a single layer, sprinkle with Parmesan cheese, and season with salt and pepper. Roast 35–40 minutes or until the fennel is cooked through and beginning to caramelize at the edges.

FOR THE CARAMELIZED LEMONS

HEAT the olive oil and butter in a large nonstick sauté pan over medium heat. Add the lemons, sugar, and salt. Arrange the lemons in a single layer and let them brown, flipping them frequently to brown evenly. The lemons are ready when they are very brown but not burned and charred, about 10 minutes. Remove from the heat and set aside.

FOR THE PAN-SEARED BRANZINO

HEAT oil in a large ovenproof nonstick sauté pan set over medium-high heat until it shimmers. Pat the fish dry with paper towels and season both sides of the fillet with salt and pepper. Place fillets skin side down in the pan and sear for about 3–4 minutes or until crisp. Then flip and continue cooking 2–3 more minutes until the fish is flaky. Transfer the fish to a plate and tent with foil to keep warm.

WIPE out the pan and add the wine and lemon juice. Deglaze the pan by scraping up any browned bits on the bottom of the pan with a wooden spoon. Cook 2 minutes to burn off the alcohol. Reduce the heat and swirl in the butter. Add the scallions, capers, tomato, and olives. Season with salt and pepper.

TO PLATE

DIVIDE the roasted fennel between 4 plates, piled in the center of each plate. Top with the fish and the caramelized lemon. Spoon the pan sauce around the fish and garnish with reserved fennel fronds.

ENTRÉES

139

HONEY-GRILLED SHRIMP WITH ROASTED CORN RELISH, CILANTRO RICE, AND SPICY CRÈME FRAÎCHE

SERVES 4

Shrimp and rice can be a simple dish, or you can pull out the stops, as we do here in typical *Hell's Kitchen* fashion. The shrimp, at once sweet, spicy, tangy, and garlicky, sits atop flavorful green rice, with sweet roasted corn relish the final flavoring element. A dollop of spicy crème fraîche, at once hot and cooling, completes the picture.

This recipe's steps are easy to break down—it's a dinner that looks more complex than it really is. First you'll marinate the shrimp a couple hours in advance and, while you roast the corn and make the rice, you can spice up the crème fraîche and have it at the ready. Then, at the last moment, you'll roast the shrimp and be set to assemble the dish.

CHIPOTLE HONEY-GRILLED SHRIMP

1–2 tablespoons honey

2 chipotle peppers in adobo sauce, chopped, plus 2 tablespoons adobo sauce

3 garlic cloves, minced

1 tablespoon water

1 tablespoon lime juice

1 tablespoon olive oil

Pinch of kosher salt

1 pound raw jumbo (16-20 count) shrimp, peeled and deveined

ROASTED CORN RELISH

1 ½ cups corn kernels (from 2 medium ears of corn)

1 tablespoons olive oil

Kosher salt and freshly ground black pepper

¼ cup red pepper, minced

1 tablespoon finely diced jalapeño chilies (including seeds)

¼ cup diced cherry tomatoes

3 tablespoons thinly sliced scallions, white and green parts

2–3 tablespoons finely chopped fresh cilantro

½ teaspoon lime zest

Pinch sugar

¼ teaspoon chili powder

¼ teaspoon cumin

FOR THE CHIPOTLE HONEY-GRILLED SHRIMP

IN a large bowl, mix the honey, chipotles, adobo sauce, garlic, water, lime juice, oil, and salt. Whisk until well combined. Add the shrimp and toss well to coat. Cover and refrigerate for at least 30 minutes and up to 2 hours.

WHILE the shrimp marinates, make the corn relish.

FOR THE ROASTED CORN RELISH

PREHEAT the oven to 450°F. In a small bowl, toss the corn kernels with 2 tablespoons olive oil and season with salt and pepper. Spread the corn in a single layer on a baking sheet. Roast, stirring once, until the corn is brown, about 20 minutes. Transfer the corn to medium bowl and stir in the red pepper, jalapeño chilies, cherry tomatoes, scallions, cilantro, lime zest, sugar, chili powder, and cumin. Let sit at room temperature while grilling the shrimp.

FOR THE CILANTRO RICE

HEAT oil in a large saucepan over moderate heat. Add onion, 2 minced garlic cloves, and ½ tablespoon serrano chili and sauté until the onion is translucent, 4–5 minutes. Add rice and stir to coat, 1–2 minutes.

RAISE the heat to medium-high, add the broth and salt, and bring to boil. Reduce heat to low; cover and cook until rice is just tender and the broth is absorbed, about 15 minutes. Remove from heat. Let stand, covered, 5 minutes. Transfer to a bowl.

WHILE the rice cooks, combine the cilantro, olive oil, white wine vinegar, the remaining minced garlic clove, cumin, and the remaining ½ teaspoon serrano chili in a blender and puree until smooth. Add the cilantro puree to the rice and toss well to combine. Season to taste.

(continued)

CILANTRO RICE

½ tablespoon olive oil

1 small white onion, chopped

3 garlic cloves, minced, divided

½ tablespoon plus ½ teaspoon minced and seeded serrano chili, divided

1 cups long-grain white rice

1½ cups chicken broth

¼ teaspoon kosher salt

½ cup coarsely chopped fresh cilantro

⅓ cup olive oil

2 tablespoons white wine vinegar

½ teaspoon cumin

SPICY CRÈME FRAÎCHE

¼ cup crème fraîche

½ teaspoon lime juice

⅛ teaspoon smoked paprika

Pinch cayenne pepper

½ teaspoon jalapeño pepper, finely diced and seeded

Kosher salt

FOR THE SPICY CRÈME FRAÎCHE

IN a small bowl, stir together the crème fraîche, lime juice, paprika, cayenne, and jalapeño until well combined. Season to taste with salt and set aside.

GRILL THE SHRIMP

PREHEAT the grill or a grill pan over high heat. Thread shrimp onto metal or soaked wooden skewers, 4–5 shrimp per skewer. Carefully oil the grill grate or grill pan. Add the skewers and grill about 2 minutes per side until the shrimp become slightly charred and are just opaque on the inside.

TO PLATE

MOUND the rice in the center of each plate. Remove the shrimp from the skewers and place on top of the rice. Drizzle the shrimp with spicy crème fraîche and serve with corn relish on the side.

CRISPY PORK BELLY, SUSHI RICE CAKE, AND LONG BEANS WITH SHISO AND KIMCHI

SERVES 4

If you like bacon, you're going to love pork belly. Both cuts come from the fatty underbelly of the pig—bacon is cured, pork belly is not. Pork belly's uncured status allows for a wide range of cooking preparations—it can be cut into chunks, braised, fried, spiced, shredded, and stuffed into buns or tacos. Pig heaven!

Pork belly is popular in Asian cuisine, particularly Korean, and it's a natural partner to the pungent, spicy fermented cabbage dish kimchi, one of Korea's national foods that's eaten with almost every meal. Sticky sushi rice is easily formed into cakes and fried to serve as a bed for the pork belly.

True to their name, long beans—also known as yard-long beans—asparagus beans, and snake beans grow up to three feet long. They are similar in appearance and taste to green beans but a bit less crisp and drier with a mild asparagus-like flavor. The beans are flavored with shiso, also known as perilla, a leaf that can be found wrapped around sushi and in other Japanese dishes. It belongs to the mint family and has a citrusy flavor. Long beans and shiso can be found in Asian markets. If unavailable, green beans and Thai basil can be substituted.

CRISPY PORK BELLY

2 garlic cloves, minced

1 tablespoon grated ginger

½ cup mirin

½ cup soy sauce

1 tablespoon honey

Pinch crushed red pepper

2 pounds boneless pork belly, skin on and scored all over

3 yellow onions, peeled and cut in half

½ cup plus 2 tablespoons white wine

3 large garlic cloves, smashed

5 whole allspice

1 large bay leaf

2 tablespoons chicken stock

FOR THE CRISPY PORK BELLY

IN a shallow dish just big enough to hold the pork belly, combine the garlic, ginger, mirin, soy, honey, and crushed red pepper, whisking to combine. Add the pork belly skin side up so that the meat is submerged in the marinade but the skin is dry. Cover and refrigerate for up to 4 hours or overnight.

PREHEAT the oven to 500°F with a rack in the upper third of the oven.

REMOVE the pork from the marinade. Place the onion halves in the center of a shallow roasting pan. Place the pork on top of the onions. Pour ¾ cup water and ½ cup white wine into the bottom of the pan and scatter the crushed garlic cloves, allspice, and bay leaf into the liquid.

PLACE the pan in upper third of oven and roast for 20 minutes, then tent the pan with foil and reduce the oven temperature to 325°F for 3½ hours or until the meat is very tender.

REMOVE the pork from the pan to rest while you make the sauce. Discard the onions, garlic, bay leaf, and allspice. Let the drippings cool off and skim any visible fat.

FOR THE SAUCE

PLACE the pan with the drippings over medium heat, add 2 tablespoons of wine, and cook 1–2 minutes until the alcohol has cooked off. Add the stock to the pan and simmer for 2 minutes. Strain the sauce and keep warm.

(continued)

SUSHI RICE CAKE

1 cup sushi rice, rinsed

1 ½ cups water

½ tablespoon mirin

½ teaspoon rice vinegar

½ teaspoon sugar

Kosher salt

Vegetable oil, for frying

LONG BEANS

1 tablespoon sesame oil

2 teaspoons minced garlic

1 pound Chinese long beans, washed and trimmed in half

¼ cup stock

1 tablespoon oyster sauce

1 teaspoon soy sauce

2 teaspoons finely minced shiso or Thai basil

FOR THE SUSHI RICE CAKE

RINSE the uncooked rice until the water runs clear.

IN a medium saucepan, combine the rice, water, mirin, vinegar, and sugar and bring to a boil. Cover and cook over low heat for 20 minutes. Fluff the rice. Transfer to a bowl and let cool. Season with salt.

IN a large nonstick skillet, heat ¼ inch of oil over medium-high heat until shimmering. For each cake, pack the rice into a ¼ cup measuring cup; unmold and flatten slightly. Cook the cakes over moderately high heat, pressing until golden brown, about 4 minutes. Turn and cook for 4 minutes longer. Serve hot.

FOR THE LONG BEANS

IN a large sauté pan or wok, heat the oil over medium-high heat. When the oil is hot but not smoking, add the garlic. Cook just until fragrant, 10 seconds. Add your long beans and sauté for 30 seconds, tossing to coat the beans with the oil. Add the stock, oyster sauce, and soy sauce. Cook the beans for 2 minutes or until they are crisp-tender. Remove from the heat, stir in the shiso, and keep warm.

TO PLATE

CUT the pork belly on the diagonal into slices about ½ inch thick. Pile the long beans in the middle of the plate. Top with the sushi rice cake, then three slices of pork belly. Spoon the sauce over the pork and garnish with the chopped chives. Serve with kimchi.

GRILLED PORK CHOP WITH SPINACH POLENTA AND SHAVED BABY ARTICHOKE SLAW

SERVES 4

Young, tender artichokes are not only edible raw; they're delicately tender and well worth seeking out when in season. They're simpler to prepare than full-sized artichokes, as they don't have that thistly "choke" that needs to be scooped out from the center. Just the stems, pointed tips, and tough outer leaves are removed, and then the artichokes are ready to be enjoyed. Using a mandoline to cut the artichokes will ensure even, paper-thin slices. If you don't have one, use your sharpest chef's knife to do the job.

Brining pork is the surest way to reliably tender, juicy, and flavorful chops. You'll need to plan an hour ahead for this. Pork chops overcook easily, so watch them carefully and remove them from the grill as soon as the temperature hits 135°F; they'll continue to cook as they rest.

PORK CHOP BRINE

¼ cup boiling water

⅓ cup kosher salt, plus more for seasoning

¼ cup sugar

2 quarts ice-cold water

4 center-cut pork rib chops, about 8 ounces each and 1 ½ inches thick

Freshly ground black pepper

SPINACH POLENTA

2 cups milk

1 cup cream

2 sprigs thyme

1 garlic clove, smashed

1 cup instant polenta

1–2 tablespoons unsalted butter, softened

2–3 tablespoons grated Parmesan cheese

5 tablespoons mascarpone cheese

3½ ounces (about 2½ cups) baby spinach

SHAVED BABY ARTICHOKES

Juice of 1 lemon, ½ tablespoon reserved

4 baby artichokes, cleaned

2 tablespoons extra virgin olive oil, more as necessary

Kosher salt and freshly ground black pepper

Zest of 1 lemon

3 tablespoons grated Parmesan cheese

Torn fresh basil leaves, for garnish

FOR THE PORK CHOPS

TO make the brine: In a large bowl, whisk together boiling water, salt, and sugar until dissolved. Add ice-cold water. Place pork chops in a zipper-lock bag and add the brine. Set the bag in a large bowl and refrigerate for 1 hour.

REMOVE pork chops from brine, pat dry with paper towels, and season with salt and pepper.

FOR THE POLENTA

COMBINE the milk, cream, thyme, and garlic in a medium saucepot. Heat over medium-high until the mixture just boils. Remove the thyme and garlic, lower the heat to medium, and add the polenta to the milk and cream in a slow, steady stream, whisking constantly. Now with a wooden spoon, continue mixing for about 5 minutes or until the mixture thickens. Remove from the heat. Stir in the butter and Parmesan, season to taste with salt and pepper, and keep warm.

WHEN the polenta is softened and smooth, stir in the mascarpone and spinach. Cook until the spinach has just begun to wilt. Cover and keep warm.

FOR THE SHAVED BABY ARTICHOKES

PREPARE a bowl of ice water with the lemon juice. Cut off the stems and pointed tips of the artichokes. Remove all of the tough outer leaves and

(continued)

drop immediately into the acidulated ice water. Removing one artichoke at a time, slice with a mandoline or thinly slice with a sharp knife. Return slices to the water.

JUST before serving, drain the artichoke slices from water and dry. In a medium bowl, whisk together the olive oil, the reserved ½ tablespoon of lemon juice, a pinch of salt, and a good amount of pepper. Add the artichoke slices and toss well to combine. Add the lemon zest and Parmesan cheese and toss to combine.

COOK THE PORK CHOPS

PREHEAT grill or a grill pan. Oil the grates or the pan. Add the chops and grill 8 minutes on one side, a quick sear on the edges, then 7 minutes on the other side, or until a meat thermometer registers 135°F. Move the chops to the outer part of the grill or lower the flame under the grill pan if they are getting too charred. Tent and allow the chops to rest before serving.

TO PLATE

PILE the polenta in the middle of each plate. Top with pork chops and finish with shaved artichokes, a drizzle of olive oil, and torn basil.

HOMEMADE PAPPARDELLE WITH WILD MUSHROOMS, POACHED EGG, AND SHAVED BLACK TRUFFLES

SERVES 4

If you want to make it onto *Hell's Kitchen*, you're going to have to learn to make pasta from scratch. If you're just looking to elevate your home cooking, pasta making is still a highly recommended skill to develop. Making pasta takes practice and patience, but once you get on a roll, it becomes a lot of fun, and soon enough you'll be cranking out shapes from wide-noodle pappardelle to skinny capellini and everything in between.

For the mushrooms, use any fresh mushrooms that are local or in season or just one favorite type if you prefer. To poach the eggs, we forego the typical whirlpool technique and instead just crack the eggs into simmering water, turn off the heat, cover the pan, and leave them until the whites are set. If black truffles are unavailable or out of your budget, feel free to omit them; the dish will still be a memorable one, and one you can serve to your vegetarian friends. Fresh truffles can be found in specialty grocers and Italian markets.

HOMEMADE PAPPARDELLE

2 cups all-purpose flour

Pinch of kosher salt

3 large eggs

½ teaspoon olive oil

Cornmeal, for dusting

SAUTÉED MIXED WILD MUSHROOM SAUCE

2–4 dried morel mushrooms or 1 ounce dried porcini mushrooms, soaked then sliced

2 tablespoons olive oil, more as needed

1 tablespoon unsalted butter

2 large shallots, chopped

1 garlic clove, minced

1¼ pounds mixed mushrooms (oyster, crimini, trumpet), cleaned and sliced

Kosher salt and freshly ground black pepper

2 tablespoons tomato paste

⅓ cup dry white wine

2 teaspoons chopped fresh thyme

Pinch chili flakes or more to taste

2 tablespoons chopped flat-leaf parsley, plus more for garnish

1 tablespooon freshly squeezed lemon juice

TO MAKE THE HOMEMADE PASTA

COMBINE the flour and salt in the bowl of a food processor fitted with a blade attachment. Pulse a few times to combine. Add the eggs and olive oil, and pulse 30–60 seconds or until the dough comes together in a ball. If it doesn't come together after a minute and looks like small pebbles, add a teaspoon of water and pulse again. Repeat until the dough comes together. If the dough is sticky, add a tablespoon of flour and process again. Repeat until the dough comes together.

TURN the dough out onto a clean surface. Knead until it comes together to form a smooth ball. Dust the dough with a little flour and place it in a small mixing bowl. Cover with plastic wrap and rest at room temperature for at least 30 minutes.

DIVIDE the dough into 4 pieces. Cover the dough with plastic wrap and work with one piece at a time.

SET pasta machine to widest setting. Flatten 1 dough piece into a 3-inch-wide rectangle. Run through machine 3 times, dusting lightly with flour if sticking. Continue to run piece through machine, adjusting to next-narrower setting after every 3 passes, until dough is about 26 inches long. Cut crosswise into 3 equal pieces. Run each piece through machine, adjusting to next-narrower setting, until the piece is a scant ¹⁄₁₆ inch thick and 14 to 16 inches long. Return machine to original setting for each piece. Arrange strips in a single layer on sheets of parchment and dust with cornmeal.

(continued)

POACHED EGGS

4 large fresh eggs

2 teaspoons vinegar

Parmesan cheese

Black truffle, optional

REPEAT with remaining dough. Let strips stand until slightly dry to touch but still pliable, about 20 minutes. Cut strips into ⅔-inch-wide pappardelle.

BRING a large pot of salted water to a boil while you cook the mushrooms.

FOR THE SAUTÉED MIXED WILD MUSHROOMS

PLACE the dried morels or dried porcinis in a bowl and cover with hot water. Soak 30 minutes, then remove from the soaking liquid. Rinse well and pat dry.

IN a large sauté pan, heat 1 tablespoon olive oil and 1 tablespoon butter over moderate heat. Add the shallots and garlic and sauté until translucent and tender, about 3 minutes. Remove shallots and garlic to a medium bowl and reserve. Add half of the mushrooms to the pan, stir so they are well coated, increase the heat, and leave in a single layer, undisturbed, for 5 minutes until the mushrooms are browned. Season to taste with salt and pepper, stir to combine, remove from the pan, and add them to the bowl with the shallots and garlic. Add remaining tablespoon olive oil to the pan and repeat with remaining mushrooms, adding them to the bowl when ready. Reduce heat to moderate and add the tomato paste and caramelize, about 5 minutes. Return all the mushrooms to the pan along with the shallots and garlic. Add wine, scraping up the brown bits from the bottom of the pan, and continue cooking until most of the liquid has cooked off. Add the thyme and chili flakes and season to taste with salt and pepper. Just before serving, fold in the parsley and lemon juice.

FOR THE POACHED EGGS

POACH the eggs just before you cook the pasta. In a 12-inch-wide sauté pan fitted with a lid, bring 4 inches of water to almost boiling. Add the vinegar to the water. Crack the eggs one at a time into a small ramekin, then place the ramekin near the surface of the hot water and gently drop the egg into the water. Repeat with each egg. With a spoon, coax the egg whites closer to their yolks. Turn off the heat and cover. Let sit for about 3 minutes or until the egg whites are cooked. Use a slotted spoon to lift eggs out of pan and transfer to a paper-towel-lined plate.

WHILE the eggs poach, cook the pasta.

COOK THE PAPPARDELLE

ADD the pappardelle to the pot of boiling water and cook until al dente, about 2 minutes. Drain, reserving ½ cup pasta water.

TRANSFER the pasta to the pan with the mushrooms. Add some of the reserved water if the pasta is too dry. Toss gently to combine.

TO PLATE

DIVIDE the pappardelle among 4 pasta bowls. Top each with 1 poached egg, a drizzle of olive oil, a shaving of Parmesan cheese, two black truffle shavings (if using), and chopped parsley. Serve with more grated Parmesan.

MUSTARD-RUBBED VEAL LOIN WITH BUTTERNUT SQUASH PUREE, SAUTÉED BABY BRUSSELS SPROUTS, AND GRAPE SAUCE

SERVES 6

Boneless veal loin roast is a tender cut that cooks in just under an hour. Note that unless you have two ovens (we can't all cook in *Hell's Kitchen*!), you'll need to roast the butternut squash before the veal, as the two cook at different temperatures. You can roast the squash and puree it up to a day ahead; reheat just before serving. While the roast is in the oven, sauté the baby Brussels sprouts and make the grape sauce. This dish is perfect for fall.

BUTTERNUT SQUASH PUREE

One 2-pound butternut squash

3 tablespoons softened butter, divided

½ teaspoon nutmeg

Kosher salt and freshly ground black pepper to taste

MUSTARD-RUBBED VEAL LOIN

2 garlic cloves, minced

1 tablespoon kosher salt, plus more to taste

2 tablespoons Dijon mustard or whole-grain mustard

1 tablespoon chopped fresh sage or 1 teaspoon dry sage

Juice of ½ lemon

3 tablespoons olive oil, divided

2 teaspoons black pepper, plus more to taste

2 pounds boneless veal loin roast, rolled and tied

BABY BRUSSELS SPROUTS

2 tablespoons extra virgin olive oil

¾ pound baby Brussels sprouts, trimmed and halved lengthwise

Kosher salt and freshly ground black pepper

2 tablespoons fresh lemon juice

FOR THE BUTTERNUT SQUASH PUREE

PREHEAT the oven 425°F. Cut the butternut squash in half lengthwise and remove the seeds. Rub the insides with 1 tablespoon softened butter and season with salt and pepper.

PLACE the squash in a shallow roasting pan cut side down. Bake 40–50 minutes or until the squash is soft.

REMOVE the squash from the oven and scoop the flesh out into a food processor. Puree until smooth; adjust seasoning if necessary.

REDUCE the oven temperature to 325°F.

FOR THE MUSTARD-RUBBED VEAL LOIN

BRING the veal loin to room temperature 30 minutes before roasting. Using the side of a chef's knife, mash the garlic with 2 tablespoons kosher salt to form a paste. In a small bowl, combine the garlic paste with the mustard, sage, lemon juice, 1 tablespoon olive oil, and black pepper. Set aside.

HEAT the remaining 2 tablespoons of olive oil in a large ovenproof skillet with 2 ½–3-inch sides, until shimmering. Add the veal loin and sear over moderately high heat until browned all over, about 6–7 minutes. Pour the mustard mixture over the veal, coating well. Transfer the pan to the oven and roast for 50–55 minutes or until an instant-read thermometer inserted in the thickest part of the roast registers 140°F.

TRANSFER to a plate or carving board, which will capture any juices from the veal as it rests. Cover loosely with foil and let rest for 10 minutes.

WHILE the veal is roasting, prepare the Brussels sprouts.

FOR THE BABY BRUSSELS SPROUTS

IN a large skillet, heat oil over medium heat. Add baby Brussels sprouts cut side down and season with salt and pepper. Cook covered for 5 minutes or until the flat side of the sprouts are just tender and beginning to brown. Uncover the pan and increase the heat to medium-high. Cook until the

(continued)

GRAPE SAUCE

½ cup red seedless grapes, cut in quarters

1 tablespoon balsamic vinegar

½ cups chicken stock

½ tablespoon cornstarch mixed with 1 tablespoon water (cornstarch slurry)

½ tablespoon unsalted butter

Kosher salt and freshly ground black pepper to taste

sprouts are tender, 2 minutes more. Remove from the heat, add the lemon juice, and season to taste. Keep warm.

FOR THE GRAPE SAUCE

HEAT a medium sauté pan over medium heat. Add the grapes and sauté until they begin to turn light brown, 2–3 minutes. Add balsamic vinegar and cook for 1 minute. Add the chicken stock and the juices from the resting meat and reduce by half. Slowly mix in the cornstarch slurry a little at a time, until the sauce begins to thicken and coats the back of a spoon. Remove the pan from the heat and swirl in the butter. Keep the sauce warm.

TO PLATE

REHEAT the butternut squash puree in a small saucepan over medium heat. Add the butter and nutmeg and season to taste. Mix well to combine.

CUT the string from the roasts and discard. Carve into ¼-inch-thick slices.

MOUNT the butternut squash puree in the center of the plate. Top with sliced veal. Scatter the baby Brussels sprouts around the veal and finish with the grape sauce.

NEW YORK STRIP WITH TRUFFLE POLENTA FRIES, TOMATO JAM, SAUTÉED SPINACH, AND RED WINE JUS

SERVES 4

Creamy polenta firms up quickly, so when it's poured from the pan and left to set for a bit, it can be cut into any number of shapes. When you slice it and fry it, you have polenta fries, a creamy, non-potato take on french fries. In another culinary about-face, sweet and tangy tomato jam stands in for the ketchup. This fanciful take on steak frites - similar to the one Mary Poehnelt of Season 11 pulled off in the show's finale—is worthy of New York strip, one of the most tender and costly of cuts.

TRUFFLE POLENTA FRIES

2 cups milk

1 cup cream

2 sprigs thyme

1 garlic clove, smashed

1 cup instant polenta

4 tablespoons unsalted butter, softened, divided

2–3 tablespoons grated Parmesan cheese

2 teaspoons truffle oil

Kosher salt and freshly ground black pepper

TOMATO JAM

½ pound plum tomatoes

2 tablespoons brown sugar

2 tablespoons sherry vinegar

2 tablespoons tomato paste

½ teaspoon lemon juice

Kosher salt and freshly ground black pepper

RED WINE JUS

2 tablespoons olive oil

2 shallots, thinly sliced

½ garlic clove, lightly crushed

small sprig rosemary

2½ tablespoons balsamic vinegar

⅞ cup dry red wine

⅞ cup beef stock or brown chicken stock, preferably homemade

Kosher salt and freshly ground black pepper

½ tablespoon butter

FOR THE TRUFFLE POLENTA FRIES

COMBINE the milk, cream, thyme, and garlic in a medium saucepot. Heat over medium-high until the mixture just boils. Remove the thyme and garlic, lower the heat to medium, and add the polenta to the milk and cream in a slow, steady stream, whisking constantly. Now with a wooden spoon, continue mixing for about 5 minutes or until the mixture is cooked. Remove from the heat. Stir in 2 tablespoons butter, Parmesan and truffle oil. Season to taste with salt and pepper.

LINE a half-sheet pan with parchment paper. Spread the polenta evenly with a spatula into the sheet pan. Cover with plastic wrap and chill for at least one hour or overnight.

PREHEAT the oven to 450°F. Melt the remaining 2 tablespoons of butter. Cut the chilled polenta into 3 x 1-inch fries and place on an unrimmed cookie sheet lined with parchment. Brush with melted butter. Bake in the center of the oven for 20 minutes, turning once halfway through, until the fries are golden and crisp.

FOR THE TOMATO JAM

ROUGH-CHOP the tomatoes. Combine the tomatoes and brown sugar in a small saucepan over medium-high heat and boil until the tomatoes have broken down and the liquid has evaporated, about 12 minutes. Deglaze with sherry vinegar, scraping up the brown bits from the bottom of the pan. Add the tomato paste, reduce heat, and simmer for 15 minutes, stirring occasionally, until reduced and thickened. Stir in the lemon juice, season to taste, and set aside.

FOR THE RED WINE JUS

IN a medium saucepan, heat the oil over moderate heat. Add the shallots and sauté for about 3 minutes until lightly browned, stirring often. Add garlic and rosemary. Continue cooking for 3 more minutes, stirring often so the shallots don't burn.

(continued)

STEAK

Four 12-ounce New York strip steaks

2 tablespoons neutral oil

Kosher salt and freshly ground black pepper

2 tablespoons unsalted butter

SAUTÉED SPINACH

2 tablespoons butter

1 teaspoon minced garlic

2 pounds baby spinach

Kosher salt and freshly ground black pepper

ADD the vinegar and cook 2 minutes or until the liquid evaporates, then add the wine and cook until reduced by two-thirds, about 10 minutes.

ADD the stock and bring to a boil. Reduce the heat to low and simmer 20 minutes or until the mixture is reduced by two-thirds. Strain through a fine mesh strainer, pressing gently to extract all of the jus, and season to taste with salt and pepper. Whisk in the butter. Set aside to keep warm.

FOR THE STEAK

LET steaks sit at room temperature for 30–45 minutes. Brush the steaks lightly with a neutral oil and season with salt and pepper. Heat a cast-iron skillet over high heat until it just starts to smoke. Sear the steak on each side, 2 ½ minutes per side for rare. About 1 minute before the steak is done, add the butter to the pan and continually baste the steak with the butter.

REMOVE the steak from the pan and allow to rest while you cook the spinach.

FOR THE SPINACH

IN a large sauté pan, melt the butter over medium heat. Add the garlic and cook for 1 minute. Add the spinach and cook, tossing to coat until the spinach is wilted. Season to taste with salt and pepper.

TO PLATE

SLICE each steak and fan it around the plate. Serve with polenta fries and spinach. Drizzle the plate and steak with red wine jus and garnish with a dollop of tomato jam.

PEPPER-CRUSTED STEAK WITH A MUSHROOM-BRANDY CREAM SAUCE, ROASTED ASPARAGUS, AND SAUTÉED POTATOES

SERVES 4

Bring out the fancy silverware—filet mignon is on the menu! To cook your steaks to perfection, resist touching them before flipping to create a crust, then leave them to rest for about as long as you cooked them before serving. A perfect filet mignon is never served above medium rare, as any *Hell's Kitchen* aficionado knows from the raw to rubbery steaks sent back to the kitchen over the years. To expedite this dish, roast the asparagus and make the sauce while the potatoes are cooking, and cook the steak at the very end.

SAUTÉED POTATOES

1 dozen purple fingerling potatoes or baby Yukon Gold potatoes

1½ tablespoons olive oil

1½ tablespoons unsalted butter

Kosher salt and freshly ground black pepper

ROASTED ASPARAGUS

1 pound asparagus, tough ends discarded and stalks peeled (if the asparagus are thick)

Olive oil

Kosher salt and freshly ground black pepper

MUSHROOM-BRANDY CREAM SAUCE

1 tablespoons unsalted butter

½ whole shallot, minced

2 small garlic cloves, thinly sliced

2 sprigs fresh thyme

1½ ounces oyster mushrooms, thinly sliced

1½ ounces trumpet mushrooms, stems diced, caps thinly sliced

2 tablespoons brandy

½ cup beef or chicken stock

⅜ cup heavy cream

Kosher salt and freshly ground black pepper

PEPPER-CRUSTED STEAK

1½ tablespoons canola oil

Kosher salt

Coarsely ground tri-colored peppercorns or black peppercorns

Four 8-ounce filets mignon

FOR THE SAUTEED POTATOES

BRING a medium pot of salted water to a boil. Add the new potatoes and boil 15 minutes or until just tender. Drain, and when the potatoes are cool enough to handle, remove the skin and slice the potatoes in half lengthwise. Set aside.

FOR THE ROASTED ASPARAGUS

WHILE the potatoes are cooking, roast the asparagus. Preheat the oven to 400°F. Place the asparagus in a single layer on a rimmed baking sheet, drizzle with olive oil, and toss to coat. Season with salt and pepper. Roast for 15–18 minutes, or until tender but still crisp.

FOR THE MUSHROOM-BRANDY CREAM SAUCE

MELT the butter in a saucepan over moderate heat. Add the shallots, garlic, and thyme sprigs. Sauté for 3 minutes until the shallots are tender. Using a slotted spoon, transfer mixture to a small bowl, leaving most of the butter in the pan. Increase heat and add the mushrooms to the pan, tossing to coat, then leave them undisturbed in a single layer for 4–5 minutes until brown. Stir and continue browning for 3 more minutes. Return the shallot mixture to the pan and stir to combine. Lift pan off the heat while you carefully add the brandy, then return the pan to the heat and cook about 1 minute until the brandy is evaporated. Add the stock and bring to a boil. Reduce heat, slowly stir in the cream, and continue at a gentle simmer until the sauce thickens and is reduced by a quarter. Season to taste with salt and pepper and keep warm.

FOR THE STEAK

SEASON the fillets with salt and press the ground peppercorns into the steak on both sides. Heat the oil in a cast-iron skillet over high heat until just smoking. Add the filet mignon and sear on both sides, 5–6 minutes total for medium rare. Transfer to a plate, tent with foil, and allow to rest for 5 minutes.

WHILE the steak is cooking, sauté the potatoes. Heat the oil and butter in a large frying pan. Add the potato halves to the pan and cook for 5 minutes until golden and crisp. Season to taste.

TO PLATE

PLACE steaks in the center of each plate. Spoon mushroom-brandy cream sauce over the steak and serve with the potato halves and asparagus.

CHICKEN MOLE WITH BLACK BEANS AND RICE AND CORN-AVOCADO SALSA

SERVES 4

Mole is a complex, multi-ingredient sauce served over meat—typically turkey or chicken—and brought out for weddings, birthdays, baptisms, Cinco de Mayo celebrations, and the like. There are several regional variations; this one, a mole poblano from the state of Puebla, is the most familiar one. Its many ingredients include cinnamon, raisins, nuts, seeds, two types of chilies (Mexico boasts countless varieties of chilies, each known not just for its heat but for its unique flavor profile), and chocolate, which lends a subtle flavor and rich, dark color to the dish. In typical Mexican fashion, beans and rice serve as an accompaniment.

CORN-AVOCADO SALSA

2 ears fresh corn

1 firm-ripe avocado, cut into small dice

¼ cup diced red onion

½ teaspoon diced jalapeño

Juice of ½ lime

1 teaspoon apple cider vinegar

2 tablespoons chopped cilantro

Kosher salt and freshly ground black pepper

CHICKEN MOLE

2 tablespoons olive oil

4 bone-in, skin-on chicken thighs, 5–6 ounces each

Kosher salt and freshly ground black pepper

½ small onion, diced

1 large garlic clove, minced

1 teaspoon cumin

1 large cinnamon stick

¼ cup tomato puree

2 tablespoons raisins

1 tablespoon whole almonds

1 tablespoon sesame seeds

1 large guajillo chili, stems removed

1 small ancho chili, stems removed

1 tablespoon peanut butter

½ cup chicken stock

¾ ounce Mexican drinking chocolate or 65 percent dark chocolate, grated

1 teaspoon kosher salt

A few turns freshly ground black pepper

BLACK BEANS AND RICE

½ cup long-grain white rice

1 tablespoon olive oil

½ small onion, chopped

¼ cup diced red bell pepper

1 garlic clove, chopped

½ teaspoon kosher salt

A few turns freshly ground black pepper

½ teaspoon ground cumin

One 15 ½-ounce can black beans, rinsed

½ teaspoon dried oregano

½ tablespoon red wine vinegar

Thinly sliced radishes

Cilantro leaves, for garnish

Lime wedges, for garnish

FOR THE CORN-AVOCADO SALSA

CUT the corn kernels off the cob. Combine the corn in a medium bowl with avocado, onion, and jalapeño. Toss to combine. Add the lime juice and cider vinegar and mix well. Fold in the cilantro and season to taste with salt and pepper. Allow to sit for 1–2 hours so the flavors develop.

FOR THE CHICKEN MOLE

IN a large Dutch oven, heat olive oil over medium-high heat. Brown the chicken on all sides, season with salt and pepper, and then transfer to a plate. Reduce heat to medium-low, add the onions, garlic, cumin, and cinnamon stick to the pot, and cook for 5 minutes. Add the tomato puree, season with salt and pepper, and cook for 5 minutes.

MEANWHILE, combine the raisins, almonds, sesame seeds, and chilies in a bowl. Pour 1 cup of boiling water over the contents of the bowl and steep for 5 minutes. Remove the nuts, sesame seeds, and chilies from the water and transfer to a bowl. Reserve the soaking liquid. Cut the chilies in half and discard the seeds. Transfer the almonds, sesame seeds, and chilies to a blender or use an immersion blender. Add the peanut butter and blend, adding just enough of the reserved liquid to create a saucelike puree.

POUR the nut-and-chili puree over the onion mixture, season with salt and pepper, and bring to a boil. Stir in the chicken stock, add the chicken pieces, and simmer for 10 minutes. Reduce the heat to low, add the chocolate, and heat until it melts and warms through, 1–2 more minutes.

FOR THE BLACK BEANS AND RICE

COOK the rice according to the package directions.

WHILE the rice cooks, heat the oil in a saucepan over moderate heat. Add the onion, red pepper, garlic, salt, and black pepper and cook, stirring occasionally, until softened, 4–5 minutes. Stir in the cumin and cook for 1 minute. Add the beans, oregano, and a ½ cup water. Cover and simmer for 10 minutes. Add the vinegar and season to taste. Serve over the rice.

TO PLATE

SERVE with thinly sliced radishes, fresh cilantro leaves, and lime wedges.

ROASTED PORK TENDERLOIN, COLLARD GREENS WITH SMOKED BACON WITH YAM AND POTATO GRATIN

SERVES 4

Pork tenderloin is lean, tender, and a delicacy; this cut is also known as pork fillet. Individual tenderloins are small, so they generally are sold two to a package. If you find a silver skin on your tenderloin, trim it off.

Though it's a fancy cut, the tenderloin is one of the easiest parts of the pig to cook; it roasts quickly, but take the greatest caution to avoid overcooking it, as it can go from tender to tough and dry in a matter of minutes. The tenderloin is marinated to further ensure a juicy outcome, so you'll need to plan at least eight hours ahead to ready the meat.

Pork and collard greens are a classic southern culinary pairing, with the collards cooked good and long and flavored with smoky bacon. Candied yams might finish such a meal; here we pair the yams with buttery Yukon Gold potatoes and cook them gratin-style to bring it up a few notches.

ROASTED PORK TENDERLOIN

¼ cup bourbon

¼ cup soy sauce

¼ cup brown sugar

¼ cup Dijon mustard

1 tablespoon finely chopped fresh ginger

3 garlic cloves, minced

Two 1-pound whole pork tenderloins, trimmed of silver skin

2 tablespoons olive oil

¼ cup chicken stock

1 tablespoon unsalted butter

COLLARD GREENS WITH SMOKED BACON

4 ounces thick cut bacon, diced

1 medium yellow onion, diced

Pinch crushed red pepper

2 garlic cloves, thinly sliced

2 bunches collard greens (about 2¼ pounds), tough stems removed and leaves roughly chopped

2 tablespoons cider vinegar

1 tablespoon molasses

Kosher salt and freshly ground black pepper

MARINATE THE PORK TENDERLOIN

PLACE the bourbon, soy sauce, brown sugar, Dijon, ginger, and garlic in a bowl and whisk to combine. Pour into a large zipper-lock bag and add the pork tenderloins. Marinate at least 8 hours or overnight.

FOR THE COLLARD GREENS

IN a large sauté pan over medium-low heat, cook the bacon until crisp and most of the fat is rendered, 8–10 minutes. Use a slotted spoon to transfer the bacon to a paper-towel-lined plate to drain, leaving the fat in the pan.

ADD the onions and crushed red pepper to the pan and sauté until the onions are tender and beginning to brown, about 8 minutes. Add the garlic and cook 1 minute. Then add the collard greens, tossing well to coat. Stir in the cider vinegar, molasses, and enough water to make the leaves float freely. Season with salt and pepper and bring to a simmer. Reduce the heat to medium-low and cook until the greens are tender, about 45 minutes.

RETURN the bacon to the pan, adjust seasoning, and stir to combine.

WHILE the collard greens cook, roast the pork tenderloin.

FOR THE YAM AND POTATO GRATIN

FILL a large bowl with cold water. One at a time, peel and slice each Yukon Gold and sweet potato into ⅛-inch-thick rounds and place in the bowl of water. Combine cream, butter, and garlic in medium saucepan and bring to simmer. Remove from heat. In a small bowl, combine the parsley, rosemary, sage, and thyme. Mix sea salt and black pepper in another small bowl.

YAM AND POTATO GRATIN
(will serve 6)

¾ pound medium Yukon Gold potatoes, peeled

¾ pound medium red-skinned yams, peeled

1 cup whipping cream

1 tablespoon unsalted butter

1 garlic clove, minced

½ tablespoon minced fresh flat-leaf parsley

½ tablespoon minced fresh rosemary

½ tablespoon minced fresh sage

½ tablespoon minced fresh thyme

Kosher salt and freshly ground black pepper

1 cup coarsely grated gruyère cheese (about 3 ounces)

PREHEAT the oven to 400°F. Arrange oven racks in the lower third and upper third.

LIGHTLY butter a 1½- to 2-quart baking dish. Drain the potatoes, then pat dry. Transfer half the potatoes to the baking dish and spread them in an even layer. Season with salt and pepper, then sprinkle with half of the herb mixture and half of the gruyère. Repeat with the remaining potatoes, salt and pepper, herb mixture, and cheese. Pour the cream mixture over the potatoes, lightly pressing the potato mixture as much as possible into the liquid.

COVER gratin tightly with foil and bake in the bottom third of the oven for 25 minutes. Move the gratin to the upper rack, uncover, and bake another 20–25 minutes or until the potatoes are very tender and the top is golden brown. The liquid will be bubbling and will become more absorbed as the gratin sets. Allow to rest at least 15 minutes before serving.

AT the same time, place a large ovenproof skillet—preferably cast iron—in the oven to heat up, about 10 minutes.

ROASTED PORK TENDERLOIN

REMOVE tenderloins from the bag and discard the marinade.

REMOVE the pan from the oven. Add the oil to the pan and swirl. Place the pork in the pan and roast in the bottom third of the oven for 10 minutes. Flip the pork and cook until the internal temperature is 140–145°F, about 8–10 minutes.

REMOVE from the pork from the pan and tent with foil to rest for 10 minutes.

ONCE the meat has rested and given up some of its juice, place the pan back on the stovetop over medium heat. Add chicken stock and pork juices and scrape up the brown bits from the bottom of the pan. Strain, then swirl in the butter. Season to taste with salt and pepper.

TO PLATE

SLICE the tenderloin on a bias and drizzle with the sauce. Serve with gratin and collard greens.

SLOW-BRAISED VEAL CHEEKS WITH SMASHED RED BLISS POTATOES AND GARLIC CONFIT

SERVES 4

Veal cheek is a tough cut that requires long cooking to coax out the tenderness and reveal a deep, rich flavor profile. Season 11's Ja'Nel Witt won the final dinner service and the title with a meal featuring her veal cheeks, a take on Southern flavors with a twist. As Ja'Nel put it, "If you don't take risks, you won't ever stand out." If there is a silver skin covering the cheeks, remove it before cooking them. Once a cut reserved for budget-minded folk, offal and other "off" cuts are having their day, making their way onto trendy restaurant menus in recent years. If your local butcher hasn't caught on to the trend, ask him or her to special order the cheeks for you.

Garlic confit—garlic cooked slowly in ample olive oil—is sweet, deliciously creamy, almost buttery, and mellowed of its sharp bite. Red bliss potatoes, smashed and enriched with crème fraîche, serve as the starch for the meal.

SLOW-BRAISED VEAL CHEEKS

2 tablespoons olive oil

4 veal cheeks, trimmed of fat and silver skin (about 4 ounces each after trimming)

Kosher salt and freshly ground black pepper

1 large carrot, peeled and chopped

2 stalks celery, chopped

1 medium onion, chopped

2 tablespoons tomato paste

1 cup dry red wine

1 cup veal stock or beef stock

1 sprig rosemary

1 sprig sage

1 sprig thyme

2 bay leaves

1 teaspoon black peppercorns

2 garlic cloves, crushed

GARLIC CONFIT

1 cup of whole garlic cloves

2 cups olive oil

Kosher salt and freshly ground black pepper

SMASHED RED BLISS POTATOES

4 red bliss potatoes, scrubbed and cut into quarters

2 tablespoons crème fraîche

2 tablespoons chicken stock, warmed

Kosher salt and freshly ground black pepper

Chopped chives, for garnish

FOR THE SLOW-BRAISED VEAL CHEEKS

HEAT the olive oil in a Dutch oven over medium-high heat. Season the veal cheeks with salt and pepper. Add the meat to the pan and sear on both sides until browned, about 5–6 minutes. Transfer the meat to a plate and set aside.

ADD the carrots, celery, and onion to the pan and sauté until the onions are translucent, 5–6 minutes. Add the tomato paste and cook, stirring often, until the paste is caramelized, about 3 minutes. Add the wine, scraping the brown bits off the bottom of the pan. Simmer 2–3 minutes so the alcohol cooks off. Return the veal cheeks to the pot, along with any juices from the plate. Add the stock, rosemary, sage, thyme, bay leaves, peppercorns, and garlic cloves. Bring to a boil, then cover with a piece of parchment paper slightly larger than the pan, so the paper is resting on the meat. Cover with the pan lid and reduce heat to low. Maintaining a very slow simmer, braise for 1½ hours until the veal cheeks are very tender.

FOR THE GARLIC CONFIT

SEPARATE the head of garlic and peel each clove. Add the garlic to a 1-quart saucepan over low heat and cover the cloves with oil by at least 1½ inches.

Cook for 35–40 minutes or until the garlic is very tender but not browned. Allow to cool completely in the oil.

FOR THE SMASHED RED BLISS POTATOES WITH CRÈME FRAÎCHE

PLACE the potatoes in a medium saucepan and add water to cover by 2 inches. Bring to a boil over high heat and cook about 20 minutes, or until the potatoes are tender when pierced with the tip of a sharp knife. Drain and return the potatoes to the pot. Add the crème fraîche, chicken stock, and salt and pepper, and smash the potatoes with a fork. Cover and keep warm.

REMOVE the veal cheeks from the Dutch oven and tent to keep warm. Strain the braising liquid and allow to stand until fat rises to the surface. Remove the fat and return to the stovetop. Bring to a boil over medium-high heat until the sauce is reduced by half. Season with salt and pepper.

TO PLATE

MOUND the smashed potatoes in the center of each plate. Top with a veal cheek and drizzle with pan sauce. Mash one or two garlic confit cloves and place on top of the meat. Serve with Rainbow-Colored Carrots with Parsley Butter (page 171) and garnish with freshly chopped chives.

CARBONARA

SERVES 4

Carbonara is a simple Italian pasta dish comprised of spaghetti, pork, cheese, and eggs. A true carbonara contains no cream and relies on eggs for its velvety texture (though many restaurant carbonaras will cheat and add cream). It's a hearty dish and a go-to weeknight meal, as many of the ingredients can already be found in a well-stocked pantry. And if you keep frozen peas and pancetta on hand, you're minutes away from carbonara making at any given moment.

If pancetta is unavailable, you can substitute an equal amount of bacon. Cook the strips and crumble the bacon before adding it to the mix. Or go really authentic Italian and search out *guanciale*, which is cured pork-jowl bacon; it's available from Italian butchers and specialty stores.

12 ounces linguine

Kosher salt

⅔ cup finely grated Parmesan cheese, plus more for garnish

¼ cup finely grated Pecorino Romano cheese

2 tablespoons finely chopped parsley

2 large eggs

3 tablespoons extra virgin olive oil

6 ounces pancetta, chopped

½ small yellow onion, cut into small dice

3 garlic cloves, peeled and thinly sliced

¼ cup dry white wine

Freshly ground black pepper to taste

½ cup fresh shucked peas or thawed frozen English peas

BRING a large pot of salted water to a boil. Add linguine and cook according to the package directions, until al dente. Drain, reserving 1 cup pasta water.

WHILE the pasta is cooking, whisk together in a large bowl the Parmesan, Pecorino Romano, parsley, and eggs. Slowly drizzle in some of the reserved pasta water, whisking until the mixture is well combined and forms a sauce for the pasta.

HEAT oil a 12-inch skillet over medium heat. Add pancetta and cook until edges are crisp, about 6 minutes. Remove the pancetta with a slotted spoon and reserve. Drain off all but 1 tablespoon of fat from the pan. Add onion and sauté until soft and translucent, about 4 minutes. Add the garlic and sauté one minute more. Add the wine and cook until almost all the liquid is evaporated. Remove the pan from the heat.

ADD the onions, pancetta, peas, and linguine to the egg-and-cheese mixture. Season with salt and pepper. Toss well to combine and serve with more Parmesan.

HALIBUT *EN PAPILLOTE* WITH PURPLE JASMINE RICE AND ISLAND SALSA

SERVES 4

Tender white-fleshed fish served *en papillote* makes a stunning visual presentation, more so when set against purple jasmine rice. A zesty tropical fruit salad adds to the effect. Cooking fish *en papillote*—wrapped in parchment to form a little package—ensures succulent fish, as the package holds in the moisture and steams the fish. Place the packages directly on your diners' plates for them to open to get the full *en papillote* effect.

Don't use light coconut milk for cooking your rice; it is made from a second extraction and therefore is less flavorful. If you really want to go light, simply swap in some water for a portion of the coconut milk.

HALIBUT EN PAPILLOTE

1 lemon, cut into 8 slices

8 teaspoons unsalted butter

Four 6-ounce halibut fillets, skin removed

PURPLE JASMINE RICE

½ cup purple jasmine rice (also called forbidden rice)

½ cup unsweetened coconut milk (not light!)

Kosher salt and freshly ground black pepper

ISLAND SALSA

1 cup pineapple, cut into small dice

1 cup jicama, cut into small dice

1 cup mango, cut into small dice

¼ cup red onion, minced

1 tablespoon jalapeño or serrano pepper, minced, or more to taste

1 teaspoon grated lime zest

2 teaspoons lime juice

1 teaspoon olive oil

Kosher salt and freshly ground black pepper

FOR THE ISLAND SALSA

IN a large bowl, combine the pineapple, jicama, mango, red onion, jalapeño, lime zest and juice, and olive oil. Season with salt and pepper and refrigerate at least 2 hours before serving.

FOR THE PURPLE JASMINE RICE

PLACE the rice in a fine mesh strainer and rinse under cold water, rubbing the kernels between your hands a few times until the water runs almost clear.

TRANSFER the rice to a medium saucepan fitted with a lid. Add the add coconut milk and ½ cup water and season with salt and pepper. Stir to combine.

BRING the rice to a boil over medium-high heat. Stir often to prevent the rice from scorching down on the bottom. Once the liquid comes to a boil, reduce the heat to a low simmer, cover, and cook for about 30 minutes or until the liquid is absorbed. Remove from heat and let the rice steam for another 10 minutes. Fluff and keep warm.

FOR THE HALIBUT

CUT four pieces of parchment paper into 11 x 15-inch rectangles. Butter the center of each paper with 1 teaspoon butter. Season the fish with salt and pepper, dot each fillet with another teaspoon of butter, sprinkle with chopped mint, and finish with two slices of lemon.

FOLD the parchment paper by taking the two long sides and meeting in the middle. Fold down a couple of times until sealed against the fish. Fold each short end and tuck underneath so the package is tightly sealed. Place on a sheet pan, seam side down, and bake about 12 minutes, or 1–2

minutes longer according to the thickness of the fish, until the fish is flaky and opaque. Remove from the oven and allow the fish to rest for 2 minutes before serving.

TO PLATE

MOUND the rice on the plate. Top with the halibut fillet. Spoon the juices over the fish and rice and serve with salsa.

CHAPTER FIVE

SIDES ARE OUR SUPPORTING CAST: A PERFECTLY COOKED VEGETABLE, STARCH, OR BREAD TO ROUND OUT A FIRST-RATE MEAL. A NEGLECTED SIDE CAN COST A HELL'S KITCHEN CONTESTANT THE TITLE, AND A CREATIVE ONE WILL KEEP A CHEF IN THE GAME. AT HOME, A SIDE IS EQUALLY IMPORTANT TO THE SUCCESS OF YOUR OVERALL DINING EXPERIENCE.

THIS CHAPTER COVERS CLASSIC COMFORT-FOOD SIDES, INCLUDING CREAMED CORN (PAGE 179) AND CREAMED SPINACH (PAGE 181) AND AN OVER-THE-TOP VARIATION ON MAC AND CHEESE FEATURING TRUFFLES (PAGE 191). TWO VARIATIONS ON GRATIN (PAGE 184 AND 187) ARE INCLUDED, AS IS A SPUDLESS VARIATION ON FRIES (PAGE 182) AND A

COUPLE OF WAYS TO COOK CARROTS (PAGES 171 AND 189). THESE ARE THE GO-TO HELL'S KITCHEN SIDES, BUT THERE'S NO NEED TO STICK TO A SCRIPT. YOU MAY ALSO PULL FROM A MULTICOMPONENT MAIN TO COMPLETE YOUR MEAL. FOR EXAMPLE, IN FALL YOU MAY TRY BRUSSELS SPROUTS (PAGE 98), OR FOR A THIRD GRATIN VARIATION, THE TRUFFLED POMMES ANNA ON PAGE 96. IF YOU'D PREFER TO PUREE YOUR CARROTS, TRY THE VERSION ON PAGE 108. POLENTA (PAGE 105, 110, OR 145) MAKES ANOTHER RELIABLE SIDE. FOR AN ALTERNATIVE TO SPINACH, YOU CAN BRAISE SOME KALE IN CIDER (PAGE 85) OR SERVE UP SMOKY COLLARD GREENS (PAGE 160). USE THE SKILLS YOU'VE LEARNED THUS FAR AND ADD A MEASURE OF KITCHEN CREATIVITY TO GO ALL OUT WITH YOUR SIDES. YOUR REWARD WILL BE A MEAL THAT TRULY SHINES.

SIDES

RAINBOW-COLORED CARROTS WITH BUTTER AND PARSLEY

SERVES 4

Before the seventeenth century, carrots were predominantly purple, making orange carrots an upstart. White and black carrots also existed, as did yellow and red carrots; it is thought that orange carrots are the result of a cross between the two. These multicolored heirloom varieties are making a culinary comeback, finding their way to farmers' markets and upscale supermarkets to satisfy this country's appetite for the sweet and earthy root. This simple side of carrots blanched and coated in butter and stock can be made with any color carrot, including good old orange if that's what you find in your crisper drawer.

6–8 rainbow carrots, greens trimmed and carrots peeled

Unsalted butter

1 tablespoon vegetable stock

Kosher salt and freshly ground black pepper

Chopped flat-leaf parsley, for garnish

BRING a medium pot of salted water to a boil. Add the carrots and blanch until just fork-tender. Drain and pat dry with paper towel.

HEAT the butter in a large sauté pan over medium heat. Add the carrots and stock, and toss the carrots to coat. Cook 2–3 minutes, then season with salt and pepper. Transfer to a plate, garnish with parsley, and serve.

DELICATA SQUASH WITH SAGE

SERVES 4

Delicata squash is a small, oval-shaped winter variety with cream- to yellow-colored skin and green stripes. Its compact size makes it easier to cut, clean, and cook than larger, heavier squashes such as butternut and, when roasted, its thin, delicate skin becomes tender enough to eat. Delicata squash weigh just one or two pounds, making them easy to pop into your shopping basket or transport home from the farmers' market. The flesh is creamy and sweet; its sweetness is concentrated when roasted. A squash half is a perfect side to a fall dish.

Two delicata squash, cut in half lengthwise, seeds removed and discarded

2 tablespoons olive oil

Kosher salt and freshly ground black pepper

2–3 tablespoons fresh chopped sage, plus more for garnish

PREHEAT the oven to 425°F.

CUT each delicata squash half into ½-inch-wide half moons. You can leave the peel on these squash. Place the squash in a single layer on a rimmed baking sheet, brush with olive oil, and season with salt and pepper. Sprinkle with sage.

BAKE until browned, about 20–25 minutes, flipping halfway through.

TEMPURA BROCCOLINI WITH LEMON AIOLI

SERVES 4

Broccolini is a more delicate version of broccoli; its stalks are more slender and the florets are smaller. Tiny yellow flowers sometimes appear among the florets; they are completely edible, as is every part of the vegetable, making it perfect for frying whole. The key to perfectly cooked tempura is maintaining the frying oil at a consistent temperature between batches; including seltzer rather than water in your batter ensures a crisp and light tempura. Aioli, based on olive oil, egg yolks, and garlic, makes for a rich and creamy dipping sauce.

TEMPURA BROCCOLINI

1 cup all-purpose flour

1 tablespoon cornstarch

1 cup cold seltzer (club soda)

Pinch of kosher salt

2 bunches broccolini, trimmed of excess leaves

4–5 cups vegetable oil

LEMON AIOLI

1 large egg yolk

1 tablespoon fresh lemon juice

1 teaspoon Dijon mustard

1 garlic clove, pressed through garlic press

1 cup vegetable oil

Kosher salt

In a medium pot, heat oil to 375°F.

FOR THE LEMON AIOLI

IN the container of an immersion blender, place egg yolk, 1 tablespoon of water, lemon juice, mustard, pressed garlic, and oil. Let sit for 30 seconds until the oil rises to the top. Lower the blender into the container all the way to the bottom. Begin blending. As the aioli begins to form, tilt the blender and slowly lift until you see all the oil is completely combined. From start to finish this should take no longer than 2 minutes. Season aioli with salt and pepper and set aside.

FOR THE TEMPURA

WHEN oil is up to temperature, combine the flour, cornstarch, seltzer, and a pinch of salt in a medium bowl. Stir just until all the ingredients are mixed. Don't overstir—the batter should still have a few lumps.

DIP the broccolini into the batter and coat well. Immediately drop the spears into the oil and fry about 1 minute or until the batter is golden and crisp. Fry a few pieces at a time, and don't overcrowd the pot. Remove the broccolini with a mesh skimmer and transfer to a paper-towel-lined plate to drain. Repeat with remaining broccolini.

TO SERVE

SPRINKLE the tempura with salt and serve immediately with aioli.

CAULIFLOWER-STUFFED NAAN WITH CILANTRO CHUTNEY

SERVES 4 6

Naan is the Indian flatbread we all love to order when we eat out; in restaurants it's cooked in a tandoor oven and comes to the table all puffed up and beautifully charred. Naan also can be cooked on the stovetop, making this bread completely doable at home. Flavorings such as garlic or onions can be cooked into naan, or the naan can be stuffed, as we do here, upping its deliciousness and turning this bread into a substantial side. Serve it as part of the Eclectic Ethnic menu (page 244) or the Asian Fusion menu (page 246). The amchur powder and other spices can be found at Indian groceries and online at kalustyans.com.

NAAN

¼ teaspoon sugar

¼ teaspoon plus ⅛ teaspoon dry active yeast

1¼ cups flour, plus more for dusting

¾ teaspoon kosher salt

¼ cup Greek yogurt

2½ tablespoons unsalted melted butter or ghee

Coarse sea salt

CAULIFLOWER

2 tablespoons olive oil

1 medium onion, finely chopped

3–4 green chilies, seeded and finely chopped

1 teaspoon grated fresh ginger

1 teaspoon amchur (dried mango) powder

2 teaspoon ground cumin

¼ teaspoon garam masala

¼ teaspoon turmeric powder

1 small head cauliflower, florets chopped

2 tablespoons chopped fresh cilantro

CILANTRO CHUTNEY

½ garlic clove, minced

1 canned green chili, minced

Pinch of kosher salt

3 cups fresh cilantro, loosely packed

1 ½ tablespoons fresh lime juice

2 tablespoons boiling water

3 tablespoons olive oil

Kosher salt and freshly ground black pepper

FOR THE NAAN

POUR ¼ cup hot water in to a medium bowl. When the water registers 110°F on an instant-read thermometer, stir in the sugar and yeast and let rest for 10 minutes.

IN a large bowl, combine the flour and kosher salt. Whisk together the yogurt and 1 tablespoon of melted butter and add it to the yeast mixture. Stir the yeast mixture into the flour and work with your hands until the dough comes together. It's okay if the dough is a bit floury and dry; it will moisten and smooth out when you knead it.

TURN the dough out onto work surface and knead the dough 5 minutes, adding a dusting of flour if the dough begins sticking to the board. The dough should be smooth. Place it in a bowl, cover with plastic wrap, and set on a warm plate for 90 minutes.

WHILE the dough is rising, make the cauliflower filling and the cilantro chutney.

(continued)

FOR THE CAULIFLOWER

HEAT olive oil in a medium skillet fitted with a lid over medium heat. Add onion, green chilies, and grated ginger and cook 2–3 minutes until the vegetables begin to soften. Add amchur, cumin, garam masala, and turmeric and cook another 2 minutes until very aromatic. Stir in the cauliflower, tossing to coat, then add ¼ cup water. Cover the pan and simmer, stirring occasionally, until the cauliflower is tender, about 10 minutes. Stir in the cilantro, season with salt and pepper, and remove from the heat.

FOR THE CILANTRO CHUTNEY

USING the side of a chef's knife, smash the garlic and chili with a pinch of kosher salt to form a paste.

IN the bowl of a small food processor or blender, combine the garlic chili paste, cilantro, lime juice, and water and blend until combined. Pour the olive oil into the cilantro in a steady steam and process until the mixture comes together and is smooth. Season to taste with salt and pepper and set aside.

TO MAKE THE STUFFED NAAN

DIVIDE the dough into 6 sections. Working with one piece at a time, roll the dough out on a lightly floured board until you have a 5-inch circle. Place 1½ tablespoons cauliflower in the center of the circle. Bring the dough up around the filling and press the edges together to seal. Gently roll the dough out again in an oval or round shape about ¼-inch thick.

REPEAT with remaining dough and filling.

HEAT a nonstick skillet over medium-high heat. Working in batches, brown the dough on both sides, 1 ½ minutes per side, until golden and cooked through.

REMOVE from the pan, brush with melted butter, and sprinkle with coarse sea salt. Slice in quarters and serve with chutney.

CREAMED CORN

SERVES 4

Grilled, boiled, or roasted corn is a reliable summer side. Cream it like they do in the South and Midwest and it's serious comfort food, paired with everything from steak to fish to chicken dishes. A tip for tidily removing kernels from the cob: set the tip of your ear of corn at the bottom of a large bowl on an angle and shave off the kernels with a chef's knife, rotating the ear as you go. If fresh on-the-cob corn isn't in season, you may substitute frozen corn; each ear equals about a ¾ cup kernels.

6 ears corn, shucked, or 3½ cups
frozen sweet corn

1 tablespoon olive oil

1 garlic clove, thinly sliced

1 shallot, thinly sliced

1 cup heavy cream

1 tablespoon chopped fresh chives

½ teaspoon kosher salt

½ teaspoon freshly ground black pepper

CUT corn from the cobs, place kernels in a bowl, and set aside.

HEAT the olive oil in a medium saucepan over medium heat. Add half of the corn, the garlic, and the shallot. Toss to coat and allow to cook, stirring occasionally, for 3 minutes. Add ¾ cup of the cream, reduce heat to low, and simmer gently for 20 minutes.

PLACE the corn mixture into a blender or use an immersion blender to puree. Add the remaining ¼ cup of cream and continue blending until the mixture is almost smooth.

RETURN the puree to the saucepan and stir in the remaining corn. Gently simmer for 10 minutes. Stir in chives and season to taste with salt and pepper.

CREAMED SPINACH

SERVES 4

Great creamed spinach starts with fresh, vibrant-looking greens—never canned—and cooked in just the water clinging to their leaves after they're washed. Creaming spinach makes this green irresistible. Fried eggs finish this *Hell's Kitchen* version; feel free to skip the eggs to match the side you're serving it with.

CREAMED SPINACH, FRIED EGG

2½ pounds fresh spinach, tough stems discarded

3 tablespoons unsalted butter

1 small onion, finely chopped

1 small clove garlic, minced

3 tablespoons all-purpose flour

1¾ cups whole milk, or a mix thereof

Pinch of freshly grated nutmeg

1 tablespoon vegetable oil

4 large fresh eggs

WASH your spinach well but no need to spin or pat it dry. Place spinach in a large pot over medium heat. Cook, covered, with just the water clinging to leaves, stirring occasionally, until wilted, about 4 to 6 minutes. Remove spinach to a colander.

WHEN the spinach is cool enough to handle, take small handfuls and squeeze out as much water as possible. Chop the spinach and set aside.

IN a small saucepan over low heat, warm the milk, stirring occasionally as it's kept warm.

MEANWHILE, cook onion and garlic in butter in medium saucepan over moderately low heat, stirring occasionally, until softened, about 5 minutes. Whisk in flour and cook for 3 minutes, mixing frequently with a wooden spoon. Add warm milk or cream in a slow stream, whisking constantly to prevent lumps, and simmer, whisking, until thickened, 4 minutes. Stir in nutmeg, spinach, and salt and pepper to taste and cook, stirring, until heated through.

KEEP warm while you fry the eggs.

PLACE a medium size nonstick frying pan, over low heat. Add the butter and let melt slowly. When all the butter has melted, but not foaming, crack the eggs one at a time into a small bowl. Gently slide each egg into the frying pan. Cook about 5 minutes until the egg white solidifies and the yolk is still runny. Salt just before serving on top of the creamed spinach.

CRISPY ZUCCHINI FRIES

SERVES 4

These "fries" are baked until crisp on the outside, tender and juicy on the inside. Zucchini fries are a lighter alternative to standard fries; they satisfy that urge for potatoes without leaving you with a heavy, carb-overload feeling, and they give you more room to enjoy your main. The recipe easily doubles to fill up more than one pan; as they are quite addictive, scaling up might be in order.

1 teaspoon olive oil, plus more for brushing and drizzling

1 pound baby zucchini, trimmed

½ cup all-purpose flour

Kosher salt and freshly ground black pepper

1 large egg, lightly beaten

1 cup panko breadcrumbs

1 teaspoon paprika

PREHEAT the oven to 425°F.

PREPARE a sheet pan with an ovenproof rack; brush the rack with olive oil.

CUT the zucchini into 3-inch sticks to resemble a medium-thick french fry.

PLACE the flour in a shallow dish and season with salt and pepper. Place the egg in another shallow dish and whisk in 1 teaspoon of oil. In a third dish combine the panko and paprika.

SEASON the zucchini with salt and pepper. Working in batches, dredge the zucchini in the flour, shaking off excess, then coat in egg-oil mixture and cover in the breadcrumb mixture.

PLACE the breaded zucchini sticks on the prepared wire rack, leaving space between each fry. Lightly drizzle with olive oil. Bake for 20 minutes or until golden and crispy.

DAUPHINOISE POTATOES

SERVES 4

Thinly sliced potatoes bathed in cream, topped with cheese, and baked au gratin make the most lush of sides, the finest in French comfort cuisine. Also known as scalloped potatoes, this dish comes from the Dauphiné region of France and pairs with just about any meat dish. This recipe requires a mandoline or a very sharp chef's knife to slice the potatoes just right.

2 pounds russet potatoes, peeled

1½ cups heavy cream

½ teaspoon kosher salt

¼ teaspoons freshly ground black pepper

1 sprig fresh sage

1 clove garlic, peeled and smashed

1 cup finely shredded Gruyère or Comté

HEAT the oven to 400°F and butter an 8-inch round baking pan.

USING a mandoline or sharp knife, slice the potatoes into ⅛-inch thick rounds.

IN a large saucepan, combine the potatoes with the cream, salt, pepper, sage, and garlic. Bring the mixture to a boil over medium-high heat, gently stirring occasionally.

ONCE the potatoes boil. remove the sage and garlic and discard Pour the mixture into the prepared baking dish. Shake the dish a bit to let the slices settle and then sprinkle with the cheese.

BAKE 40 minutes or until the top is golden brown, the cream has thickened and the potatoes are very tender when pierced with a knife. There still may be some liquid but it will set as it cools. Allow to rest at least 15 minutes before serving.

POTATO LEEK GRATIN

SERVES 4

Another variation on the gratin theme (see page 184 for the classic Dauphinoise Potatoes recipe), this one is flavored by mildly oniony leeks. To clean leeks, trim the root end and remove the dark tops (save them for stock), leaving just the white and light green parts. Cut the leeks into sections three to four inches long then cut those sections in half and immerse them in a bowl of water, fanning them out and leaving the leeks to float and the dirt to sink to the bottom. For particularly dirty leeks, repeat the cleaning for a second time with fresh water.

1½ pounds peeled Yukon Gold potatoes

Kosher salt and freshly ground black pepper

2 tablespoons unsalted butter, plus more for greasing the pan

2 large leeks, white and light green parts only, trimmed, washed and halved lengthwise, then thinly sliced crosswise

Leaves from 2 sprigs of thyme

1 cup heavy cream

1 large garlic clove, minced

1 bay leaf

¼ teaspoon freshly ground nutmeg

1 cup Asiago, grated

1 cup fresh breadcrumbs

2 tablespoons finely grated Parmesan

1 tablespoon unsalted butter, melted

HEAT oven to 400°F and butter a 2-quart gratin dish.

MELT the 2 tablespoons butter in a large skillet over medium heat. Add leeks, remaining salt and pepper, and thyme. Cook, stirring, until leeks are tender and golden, about 7 minutes.

ADD cream, garlic and bay leaf to the skillet, scraping up browned bits of leeks from the bottom of the pan. Simmer gently for 5 minutes. Stir in nutmeg.

WHILE the cream is heating, use a mandoline or sharp knife, and slice the potatoes into ⅛-inch thick rounds. Toss with salt and pepper. Layer half of the the rounds in the gratin dish. Top with all of the leeks and finish with a layer of the remaining potatoes. Pour the cream over the leeks and potatoes and top with the Asiago.

IN a small bowl, combine the breadcrumbs, Parmesan, and melted butter, and season with salt and pepper.

COVER the pan with aluminum foil and bake for 40 minutes. Remove the foil and sprinkle the breadcrumb mixture over the top. Return the gratin to the oven, uncovered, and bake an additional 12-15, or until until the cheese is bubbling and the top is golden brown. Allow to rest at least 10-15 minutes before serving.

GINGER CARAMELIZED CARROTS

SERVES 4

Did you know that Americans eat more carrots than any other people in the world? Here's a second take on the darling of America's vegetables, given a sweet bite with crystallized ginger, caramelized with honey, and finished with lemon juice and mint to bring all the flavors together.

1 pound small, thin carrots, peeled

2 tablespoons unsalted butter

1 tablespoon honey

1 tablespoon finely chopped crystallized ginger

Kosher salt and freshly ground pepper to taste

1 teaspoon fresh lemon juice

1 tablespoon chopped fresh mint

PREHEAT the oven to 425°F.

ROLL cut the raw carrots. Put the butter in a roasting pan just large enough to hold the carrots in a single layer and place in the preheating oven. Watch carefully to prevent burning. When the butter has melted, remove the pan from the oven and stir in the honey and crystallized ginger. Add the carrots and toss to coat them evenly. Season with salt and pepper and spread the carrots out in a single layer.

ROAST the carrots, stirring 2 times until golden, glazed, and fork-tender, about 30 minutes.

REMOVE the pan from the oven and sprinkle with lemon juice and mint.

TRUFFLE MAC AND CHEESE

SERVES 4

Comfort food reaches new heights in this take on classic mac and cheese enriched with truffle oil. Cavatappi is a corkscrew-shaped macaroni, and mezzi rigatoni is a squat variation; they can be found in Italian markets or specialty stores. If unavailable, regular rigatoni, elbow macaroni, or whichever pasta shape you prefer for your mac and cheese will work. We include panko, Japanese breadcrumbs, which are coarser and lighter than those normally used in the United States. They can be found in Japanese grocers, international food stores, and some supermarkets. Truffle oil can be found in specialty grocers and Italian markets; read more about this delicacy on page 68.

¾ pound cavatappi or mezzi rigatoni

1 tablespoon truffle oil or more to taste

3 tablespoons unsalted butter

¼ teaspoon paprika

Leaves from 2 sprigs fresh thyme

1 large shallot, minced

1 small bay leaf

3 tablespoons all-purpose flour

Pinch cayenne pepper

2¼ cups whole milk, scalded

1½ cups grated gruyère cheese, about 3 cups

1½ cups grated extra sharp cheddar

Pinch freshly ground nutmeg

Kosher salt and freshly ground black pepper

1 large garlic clove, finely minced

2 tablespoons chopped fresh parsley

1 cup panko breadcrumbs

PREHEAT the oven to 375°F.

BRING a large pot of salted water to a boil. Add the pasta and cook according to package directions until al dente. Drain well and toss with truffle oil.

MEANWHILE, melt butter in a 3-quart saucepan over medium-low heat. Add paprika, thyme leaves, shallots, and bay leaf. Cook until the shallots are soft, about 5 minutes. Remove the bay leaf and whisk in the flour and cayenne. Cook for 2 minutes over low heat, stirring. Slowly whisk in the hot milk and simmer, stirring constantly with a wooden spoon until thickened and creamy. Remove from the heat and stir in the gruyère, cheddar, and nutmeg. Season with salt and pepper.

ADD the pasta to the sauce and toss stir well to combine. Pour into a 2-quart baking dish.

COMBINE the garlic, parsley, and breadcrumbs in a small bowl. Sprinkle the crumbs over the pasta and bake for 35 minutes or until the sauce is bubbly and the crumbs are golden brown. Serve hot.

CHAPTER SIX

YOU DON'T HAVE TO BE A PASTRY CHEF TO MAKE IT INTO HELL'S KITCHEN, BUT YOU DO NEED TO KNOW YOUR DESSERTS. THE RECIPES IN THIS CHAPTER WILL GUIDE YOU THROUGH THE SWEETEST OF ENDEAVORS WITH A GOAL OF PROVIDING A SOLID FOUNDATION IN RESTAURANT-QUALITY DESSERT MAKING.

YOU'LL START OUT WITH THE FRENCH CLASSIC CRÈME BRÛLÉE (PAGE 194) AND LEARN HOW TO MAKE PIE CRUST FROM SCRATCH TO USE IN RECIPES INCLUDING DRUNKEN APPLE PIE (PAGE 201) AND PASSION FRUIT TART (PAGE 221). YOU'LL MAKE A PURIST'S NEW YORK-STYLE CHEESECAKE (PAGE 206), AND YOU'LL GET FAMILIAR WITH THE ART OF CAKE BAKING (NO CAKE MIX FOR THE HELL'S KITCHEN CROWD!) WITH A LIGHT, FLUFFY COCONUT LAYER CAKE (PAGE 205), CLASSIC RED VELVET CAKE WITH A TWIST (PAGE 208), AND TWO TYPES OF CELEBRATION-WORTHY MOLTEN CHOCOLATE CAKE (PAGE 217 AND 219). AND THERE ARE THREE VARIATIONS ON PANNA COTTA (PAGES 210 TO 213) THAT WILL WOW YOUR GUESTS WITH THEIR SIMPLE ELEGANCE. FROZEN TREATS INCLUDING THE OFFBEAT WHITE PEPPER ICE CREAM (PAGE 196), EARTHY

CINNAMON ICE CREAM (PAGE 198), TANGY BUTTERMILK SHERBET (PAGE 221), AND TWO GRANITAS (PAGE 211 AND 212) COMPLETE THE RECIPES AS A CROWNING TOUCH.

AS WITH THE ENTRÉES, MANY OF THESE DESSERTS ARE MADE UP OF MORE THAN ONE COMPONENT AND CAN TAKE SOME QUALITY KITCHEN TIME TO PUT TOGETHER. THE GOOD NEWS IS THAT IF TIME IS SHORT OR SIMPLICITY IS YOUR OBJECTIVE, IT'S EASY TO PICK AND CHOOSE. FOR EXAMPLE, CINNAMON ICE CREAM, CARAMELIZED APPLES, AND WALNUT SABLÉ (PAGE 198) CAN BE MADE WITHOUT THE SABLÉ, AND THE CHOCOLATE MOLTEN CAKE WITH MALTED MILK ICE CREAM AND MARCONA ALMOND BRITTLE (PAGE 217) WILL STILL BE A SHOWSTOPPER WITHOUT THE BRITTLE. (OR, CONVERSELY, YOU CAN SNACK ON THE SABLE OR BRITTLE SOLO.) ICE CREAM, AS ANY HUMAN KNOWS, IS PERFECT ON ITS OWN, AND A HIGH-QUALITY, STORE-BOUGHT VARIETY IS PERFECTLY ACCEPTABLE TO SCOOP OVER YOUR CAKE, PIE, OR THE LIKE. IT'S DESSERT, AFTER ALL—WHAT'S NOT TO LOVE?

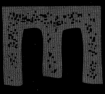

DESSERTS

CHAI CRÈME BRÛLÉE

SERVES 10

Crème brûlée, translated to "burnt cream," is a silky cream custard finished with a thin crust of caramelized sugar. The custard base is a simple mix of cream, egg yolks, and sugar that's poured into ramekins, placed into a water bath, and cooked until just set; it's then cooled and given its signature finish by sprinkling the top with sugar and letting it go for a quick turn under the broiler to caramelize it. (Or if you have a culinary blowtorch, you can use it to caramelize the topping with a bit of added kitchen flair.)

Here, *Hell's Kitchen* has once again taken a classic and evolved it, expanding on the custard's basic vanilla bean flavoring to include ginger, cinnamon, cardamom, cloves, and other chai spices for a warming, sweet, and spicy finish.

3 cups heavy cream

1 vanilla bean

1-inch piece fresh ginger, peeled and coarsely chopped

1 cinnamon stick

2 cardamom pods

4 cloves

2 chai teabags

10 large egg yolks

½ cup sugar, plus more for topping

PUT the cream into a saucepan with the vanilla bean, ginger, cinnamon stick, cardamom pods, and cloves, bring to a boil, and immediately turn off. Add the teabags and let steep for 15 minutes. As the chai steeps, prepare a pot of boiling water. Strain the custard and discard the teabags, ginger, and spices but reserve the vanilla bean. Split the bean lengthwise and add its seeds to the cream. Preheat the oven to 325°F. In a mixer on medium-high speed, beat the egg yolks and sugar until light and fluffy. Slowly mix in the warm cream mixture. Pour carefully into 10 x 4-ounce ramekins. Place in a baking pan and carefully pour the boiling water into the pan until it reaches halfway up the side of the ramekins. Bake in the water bath for around 20 minutes, until the outside of the custard is setting. Refrigerate for at least 4 hours, preferably overnight. Up to 2 hours before serving, preheat the broiler to its highest setting and sprinkle the custard with 2 teaspoons of sugar in an even layer. Put the crème brûlée under the heat as close as you can get it and watch carefully for the sugar to melt and caramelize. Pull out and cool completely so the top hardens before serving.

FIG BREAD PUDDING WITH WHITE PEPPER ICE CREAM

MAKES AN 8 X 8-INCH BREAD PUDDING

"Sweet or spicy?" asked Cibo Matto, a Japanese musical group known for their off-beat food-related lyrics back in the nineties. If you grew up wondering about white pepper ice cream, the answer is "both"; the peppercorns insert a note of heat to a sweet ice cream custard base.

Black peppercorns are picked when almost ripe and dried in the sun, which turns the husks black; white peppercorns fully ripen on the vine and then their husks are removed, with just the inner white seed remaining. In savory cuisine, white pepper makes its way into light-colored dishes such as mashed potatoes and cream sauces to maintain a consistent color; white pepper ice cream is a spicy-sweet extension of the concept that works brilliantly here atop this figgy twist on classic bread pudding.

WHITE PEPPER ICE CREAM

2 cups whole milk

1 cup heavy cream

¾ cup granulated sugar, divided

30 crushed white peppercorns

10 whole white peppercorns

5 yolks

¼ teaspoon salt

FIG JAM

½ pound figs, stemmed and cut into sections

⅓ cup granulated sugar

2 tablespoons freshly squeezed lemon juice

¼ cup water

2 tablespoons boiling water, plus extra

FOR THE WHITE PEPPER ICE CREAM

IN a medium-sized, heavy-bottomed saucepan, whisk the milk, cream, ½ cup of sugar, and crushed and whole peppercorns together. Over medium-high heat, bring the mixture to a steady simmer. Turn off the heat, cover, and let sit for 15 minutes to steep. Once steeped, in a medium-sized bowl, whisk the yolks, ¼ cup sugar, and salt until frothy and combined. Bring the milk mixture back to a simmer and temper the yolk mixture by adding a little of the warm milk/cream to the yolks and whisking. Continue adding the milk to the yolks, a little at a time, until the temperature of the yolks has risen. Then, whisking constantly, carefully pour the tempered yolks into the saucepan of milk on the stove. Stir the custard constantly with a wooden spoon or a heatproof spatula over medium heat until—once coated in custard—your finger leaves a trail on the spoon. Do not boil.

STRAIN the custard into a medium-sized bowl and place in the refrigerator until chilled. This can take several hours, and can be speeded up by placing the bowl in the freezer. If you do place it in the freezer, stir the mixture periodically to ensure it does not freeze solid. Once chilled, transfer the custard to your ice cream maker and freeze the custard, following the manufacturer's instructions. Transfer to a freezerproof container and store in the freezer until ready to use.

FOR THE FIG JAM

IN a heavy-bottomed, medium-sized saucepan, combine the figs, sugar, lemon juice, and ¼ cup water. Bring to a boil over medium-high heat, stirring constantly. Reduce heat to medium, cover, and simmer for 20 minutes, stirring occasionally until the mixture thickens. When the mixture gets quite thick, stir constantly to keep it from burning. Take the mixture off the heat and place in a blender with 2 tablespoons of boiling water. Blend until the jam loosens to your liking, adding additional hot water if necessary. Set aside and cool to room temperature, then refrigerate until ready to use.

BREAD PUDDING CUSTARD

One half loaf of challah bread or brioche, about 6–7 cups, sliced into 1 x 1-inch pieces

2 large eggs

2 yolks

1½ teaspoon pure vanilla extract

¾ cup light brown sugar

2 cups whole milk

1 cup heavy cream

4 tablespoons unsalted butter, melted

Confectioners' sugar, for dusting

FOR THE CUSTARD

SPRAY an 8 x 8-inch pan with cooking spray, or grease with butter. Place cubed bread in the prepared pan. In a medium-sized mixing bowl, add the eggs, yolks, and vanilla and whisk until combined. Add the sugar and whisk again. Add the milk and cream and whisk again. Add the melted butter and whisk a final time. Pour the custard over the bread and lightly push down with your fingers until the bread is covered in custard. Cover in plastic wrap and place in the refrigerator for several hours or overnight.

PREHEAT the oven to 350°F. Spoon the fig jam all over the surface of the pudding and, using your fingers, work it gently between the pieces of bread. Bake in the preheated oven for about an hour, rotating every 20 minutes until the pudding puffs and is golden and the custard is set.

TO PLATE

SIFT confectioners' sugar over the bread pudding and cut it into slices. Serve each on a serving plate with a scoop of white pepper ice cream and an additional dusting of confectioners' sugar.

CINNAMON ICE CREAM, CARAMELIZED APPLES, AND WALNUT SABLÉ

SERVES 5

Cinnamon, apples, and walnuts are natural partners, and this dessert offers a play on the apple crumble effect: apples are caramelized, topped with cinnamon-infused ice cream, and finished with a buttery, crumbly sablé (a French shortbread-style cookie). This fancy dish aims to impress, but each element can be prepared a day or two ahead and none require advanced techniques. You could also go solo with the sablés or ice cream for a pared-down everyday treat.

WALNUT SABLÉ COOKIES

1 cup all-purpose flour

½ cup cake flour

¼ teaspoon baking powder

¼ teaspoon salt

1 cup toasted and chopped walnuts

1 stick (8 tablespoons) unsalted butter, room temperature

½ cup granulated sugar

2 yolks

¾ teaspoon pure vanilla extract

CINNAMON ICE CREAM

2 cups whole milk

1 cup heavy cream

½ cup granulated sugar

7 sticks of cinnamon

½ teaspoon ground cinnamon

5 yolks

¾ teaspoon pure vanilla extract

¼ cup light brown sugar

¼ teaspoon salt

CARAMELIZED APPLES

3 apples, any variety, peeled, cored, and each cut into 8 pieces

Juice of one lemon

1 cup granulated sugar

⅓ cup water

2 tablespoons unsalted butter

FOR THE WALNUT SABLÉ COOKIES

WHISK the all-purpose flour, cake flour, baking powder, and salt in a medium mixing bowl. Whisk in the chopped walnuts and set aside. In the bowl of a stand mixer fitted with the paddle attachment, cream the butter and sugar at medium speed until combined, about two minutes. Add the yolks and vanilla and mix until combined, scraping the bowl as needed. Add the dry ingredients and mix until just combined. Roll the dough into a cylinder/log shape about 3 inches wide. Wrap in plastic wrap and place in the refrigerator for about two hours until firm, or overnight.

PREHEAT the oven to 350°F. Slice the log into ¼-inch rounds and place the cookies on 2 (or more) parchment lined baking sheets. Place the sheets in the refrigerator for 10 minutes and then bake the cookies 1 tray at a time for 10 minutes, rotating after 5 minutes, until the cookies are lightly browned. Let cool on a rack before placing in an airtight container to store.

FOR THE CINNAMON ICE CREAM

IN a medium-sized, heavy-bottomed saucepan, whisk the milk, cream, granulated sugar, cinnamon sticks, and ground cinnamon together. Over medium-high heat, bring the mixture to a steady simmer. Turn off the heat, cover, and let sit for 15 minutes to steep. Once steeped, in a medium-sized bowl, whisk the yolks, vanilla, brown sugar, and salt until frothy and combined. Bring the milk mixture back to a simmer and temper the yolk mixture by adding a little of the warm milk/cream to the yolks and whisking. Continue adding the milk to the yolks a little at a time, until the temperature of the yolks has risen. Then, whisking constantly, carefully pour the tempered yolks into the saucepan of milk on the stove. Stir the custard constantly with a wooden spoon or a heatproof spatula over medium heat until the custard coats the back of the spoon and your finger leaves a trail on the coated spoon. Do not boil.

STRAIN the custard into a medium-sized bowl and place in the refrigerator until chilled. This can take several hours but can be speeded up by placing the bowl in the freezer. If you do place it in the freezer, stir the mixture periodically to ensure it does not freeze solid. Once chilled, transfer the custard to your ice cream maker and freeze the custard, following the manufacturer's instructions. Transfer to a freezerproof container and store in the freezer until ready to use.

FOR CARAMELIZED APPLES

TOSS sliced apples and lemon juice in a small container and let sit until ready to use. Combine sugar and water in a medium-sized, heavy-bottomed saucepan over medium heat and allow the sugar and water to caramelize and reach a deep amber color. Add butter. Once the butter has fully melted, add the apples. Cook the apples until a fork is easily stuck through them, about five minutes. There may be some seizing—hardening of the caramel—when the apples are added. If the caramel seizes, keep cooking until the caramel melts, lowering the temperature to medium if necessary. Place the apples and caramel in a small container and place in the refrigerator until ready to use.

TO PLATE

PLACE about 5 pieces of caramel apple on each of five serving plates. Sprinkle crumbled walnut sablé cookies on top and around the apples and place an entire cookie on each plate as well. Place a scoop of cinnamon ice cream on the plates and perhaps some additional caramel (from the apples) on top of the ice cream.

DRUNKEN APPLE PIE

SERVES 8

There's nothing better than a good old-fashioned apple pie spiced with the trinity of cinnamon, nutmeg, and allspice; brighten it up with a swig of bourbon and it's a dessert designed for adults. Add a scoop of cinnamon ice cream and it will be over the top, or try the white pepper ice cream (page 196) or buttermilk sherbet (page 221) for something a little different.

PASTRY DOUGH

2½ cups all-purpose flour, plus more for rolling

1 teaspoon sugar

1 teaspoon kosher salt

2½ sticks unsalted butter, cut into ¼-inch cubes

6–8 tablespoons iced water, as needed

PIE FILLING

8 medium Granny Smith apples

½ cup sugar

2 tablespoons cornstarch

1 teaspoon cinnamon

½ teaspoon nutmeg

½ teaspoon ground allspice

¼ teaspoon salt

2 tablespoons bourbon

1 egg white

sugar for sprinkling

FOR THE CRUST

PLACE the butter in the freezer until needed. Put the flour, sugar, and salt in a food processor. Mix well. Add butter and pulse until the mixture resembles coarse breadcrumbs. Sprinkle 2 tablespoons water over the mixture and pulse again until the mixture starts to come together. Tip it into a bowl and sprinkle on 4–6 more tablespoons of water, one tablespoon at a time, mixing lightly with a fork until the dough is moist enough to be shaped into 2 disks. Wrap each disk in plastic wrap and refrigerate for at least an hour.

FOR THE FILLING

PREHEAT the oven to 425°F. Peel, core, and cut the apples into ¼-inch slices. In a large bowl, whisk together sugar, cornstarch, cinnamon, nutmeg, allspice, and salt. Add the apples and bourbon and toss gently until well mixed. On a lightly floured surface, roll out one disk of dough and transfer to line a 9-inch pie plate, leave a small overhang. Add apple filling. Roll out the second disk of dough. Lay it carefully across the filling and trim, seal, and flute the pie edges. Make slits in the top with a sharp knife to let steam escape. Beat the egg white until foamy. Brush the pie with egg white and scatter sugar over the top. Bake for 15 minutes at 425°F, then reduce temperature to 375°F and continue to cook for about 45 minutes, checking that the top does not overbrown and the juices are bubbling. If necessary, cover the pie loosely with foil during the last 20 minutes of cooking.

BANANAS FOSTER

SERVES 6

This restaurant treat is surprisingly easy to make at home. Bananas are cooked in a cinnamon-spiced, brown-sugar-sweetened cream, then a generous amount of rum is added to the cream and ignited (known as *flambé*), deepening the flavor of the dessert and bringing some drama, reminiscent of many a dish to come out of *Hell's Kitchen*. Make sure to use a long kitchen match so you can stay a safe distance from the flames, and keep the pan's lid nearby to extinguish any flames that don't die down quickly. Or if you'd rather not light the pan, you may skip over the step of flambéing and reduce the amount of rum a bit. Vanilla ice cream is the natural partner to Bananas Foster.

6 firm, ripe bananas

1 stick salted butter

1 cup packed dark brown sugar

½ teaspoon cinnamon

¼ teaspoon allspice

½ cup heavy cream

½ cup dark rum

PEEL and halve bananas. Melt butter in a large nonstick skillet over medium heat. Stir in brown sugar, cinnamon, and allspice and stir until sugar dissolves. Add cream and bring sauce to a simmer. Cook the sauce until bubbles appear, then add the bananas and cook for another minute until the bananas are heated through. Remove them to a warmed serving dish. Add the rum and carefully ignite. Keep cooking until flame disappears, and cook a further 2 minutes until sauce becomes syrupy. Pour sauce over bananas. Serve immediately with ice cream.

WARM RASPBERRY FRITTERS

SERVES 8

The fritter—a simple flour-and-egg batter that, as its name implies, is fried—can be either sweet or savory and is known to many cultures in various forms, from the pakora of India to Japanese tempura and classic American corn fritters. The breading holds the key ingredient together—in this recipe, it's the unconventional yet delightful choice of raspberries. A burst of juicy berry flavor in each crispy bite makes these fritters downright addictive. Keeping the oil at a consistent temperature avoids dense and greasy fritters and ensures that your fritters brown evenly and come out perfectly crisp.

1 cup all-purpose flour

½ teaspoon kosher salt

4 eggs (2 whole, 2 separated)

½ pint milk

2 tablespoons vegetable oil plus more for frying

½ cup sugar

3 cups of raspberries (two 6-ounce boxes)

Granulated sugar to serve

SIFT the flour and salt into a bowl. Separate 2 eggs and set 2 whites aside. Make a well in the flour mix and place 2 eggs and 2 egg yolks into the center. Mix with a whisk, incorporating the flour and slowly pouring in the milk until the batter is smooth. Add the oil and sugar and let the batter stand for 30 minutes. In a mixer, whisk the remaining egg white on medium-high until stiff peaks form; fold the egg whites gently into the batter. Heat oil in a deep fryer or heavy-bottomed pan to 360°F. Dip the raspberries into the batter, then carefully drop into hot oil and cook, turning once, until golden brown, around 2 minutes. Remove to a paper-towel-lined plate to drain. Lightly roll in a bowl of sugar to serve. To plate, heap around 10 fritters on a plate. Sprinkle with extra sugar if needed.

OPTIONAL: serve with vanilla ice cream.

COCONUT LAYER CAKE

SERVES 8

Coconut cake is a classic in the South where it's served sky-high, sandwiched with a snow-white frosting, and anointed with sweetened flaked coconut. Guaranteed to satisfy the staunchest sweet tooth!

The layers of this cake are fantastically moist, and they can be made a day or two ahead: cool completely, then wrap them well in plastic and refrigerate. Bring to room temperature before frosting and serving your celebration-worthy creation.

CAKE

3 cups cake flour

4 teaspoons baking powder

¾ teaspoon salt

1 cup butter, at room temperature, plus more for greasing cake pans

1½ cups sugar

4 eggs

1 tablespoon vanilla essence

1 cup coconut milk

1 cup shredded, sweetened coconut, finely chopped

COCONUT FROSTING

3 sticks unsalted butter at room temperature

4 cups confectioners' sugar, sifted

¼ teaspoon kosher salt

2 teaspoons coconut extract

Toasted coconut

½ cup sweetened flaked coconut

FOR THE CAKE

PREHEAT the oven to 350°F. Line the base of two 8-inch round cake pans with baking parchment and lightly grease sides and bottom of the pans. Sift together the flour, baking powder, and salt and set aside. In a mixer on a medium-high speed, cream the butter and sugar until light and fluffy, 2–3 minutes. Add the eggs one at a time, beating well after each addition. Mix in the vanilla, coconut milk, and shredded coconut. Add the flour mix and stir until just combined. Spoon the batter into two 9-inch round pans and level. Bake for 25 minutes or until a toothpick inserted into the center comes out clean. Cool for 10 minutes and remove from pans. Cool completely before frosting.

FOR THE FROSTING

IN a mixer on a medium-high speed, beat the butter until smooth, around 1 minute. Add the confectioners' sugar in 4 stages and beat until well mixed, around 2 more minutes. Add the salt and coconut extract. Continue to beat until light and fluffy.

FOR THE TOASTED COCONUT

PREHEAT the oven to 325°F. Scatter the coconut on a baking sheet and toast, stirring occasionally, for around 6 minutes or until coconut has browned.

TO ASSEMBLE

WITH a serrated knife, cut both cakes in half to make 4 layers. Spread just under a cup of frosting on each layer and sandwich all 4 layers together. Use the rest of the frosting on the top and sides, smoothing with an icing spatula or butter knife. To finish, scatter the toasted coconut on the top of the cake.

VANILLA BEAN CHEESECAKE

SERVES 8

This is a classic New York–style cheesecake based in cream cheese (as opposed to Italian style, which uses ricotta cheese). It's a purist's cheesecake, flavored only with vanilla and set into a simple crisp graham cracker crust.

An excellent cheesecake is dense but never heavy, firm but not rigid; these standards are achieved by baking the cheesecake in a water bath (known as a *bain-marie*, the same setup we used for baking the crème brûlée on page 194) until just set with a bit of wiggle left to it.

A perfect cheesecake can stand on its own, no embellishments required. Purists pass on elaborate flavorings—no cookie crumbs, raspberry swirl, or pumpkin for them—and insist that theirs be served plain. Those less rigid will allow for simple handful of berries and a drizzle of fruit syrup to finish their cheesecake.

CRUST

2 cups graham cracker crumbs (around 14 cookies)

¼ teaspoon salt

10 tablespoons unsalted butter, melted

¼ cup sugar

FILLING

24 ounces cream cheese, room temperature

1 cup packed light brown sugar

4 large eggs

1 cup sour cream

1 tablespoon pure vanilla extract

2 vanilla seeds, split lengthwise and seeds scraped

FOR THE CRUST

PREHEAT the oven to 350°F. Place the graham crackers into a plastic bag and crush with a rolling pin. In a bowl, combine graham cracker crumbs, salt, butter, and sugar. Stir until combined. Press onto the bottom of a 9-inch springform pan. Bake for 10 minutes and let cool. Cover the outside of the pan with heavy-duty aluminum foil.

FOR THE FILLING

BOIL a pot of water while you mix the filling. Beat the cream cheese in the bowl of an electric mixer with the paddle attachment on medium-high until smooth, around 2–3 minutes. Scrape down sides with a spatula and add brown sugar. Beat again until combined. Beat in eggs one at a time. Next beat in the sour cream, vanilla extract, and seeds. Pour filling over crust. Place the springform pan into a larger pan and pour the boiling water into larger pan until it comes halfway up the side of the cheesecake pan. Bake on the center oven rack in the water bath for around 1 hour, or until just set; the center of the cheesecake should jiggle. Once done, turn off the oven and let the cheesecake sit for 30 minutes. Remove from oven, cool, and then refrigerate for at least 10 hours.

RED VELVET CAKE WITH MASCARPONE FROSTING

SERVES 8-10

This Southern-style cake, red in color but chocolate in flavor, has achieved nation-wide fame in recent years, with red velvet making its way into cupcakes, lattes, our country's iconic sandwich cookie, and more. The red in red velvet is achieved by adding red food coloring, though back when food was rationed during World War II, beet juice did the trick, and some recipes still call for the ruby-red root for color.

Traditional red velvet cake is filled and topped with a cream cheese frosting; here *Hell's Kitchen* takes a twist on the classic and swaps in mascarpone—a fresh, Italian, cream-based cheese (best known as the star ingredient in tiramisù)—and tops the cake with fresh berries for a fruity finish. Make this cake as part of the Stylish Versions of Everyday Dishes menu (page 241).

CAKE

1¾ cups all-purpose flour

¼ cup cocoa powder

1 teaspoon kosher salt

1 teaspoon baking soda

½ cup butter, plus more for greasing cake pans

1 cup sugar

2 large eggs

2 teaspoons vanilla extract

2 tablespoons red food coloring

½ cup buttermilk

¼ cup sour cream

1 tablespoon white wine vinegar

FROSTING

8 ounces mascarpone

1 cup heavy cream

¼ cup sugar

One 6-ounce box blueberries

One 6-ounce box raspberries

FOR THE CAKE

PREHEAT the oven to 350°F. Prepare two 9-inch round cake pans by buttering lightly. In a large bowl, sift flour, cocoa powder, salt, and baking soda together and set aside. In a mixer on medium-high, beat butter and sugar with the paddle attachment until light and fluffy, 3–5 minutes. Add the eggs one at a time until they are well mixed. Beat in vanilla and red food coloring until incorporated. In a medium bowl with a wire whisk, beat together buttermilk, sour cream, and vinegar. Alternating in two stages, add the flour mix and the buttermilk mix until just incorporated. Don't overmix. Divide batter equally between the two pans and bake for around 20 minutes, or until a toothpick inserted in the center of the cake comes out clean. Transfer to a wire rack to cool completely before frosting.

FOR THE FROSTING

IN a mixer on a low-high speed with the paddle attachment, beat the marscapone, cream, and sugar until smooth, around 1 minute. Turn up to medium-high and beat until stiff peaks form, around 1 more minute. Don't overbeat or frosting will go grainy.

TO ASSEMBLE

PLACE one cake on a serving plate. Add half the frosting and use a small spatula to spread it evenly. Scatter half the blueberries and raspberries. Top with the second cake and smooth the rest of the frosting evenly over the top. Finish with the remaining berries.

COCONUT WHITE CHOCOLATE PANNA COTTA WITH CHAMPAGNE-POACHED FRUIT AND MANGO SORBET

MAKES SIX 4-OUNCE PANNA COTTAS

Panna cotta—an Italian cream-based dessert (the name translates to "cooked cream") thickened with gelatin—boasts a showy presentation but is relatively simple to make, requiring just minutes. A perfect panna cotta has the right proportion of liquid to gelatin to gently set it; it's not quite firm, but jiggles when touched. For a flavor accent, we use coconut milk in place of the standard dairy milk, and white chocolate sweetens the deal. We finish ours with fruit poached in a ginger-infused champagne syrup; if time is short, you can skip the syrup and go for a simple sprinkle of shredded coconut and seasonal fresh fruit.

COCONUT WHITE CHOCOLATE PANNA COTTA

2½ tablespoons cold water

1 envelope powdered gelatin, about 2¼ teaspoons

1 cup heavy cream

1½ cup coconut milk

3 ounces (½ cup) chopped white chocolate

½ teaspoon salt

½ teaspoon coconut extract

CHAMPAGNE SYRUP

1 cup champagne, or dry white wine

6 tablespoons granulated sugar

½ teaspoon minced ginger

½ teaspoon pure vanilla extract

FRUIT

12 ounces (1 pint) strawberries, sliced

2 kiwi, peeled and chopped

1 mango, cubed

Mango Sorbet (store-bought or homemade)

FOR THE COCONUT WHITE CHOCOLATE PANNA COTTA

PLACE cold water in a small bowl and sprinkle the gelatin over it. Let stand for 5 minutes to soften the gelatin. Place the heavy cream, coconut milk, chocolate, and salt in a heavy-bottomed, medium-sized saucepan over medium to medium-high heat. Stir until the sugar dissolves, the chocolate melts, and the mixture simmers. Continue to simmer for 5–7 minutes. Remove from the heat. Add the gelatin and stir to melt. Add the coconut extract. Strain the panna cotta through a sieve and pour into 6 wine glasses or other decorative vessels. Cool slightly. Refrigerate until set, at least 6 hours.

FOR THE CHAMPAGNE-POACHED FRUIT

IN a small saucepan over medium-high heat, add the champagne, sugar, ginger, and vanilla. Bring to a simmer and simmer constantly until reduced to a syrupy consistency, about 10 minutes. Add the fruit and simmer for 2–3 minutes. Remove from the heat and transfer the poached fruit and syrup to a container, bring to room temperature on the counter, and then place in the refrigerator until ready to use.

TO PLATE

PLACE the panna cotta–filled wine glasses on serving plates. Top each glass with a tablespoon or two of poached fruit and place a scoop of mango sorbet on each plate with a bit of additional fruit placed decoratively on top. Alternatively, if you would like to remove the panna cotta from the glasses, run a paring knife just around the edge of the panna cotta and invert the glass on to a serving plate. The panna cotta should pop right out. If it does not, nudge it out with the paring knife, or try briefly dipping the glass in very hot water before inverting it.

CRÈME FRAÎCHE PANNA COTTA WITH HONEY GRANITA AND QUINCE

MAKES SIX 4-OUNCE PANNA COTTAS

A simple panna cotta is made with cream, milk, sugar, and gelatin; on page 210 we upped the ante by swapping in coconut milk and adding white chocolate. Here the addition of crème fraîche offers another layer of lusciousness to this already creamy dessert. It's served with the Sicilian semi-frozen dessert known as granita, which here is made from a simple mix of honey and water, frozen in 30-minute increments and raked with a fork each round until the mixture is at once frozen, flaky, and scoopable. Quince paste, also known as quince cheese or *dulce de membrillo*, is a sweet and sticky jelly formed into a block that's traditionally served with Spanish cheeses; here it's blended into a puree that serves as the final flourish to the panna cotta. Quince paste can be found in Spanish and international groceries.

CRÈME FRAÎCHE PANNA COTTA

2½ tablespoons cold water

1 envelope powdered gelatin, about 2¼ teaspoons

1½ cup milk

1 cup heavy cream

½ cup granulated sugar

½ teaspoon salt

1 cup crème fraîche

1 teaspoon pure vanilla extract

HONEY GRANITA

½ cup honey

2½ cups water

QUINCE PUREE

¼ cup boiling water, plus a little more

8 ounces quince paste (found in specialty grocery stores)

FOR THE CRÈME FRAÎCHE PANNA COTTA

PLACE cold water in a small bowl and sprinkle the gelatin over it. Let stand for 5 minutes to soften the gelatin. Place the milk, cream, sugar, salt, and crème fraîche in a heavy-bottomed, medium-sized saucepan over medium to medium-high heat. Stir until the sugar dissolves and the mixture simmers, 5–7 minutes. Remove from the heat. Add the gelatin and stir to melt. Add the vanilla extract. Strain the panna cotta through a sieve and pour into 6 wine glasses or other decorative vessels. Cool slightly. Refrigerate until set, at least 6 hours.

FOR THE HONEY GRANITA

HEAT honey and water in small heavy-bottomed saucepan over medium-high heat until honey dissolves and water simmers. Pour mixture into an 8 x 8-inch nonstick metal baking pan. Place in the freezer and freeze for about 30 minutes. Remove from the freezer and, using a fork, stir the granita, incorporating all the icy bits into the not-so-icy bits. Continue freezing and stirring/scraping every half hour until the mixture is frozen and flaky. Transfer to a small container and freeze until ready to use.

FOR THE QUINCE PUREE

COMBINE the hot water and paste in a small bowl and whisk vigorously to loosen the paste. Add additional hot water as needed to achieve a thick but pourable, puree-like consistency. Set aside at room temperature until ready to use.

TO PLATE

PLACE the panna cotta–filled wine glasses on serving plates. Place a scoop of granita on each plate and dribble a bit of puree decoratively on top, or place the puree directly on the panna cotta. Alternatively, if you would like to remove the panna cotta from the glasses, run a paring knife just around the edge of the panna cotta and invert the glass on to a serving plate. The panna cotta should pop right out. If it does not, nudge it out with the paring knife or try dipping the glass briefly in very hot water before inverting it.

BERRY PUDDING PANNA COTTA

MAKES SIX 4-OUNCE BERRY PUDDINGS

There's no limit to the creativity that has come out of *Hell's Kitchen*; in a third innovative take on the classic cooked-cream dessert, this panna cotta is enriched with crème fraîche and poured over cubes of cake and berry compote and left to set into three distinct layers. The raspberry granita makes for a cooling, sweet, and tangy finish, though if time is short, a sprinkle of fresh berries would be a simple stand-in. Feel free to make just the granita and serve it on its own for a simple, refreshing summertime treat.

RASPBERRY GRANITA

½ cup water

⅓ cup granulated sugar

3½ ounces (about 1½ cups) raspberries

Juice of one lemon

BERRY COMPOTE AND SOAKING LIQUID

6 tablespoons granulated sugar

5 tablespoons lemon juice

4½ cups, about 16 ounces, mixed berries

1½ teaspoons pure vanilla extract

CRÈME FRAÎCHE PANNA COTTA

2½ tablespoons cold water

1 envelope powdered gelatin, about 2¼ teaspoons

1½ cup milk

1 cup heavy cream

½ cup granulated sugar

½ teaspoon salt

1 cup crème fraîche

1 teaspoon pure vanilla extract

6 slices of store-bought pound cake, cubed

Mint leaves, for garnish

FOR THE RASPBERRY GRANITA

IN small heavy-bottomed saucepan over medium-high heat, boil the water and sugar until the sugar dissolves. Remove from the heat and let cool. Mash the raspberries in a small bowl with a potato masher. Add the raspberries and lemon juice to the sugar water and mix to combine. Pass through a sieve into an 8 x 8-inch nonstick metal baking pan. Place in the freezer and freeze for about 30 minutes. Remove from the freezer and, using a fork, stir the granita, incorporating all the icy bits into the not-so-icy bits. Continue freezing and stirring/scraping every half hour until the mixture is frozen and flaky. Transfer to a small container and freeze until ready to use.

FOR THE BERRY COMPOTE AND SOAKING LIQUID

STIR the sugar and lemon juice together in a large skillet until sugar is dissolved. Add berries and cook over medium heat, tossing gently (try to keep most of the berries from breaking up) until berries are warm and juices begin to be released, 2–3 minutes. Add vanilla and stir.

TRANSFER to a small container and bring to room temperature.

REMOVE a rounded ½ cup of berries and juice and transfer to a blender and puree. This is the soaking liquid. Set aside in a shallow container.

FOR THE CRÈME FRAÎCHE PANNA COTTA

NOTE: Do not make the panna cotta until after the cake and berries have chilled in the refrigerator for an hour or so and become firm in their serving vessels.

PLACE cold water in a small bowl and sprinkle the gelatin over it. Let stand for 5 minutes to soften the gelatin. Place the milk, cream, sugar, salt, and crème fraîche in a heavy-bottomed, medium-sized sauce pan over medium to medium-high heat. Stir until the sugar dissolves and the mixture simmers, 5–7 minutes. Remove from the heat. Add the gelatin and stir to melt. Add the vanilla extract. Strain the panna cotta through a sieve and use immediately.

TO ASSEMBLE

PLACE the cake cubes in the soaking liquid and divide evenly between 6 short, wide glasses/serving vessels. Place a ¼ cup of berry compote over the cake. Press down lightly and refrigerate until cold and firm, about an hour.

Once chilled, slowly pour the warm panna cotta over the top of the berry compote. You should have a solid layer of panna cotta with a berry and cake layer below it. Place in the refrigerator for at least six hours before serving.

TO PLATE

PLACE each berry pudding on a serving plate, add a scoop of granita to the plate, garnish with a sprig of mint and a tablespoon or two of extra berries, and serve.

CHOCOLATE EMPANADAS WITH MACERATED STRAWBERRIES

MAKES 10 EMPANADAS

The Latin American pastry pocket known as the empanada—typically filled with meat, cheese, or vegetables—was developed as a tidy little portable meal for working folk. At *Hell's Kitchen*, we don't restrict our empanadas to lunch or dinner; these sweet empanadas, filled with Kahlúa-spiked chocolate ganache and topped with strawberries made tipsy with tequila, make for a unique dessert and a clever way of bringing chocolate and berries together. If you're planning in advance, the empanadas can be filled ahead of time and refrigerated for a day or two before frying.

CHOCOLATE FILLING

1½ cups chopped bittersweet chocolate

¾ cup heavy cream

6 tablespoons Kahlúa, or other coffee-flavored liqueur

MACERATED STRAWBERRIES

2 cups sliced strawberries

¼ cup fresh mint, chopped

¼ cup honey

Tequila, to taste, optional

EMPANADAS

10 empanada wrappers, such as Goya Discos (found in the grocery store's freezer section and placed in the refrigerator to defrost prior to using)

1 egg, lightly beaten for egg wash

2 teaspoons cinnamon, for decorating

¼ cup granulated sugar, for decorating

Vegetable oil, for frying

Store-bought vanilla ice cream, optional

FOR THE FILLING

PLACE the chocolate in a medium-sized, heatproof bowl and set aside. Pour the heavy cream into a small saucepan and warm it over medium-high heat until bubbles just begin to form around the edges of the pot. Remove the cream from the heat and pour it over the bowl of chocolate. Let cream and chocolate sit for about a minute and then gently stir until the chocolate melts and the two are fully incorporated. Add the liqueur and stir again. Transfer the bowl to the refrigerator until the filling hardens enough so that it is more spreadable than pourable, at least 1 hour, preferably overnight. To speed the process, you can place the bowl in the freezer, but remove and stir it periodically to ensure that it does not freeze solid.

FOR THE MACERATED STRAWBERRIES

MIX the strawberries, mint, honey, and tequila (if using) together in a small bowl and let sit at least until the berries begin releasing juice, about 30 minutes or so. Set aside.

FOR THE EMPANADAS

ONCE the chocolate is chilled, remove the empanada skins from their packaging. Separate each skin and lay flat on a work surface. Working with one skin at a time, brush it with egg wash. Place 2 tablespoons of the filling in the center of each skin. Fold the skin over itself, forming a half moon, and seal the rounded edges together with your fingers. Working from there, continue sealing the skin together by pressing down from the edges towards the chocolate: the skins should lie flat, save for the pocket of filling. Brush additional egg wash on top of the rounded edge and crimp the rounded edge by gently rolling the edge up on itself. The edge must be very well sealed or the chocolate will escape when the empanada is fried. Refrigerate until quite cold, 30 minutes or so.

MIX the cinnamon and sugar together in a small bowl and set aside. Cover a plate with paper towels and set aside.

TO fry the empanadas, fill a large, heavy-bottomed pot with about 3 inches of vegetable oil and, using a candy thermometer, bring the oil to 350°F. Fry 3 empanadas at a time in the oil—do not overcrowd them—until golden brown, about 4 minutes, flipping them over after 2 minutes. Remove the empanadas from the oil, place on the prepared plate, and immediately sprinkle with cinnamon sugar.

TO PLATE

PLACE an empanada or two on a plate. Place a scoop of vanilla ice cream on the plate (if using) and top with the macerated strawberries and juice.

CHOCOLATE MOLTEN CAKE WITH MALTED MILK ICE CREAM AND MARCONA ALMOND BRITTLE

MAKES FOUR 7-OUNCE CAKES

Chocolate molten cake, served piping hot and oozing with rich melted chocolate, is an ever-popular celebration food, a perennial choice for birthdays, anniversaries, and other milestones. You'll find it featured in the Date Night menu (page 243). For the moistest result, remove the cakes from the oven when they are just set but the centers still look a little wet and wobbly. Marcona almonds, native to Spain, are a rounded, more delicate, and upscale version of the nut and elevate the simple brittle that crowns the cakes. Marcona almonds can be found in specialty grocers and various online sources including Nuts.com.

MALTED MILK ICE CREAM

2 cups whole milk

1 cup heavy cream

½ cup granulated sugar

¼ teaspoon salt

¾ cup malt powder

5 yolks

¼ cup light brown sugar

2 teaspoons pure vanilla extract

MARCONA ALMOND BRITTLE

1 cup granulated sugar

½ cup light corn syrup

½ cup water

1 cup unsalted Marcona almonds, toasted and chopped (if you use salted ones, omit half of the salt called for in the recipe)

½ teaspoon salt

1 teaspoon baking soda

1 tablespoon butter

CHOCOLATE MOLTEN CAKES

⅓ cup sugar

1 large egg

3 yolks

½ teaspoon pure vanilla extract

1 stick (8 tablespoons) unsalted butter

5 ounces bittersweet chocolate

3 tablespoons all-purpose flour

¼ teaspoon salt

FOR THE MALTED MILK ICE CREAM

WHISK the milk, cream, granulated sugar, salt, and malt powder in a large, heavy-bottomed saucepan. Bring to a simmer over medium heat. Meanwhile, in a medium-sized bowl, whisk the yolks, brown sugar, and vanilla until frothy and combined. Once the milk mixture is simmering, temper the yolk mixture by adding a little of the warm milk to the yolks and whisking. Continue adding the milk to the yolks a little at a time until the temperature of the yolks has risen. Then, whisking constantly, carefully pour the tempered yolks into the saucepan of milk on the stove. Over medium heat, stir the custard constantly with a wooden spoon or a heatproof spatula until—once coated in custard—your finger leaves a trail on the spoon. Do not boil.

STRAIN the custard into a medium-sized bowl and place in the refrigerator until chilled. This can take several hours, but can be speeded up by placing the bowl in the freezer. If you do place it in the freezer, stir the mixture periodically to ensure it does not freeze solid. Once chilled, transfer the custard to your ice cream maker and freeze the custard, following the manufacturer's instructions. Transfer to a freezerproof container and store in the freezer until ready to use.

FOR THE MARCONA ALMOND BRITTLE

SPRAY a parchment-lined baking sheet lightly with cooking spray and set aside. Combine the sugar, corn syrup, and water in a medium-sized, heavy-bottomed saucepan and bring to a boil over medium-high heat. Cook the sugar without stirring, lifting the pan off the heat and swirling its contents periodically to ensure the sugar cooks evenly. Continue to cook until the mixture becomes a deep amber color (or lighter amber if you prefer a lighter, more sweet-tasting, and less burnt-caramel-tasting brittle). Remove the pan from the heat and immediately add the nuts. Stir and add the salt, baking soda, and butter. Stir again until incorporated.

(continued)

POUR the mixture into the parchment-lined pan and, using a small offset spatula, smooth the mixture out over the parchment until it is about ¼-inch thick. Place the baking sheet in the freezer for about 20 minutes or leave out on the counter for an hour until the brittle has hardened. Crack it into pieces and place in an airtight container.

FOR THE CHOCOLATE MOLTEN CAKES

PREHEAT the oven to 350°F. Lightly spray four 7-ounce ovenproof ramekins with cooking spray, or lightly grease with butter. Set aside. In the bowl of a stand mixer fitted with the whisk attachment, whisk the sugar, egg, yolks, and vanilla until thick and ribbony, about 10 minutes. Meanwhile, melt the butter and chocolate together in a small saucepan over medium heat. Set aside to cool slightly. Remove the bowl from the mixer and gently whisk in the melted butter and chocolate.

GENTLY fold in the flour and salt using a rubber spatula. Divide the batter evenly between the 4 ramekins, place on a baking sheet, and bake for 10–12 minutes, rotating after 5 minutes. Do not overbake. Once removed from the oven, let the cakes sit for one minute on a wire rack. Run a paring knife gently around the upper edge of the cakes and invert the cakes on to individual serving plates, leaving the ramekins on top for about 20 seconds more. Lift off the ramekins and serve immediately. Alternatively, you can serve the cakes directly from the ramekins.

TO PLATE

PLACE each cake on a serving plate and add a scoop of malted milk ice cream. Stick a piece of brittle decoratively into each ice cream scoop.

CARAMEL-FILLED CHOCOLATE MOLTEN CAKES

MAKES FOUR 7-OUNCE CAKES

Hot-from-the-oven molten chocolate cake envelops a core of melty caramel, bringing an already luxurious treat to a new level of decadence. A second and third shot of caramel—caramel ice cream, followed by a drizzle of additional caramel—finishes the dish. This flavorful caramel is based on real butter, cream, and sugar; the addition of corn syrup keeps the caramel soft. The caramel is formed into balls and frozen before adding to the batter so it melts slowly as it bakes into the cakes, revealing a sticky-sweet treat when you dig in.

CARAMEL

½ cup corn syrup

1 cup granulated sugar

⅓ cup water

3 tablespoons salted butter

¾ cup heavy cream

CHOCOLATE MOLTEN CAKES

⅓ cup sugar

1 large egg

3 yolks

½ teaspoon pure vanilla extract

1 stick (8 tablespoons) unsalted butter

5 ounces bittersweet chocolate

3 tablespoons all-purpose flour

¼ teaspoon salt

FOR THE CARAMEL

COMBINE the corn syrup, sugar, and water in a medium-sized, heavy-bottomed saucepan and stir gently. Place the pan over medium-high heat and cook the mixture without stirring, lifting the pan and swirling the mixture periodically to ensure the sugar cooks evenly. Once the mixture begins to caramelize and becomes a light amber color, about 8–10 minutes, you may remove it from the heat if the color is to your liking. If you like a darker caramel with an almost burnt flavor, continue to cook the sugar until it reaches a dark amber color.

REMOVE the pot from the heat, add the butter, and stir. Once melted, carefully add the cream, as the mixture may bubble up. The caramel may seize up at this point, but once it is returned to the heat, it will smooth out again. Return the pan to the heat and stir the caramel until smooth. Attach a candy thermometer and cook the caramel until the thermometer reads 240°F. Transfer the caramel to a container, let cool slightly, and place in the refrigerator. Once hardened, create four 2-tablespoon balls of caramel. Grease a small plate with cooking spray or butter and place the balls on the plate. Place the plate in the freezer until the balls are frozen, at least one hour. Periodically check on the balls, rotating them so that they don't freeze solid to the plate.

FOR THE CHOCOLATE MOLTEN CAKES

PREHEAT the oven to 350°F. Lightly spray four 7-ounce ovenproof ramekins with cooking spray, or lightly grease with butter. Set aside. In the bowl of a stand mixer fitted with the whisk attachment, whisk the sugar, egg, yolks, and vanilla until thick and ribbony, about 10 minutes. Meanwhile, melt the butter and chocolate together in a small saucepan over medium heat. Set aside to cool slightly. Remove the bowl from the mixer and gently whisk in the melted butter and chocolate. Gently fold in the flour and salt using a rubber spatula. Divide the batter evenly between the 4 ramekins. Press a frozen caramel ball into each cake and bake for 10–12 minutes, rotating after 5 minutes. Do not overbake. Serve immediately directly from the ramekins.

(continued)

IF you want to remove the cakes from the ramekins, be warned that the caramel will ooze out of the cakes immediately after the ramekins are removed. To do so, once removed from the oven, let the cakes sit for 1 minute on a wire rack. Then run a paring knife gently around the upper edge of the cakes and invert the cakes onto individual serving plates, leaving the ramekins on top for about 20 seconds more. Lift off the ramekins and serve immediately.

TO PLATE

PLACE cakes, still in their ramekins, on 4 small serving plates. It can be nice to add a scoop of caramel ice cream on the side of this dish and drizzle with any additional caramel.

PASSION FRUIT TART WITH BUTTERMILK SHERBET

MAKES ONE 9-INCH TART OR FIVE 4½-INCH MINI-TARTS

Most of us are familiar with lemon curd (see the lemon meringue tart recipe on page 226); passion fruit curd, the base of this tart, is something a little different but shares lemon's sweet-tart taste profile. Passion fruit is a tropical fruit that's colored yellow to dark purple depending on its stage of ripeness; its unassuming exterior reveals impressive sacs of edible dark-colored seeds encased in a yellow-orange pulpy juice. The curd from the fruit is set into a sweet pastry base and the tart is topped with a scoop of tangy-sweet and refreshing buttermilk sherbet.

BUTTERMILK SHERBET

1 cup heavy cream

½ cup sour cream

2 cups buttermilk

1 cup sugar

Juice of ½ lemon

PASSION FRUIT CURD

1 cup passion fruit juice

2 tablespoons freshly squeezed lemon juice

1 cup granulated sugar, divided

2 large eggs

3 yolks

4 teaspoons cornstarch

¼ teaspoon salt

5 tablespoons unsalted butter

SWEET TART DOUGH

1½ cup all-purpose flour

⅓ cup sugar

¼ teaspoon salt

1 stick (8 tablespoons) unsalted butter, room temperature, cubed

1 egg, lightly beaten

Confectioners' sugar for dusting

FOR THE BUTTERMILK SHERBET

COMBINE the cream, sour cream, buttermilk, sugar, and lemon juice in a blender, and blend until thoroughly combined. Transfer to an ice cream machine and freeze the sherbet in your ice cream maker, following your manufacturer's instructions. Transfer the sherbet to a container with a lid and place in the freezer until ready to use.

FOR THE PASSION FRUIT CURD

IN a heavy-bottomed saucepan, whisk the passion fruit juice, lemon juice, and ½ cup of sugar. Bring to a simmer over medium heat, whisking occasionally to ensure the sugar melts. In a medium-sized bowl, combine the eggs, yolks, ½ cup sugar, cornstarch, and salt and whisk vigorously until thickened and smooth.

WHEN the juice is simmering, temper the egg-and-yolk mixture by adding a little of the warm juice and whisking. Continue adding the juice to the eggs/yolks a little at a time until the temperature of the eggs/yolks has risen. Then, whisking constantly, carefully pour the tempered eggs/yolks into the saucepan of juice on the stove.

BRING the mixture almost to a boil over medium heat, whisking constantly. Continue whisking until the cream coats the back of the spoon and has thickened considerably. Remove the mixture from the heat and add butter; stir until the butter melts and is well combined. Scrape the curd into a medium-sized bowl and cover the surface of the curd with plastic wrap. Refrigerate until firm, about 2 hours or overnight. Whisk aggressively to loosen before using.

FOR THE SWEET-TART DOUGH

PLACE flour, sugar, and salt in a food processer and process until combined. Add the cubed butter and pulse until pea-sized chunks form. Add the beaten egg and pulse until the dough begins to come together. Transfer the dough to a sheet of plastic wrap and, using the wrap, form the dough into a disc and wrap tightly. Alternatively, divide the dough into 5 pieces (use a scale to

(continued)

do this exactly, or eyeball it), form each piece into a mini disc and wrap each disc in plastic wrap. Refrigerate the dough for at least 1 hour or overnight.

ONCE chilled, remove the dough from the refrigerator and let rest at room temperature for a few minutes. Once softened a bit, transfer the large disc to a 9-inch tart pan with a removable bottom, or the 5 small discs to five 4½-inch mini-tart pans with removable bottoms. Using your fingers, evenly press the dough into the bottom and sides of the tart pan(s). Return the dough-lined pans to the refrigerator and chill for an hour.

PREHEAT the oven to 375°F. Remove the tart pan(s) from the refrigerator and press tin foil over the bottom and sides of the dough (do not cover the top edge of the crust in foil), forming a tight seal. Place the tart(s) on a baking sheet and bake 18 minutes, rotating after 9 minutes, until the top of the edge of the crust begins to brown and the bottom no longer looks wet and shiny when you lift the tin foil. Remove the tin foil and bake for 10 minutes more until the crust is nicely browned. Set aside to cool before filling.

TO ASSEMBLE

PREHEAT the oven to 350°F. Spread the whisked curd over the bottom of the 9-inch tart shell, or put ⅕ of the curd into each mini-tart, spreading it evenly over the bottom. Bake the tart(s) for 10 minutes, rotating after 5 minutes. Let cool on a cooling rack to room temperature and then place in the refrigerator until cool.

TO PLATE

REMOVE the tart(s) from the pan(s), using a paring knife to ease the pan bottom and sides off if necessary. Transfer slices or mini-tarts to serving plates. Dust with confectioners' sugar and serve with a scoop of buttermilk sherbet.

MAKING PASTRY CRUST LIKE A PRO

Learning the basics of pastry making can be a valuable investment, as homemade pie crust is head-and-shoulders above anything you'll buy in a store. Soon you'll be pumping out one perfect crust after the next, and you'll be known throughout town for your pie-making skills. Pastry dough is something you can make well in advance; wrapped tight in plastic, it keeps in the freezer for several months.

Several recipes in this chapter require making pastry dough—a standard pastry dough for the apple pie (page 201), a sweet-tart dough enriched with sugar for the passion fruit tart (page 221) and lemon meringue tart (page 226), and a sablé Breton crust based in salted butter for the raspberry crémeux tart (page 223).

Chef-quality pie crust starts with high-quality flour, and real butter is a must. Chilled butter, cut into chunks and rubbed into the dough or pulsed in a food processor, yields a flaky crust that skips the need for shortening. To further ensure flaky results, the dough must be chilled before rolling it out to allow the fat to melt slowly and gently into the pastry.

Rolling out pastry is an acquired skill, one that requires a bit of practice to reach perfection. First you'll need to liberally flour your work surface and rolling pin so the dough doesn't stick or tear, then start rolling, working from the center, keeping the work surface floured as you go and slipping a long spatula underneath to prevent the dough from sticking every few passes. When the dough is rolled out to the required size, wrap it around the rolling pin to transport it, gently insert it into the pie plate, and use kitchen scissors to trim the dough, then proceed with the recipe as instructed, either blind-baking it (baking the crust without the filling) or filling, baking, and bringing your pie to the table.

If you're looking for a pie crust that's made in minutes, try the simple graham cracker crust that serves as the base of the cheesecake (page 206) and chocolate caramel tart (page 229). It's not a true pastry, but it's still pretty darn delicious!

PINEAPPLE TARTE TATIN

SERVES 8

Tarte Tatin is a French-style upside-down tart made with caramelized fruit. The classic is made with apples; here we switch it up with pineapple, a play on good old American pineapple upside-down cake but with a base of puff pastry. Swapping in no-sugar-added canned pineapple is completely acceptable if fresh isn't available or time is short, and using store-bought puff pastry makes this recipe completely doable for cooks of all skill levels (puff pastry is one of the most challenging pastries to pull off at home). Choose a puff pastry made with butter rather than vegetable oil for the most flavorful, flaky, and—true to the name—puffy results.

All-purpose flour, for rolling

12 ounces puff pastry

6 tablespoons butter at room temperature

⅔ cup light brown sugar, loosely packed

3 cups (1 pound 3 ounces) fresh pineapple, peeled, cored, and chopped into 1-inch pieces

1 vanilla bean, halved and scraped

PREHEAT the oven to 400°F. Dust the rolling pin and surface with flour, roll out the puff pastry sheet, and, using a sharp knife, cut into a 10 ½-inch round. Transfer to a wax-paper-lined baking sheet and chill. Smear the butter evenly around the bottom of a 10-inch ovenproof skillet. Sprinkle the sugar evenly on top. Add the pineapple and cook, stirring occasionally, on a medium-high heat for around 20 minutes until a golden brown caramel sauce develops. Carefully lay the pastry over the top of the pineapple, being careful not to touch the hot caramel (using a wooden spoon to tuck the edges right under the fruit). Bake for about 20 minutes until the pastry is golden brown and the caramel is bubbling around the edges. Remove from the oven and cool for 5 minutes. Using potholders, carefully invert onto a plate larger than the skillet. Serve immediately.

LEMON MERINGUE TART

MAKES ONE 9-INCH TART OR FIVE 4½-INCH MINI-TARTS

Based on lemon curd, an intensely lemony English dessert topping that uses both the juice and zest of the fruit, this classic tart is a rich yet light palate cleanser, perfect after a heavy meal. The curd is set into a base of sweet pastry and topped with a delicate, fluffy meringue topping. For a final hit of lemon, the tart is topped with a scoop of lemon sorbet. If Meyer lemons are available, you might want to try them out in your curd; this cross between a lemon and mandarin is sweeter and less acidic than a standard lemon, and its delicate floral aroma makes it a fruit worth seeking out when in season.

SWEET-TART DOUGH

1½ cup all-purpose flour

⅓ cup sugar

¼ teaspoon salt

1 stick (8 tablespoons) unsalted butter, room temperature, cubed

one egg, lightly beaten

LEMON CURD

½ cup freshly squeezed lemon juice

⅔ cup granulated sugar

4 large eggs

1 yolk

¼ cup lemon zest

5 tablespoons unsalted butter, cubed

MERINGUE

5 egg whites

¼ teaspoon cream of tartar

⅛ teaspoon salt

½ cup plus 2 tablespoons sugar

FOR THE SWEET-TART DOUGH

PLACE flour, sugar, and salt in a food processor and process until combined. Add the cubed butter and pulse until pea-sized chunks form. Add the beaten egg and pulse until the dough begins to come together. Transfer the dough to a sheet of plastic wrap and, using the wrap, form the dough into a disc and wrap tightly. Alternatively, divide the dough into 5 pieces (use a scale for precision, or eyeball it), form each piece into a mini-disc, and wrap each disc in plastic wrap. Refrigerate the dough for at least 1 hour or overnight.

ONCE chilled, remove the dough from the refrigerator and let rest at room temperature for a few minutes. Once softened a bit, transfer the large disc to a 9-inch tart pan with a removable bottom, or the 5 small discs to five 4½-inch mini-tart pans with removable bottoms. Using your fingers, evenly press the dough into the bottom and sides of the tart pan(s). Return the dough-lined pans to the refrigerator and chill for 1 hour.

PREHEAT the oven to 375°F. Remove the tart pan(s) from the refrigerator and press tin foil over the bottom and sides of the dough (do not cover the top edge of the crust in foil), forming a tight seal. Place the tart(s) on a baking sheet and bake 18 minutes, rotating after 9 minutes, until the top of the edge of the crust begins to brown and the bottom no longer looks wet and shiny when you lift the tin foil. Remove the tin foil and bake for 10 minutes more until the crust is nicely browned. Set aside to cool before filling.

FOR THE CURD

IN a medium-sized, heavy-bottomed saucepan, over medium heat, combine the juice, sugar, eggs, yolk, and zest. Whisk constantly until the mixture thickens considerably and coats the back of a spoon. Take off the heat and strain the curd through a sieve into a small bowl. Add the butter and mix with a heatproof rubber spatula. Cover the curd's surface with plastic wrap, and place in the refrigerator for at least 2 hours or overnight. Whisk to loosen before using.

(continued)

FOR THE MERINGUE

IN the bowl of a stand mixer fitted with the whisk attachment, whisk the egg whites, cream of tartar, and salt on medium-high speed until frothy. Slowly add the sugar until stiff peaks form. Use immediately.

TO ASSEMBLE

PREHEAT the oven to 350°F. Spread the whisked curd evenly over the bottom of the 9-inch tart shell, or put ⅕ of the curd into each mini-tart. Using a small offset spatula, spread the top of the tart(s) with meringue so that it completely covers the curd and touches the edges of the prebaked tart shell. Bake the tart(s) for 8–13 minutes, rotating after 8 minutes, until the meringue is nicely browned. Let tart(s) cool on a cooling rack to room temperature and then place in the refrigerator until chilled.

TO PLATE

REMOVE the tart(s) from the pan(s), using a paring knife to ease the pan bottom and sides off if necessary. Transfer slices or mini-tarts to serving plates. A scoop of lemon sorbet on the side can be a nice complement to this tart.

CHOCOLATE CARAMEL TART WITH CARAMELIZED BANANA ICE CREAM

MAKES ONE 9-INCH TART

Chocolate, caramel, and banana are a divinely sweet match; when you caramelize the bananas, it's one step closer to heaven. While there are several steps to this recipe, they're all completely doable—the crust is no more than graham cracker crumbs bound together with butter, the caramel and chocolate aren't difficult to master, and if ice cream isn't yet in your culinary repertoire, feel free to sub in store-bought banana ice cream.

If you stumble over the word *ganache*, don't be daunted—it's a simple mix of cream poured over chopped chocolate and stirred until smooth; a dab of butter is added to give it some shine. Ganache is versatile—it's used to fill and top cakes, it's the base for chocolate truffles, and it's poured atop ice cream, so learning the simple technique is well worth taking the time to master.

CARAMELIZED BANANA ICE CREAM

4 tablespoons unsalted butter

4 very ripe, medium-sized bananas, cut into ½- to 1-inch coins

7 tablespoons light brown sugar, divided

¾ teaspoon salt, divided

1½ cups whole milk

¾ cup heavy cream

1 teaspoon pure vanilla extract

1 teaspoon freshly squeezed lemon juice

GRAHAM CRACKER CRUST

11 whole graham crackers, broken into pieces

2 tablespoons light brown sugar

6 tablespoons unsalted butter, melted

CARAMEL

½ cup corn syrup

1 cup granulated sugar

⅓ cup water

3 tablespoons salted butter

¾ cup heavy cream

GANACHE

⅔ cup chopped bittersweet chocolate

⅓ cup heavy cream

1 tablespoon unsalted butter

Maldon sea salt, for decorating

FOR THE CARAMELIZED BANANA ICE CREAM

MELT the butter in a large skillet over medium to medium-high heat until the foam begins to subside. Add the bananas, 5 tablespoons sugar, and ¼ teaspoon salt and cook the bananas, stirring frequently, until the sugar melts and begins to caramelize, about 10 minutes.

PLACE the caramelized bananas in a blender and add 2 tablespoons sugar, ½ teaspoon salt, milk, heavy cream, vanilla, and lemon juice. Blend the mixture until thoroughly combined. Transfer the mixture to a medium-sized bowl and place in the refrigerator until chilled. This can take several hours but can be sped up by placing the bowl in the freezer. If you do place it in the freezer, stir the mixture periodically to ensure it does not freeze solid. Once chilled, freeze the mixture in your ice cream maker, following the manufacturer's instructions. The ice cream is best eaten right from the machine while it is still soft, but you can transfer it to a freezerproof container and freeze it as well.

FOR THE GRAHAM CRACKER CRUST

PREHEAT the oven to 350°F. Combine the crackers and sugar in a food processor and process until finely ground. Add warm melted butter and pulse until moist clumps form, scraping down the bowl as needed. Transfer the mixture to a 9-inch tart pan with a removable bottom and firmly press the crumbs into the bottom and sides of the pan. If needed, use the bottom of a dry measuring cup to help you achieve a flat, even bottom and sides. Freeze the crust until firm, at least 30 minutes. Bake the crust until golden and fragrant, about 8 minutes, rotating after 4 minutes. Set aside to cool completely on a rack.

(continued)

FOR THE CARAMEL

COMBINE the corn syrup, sugar, and water in a medium-sized, heavy-bottomed saucepan and stir gently. Place the pan over medium-high heat and cook the mixture without stirring. Instead, lift the pan and swirl the mixture periodically to ensure the sugar cooks evenly. Once the mixture begins to caramelize and becomes a light amber color after about 8–10 minutes, you may remove it from the heat. If you like a darker caramel with an almost burnt flavor, continue to cook the sugar until it darkens.

REMOVE the pot from the heat, add the butter, and stir. Once melted, carefully add the cream, as the mixture may bubble up. The caramel may seize up at this point, but once it is returned to the heat it will smooth out again. Return the pan to the heat and stir the caramel until smooth. Attach a candy thermometer and cook the caramel until the thermometer reads 240°F. Immediately pour the caramel into the cooled crust and refrigerate in order to set the caramel, about an hour or chill in the freezer for 30 minutes.

FOR THE GANACHE

PLACE the chocolate in a medium-sized heatproof bowl and set aside. Pour the heavy cream into a small saucepan, and warm it over medium-high heat until bubbles just begin to form around the edges of the pot. Remove the cream from the heat and pour it over the bowl of chocolate. Let the cream and chocolate sit for about a minute and gently stir until the chocolate melts and the two are fully incorporated.

ADD the butter and stir again until melted. Immediately pour the ganache over the firm caramel in the tart shell and, using a small offset spatula, smooth the ganache. Sprinkle the tart with Maldon sea salt and place in the refrigerator to firm up, at least 1–2 hours. Prior to serving, allow the tart to sit at room temperature for 20 minutes or so to allow the caramel to soften a bit.

TO PLATE

REMOVE the tart from the pan, using a paring knife to ease the pan bottom and sides off if necessary. Place a scoop of ice cream next to, or on top of, a slice of tart.

RASPBERRY CRÉMEUX TART WITH A SABLÉ BRETON CRUST AND RASPBERRY SORBET

MAKES ONE 9-INCH TART OR FIVE 4½-INCH MINI-TARTS

Crémeux, French for "creamy," is a rich pudding typically made from chocolate or fruit. This raspberry crémeux is enriched with egg yolks and plenty of butter and held together with gelatin, then poured into a shortbread crust known as sablé Breton. This crust is made with salted butter and hails from Brittany, France. Raspberry sorbet, which is surprisingly creamy for a fruit-based frozen dessert, is the crowning touch. Pistachio ice cream would also be lovely here.

RASPBERRY PUREE

2½ cups raspberries

⅓ cup granulated sugar

2 tablespoons freshly squeezed lemon juice

SABLÉ BRETON CRUST

1 cup all-purpose flour

1¼ teaspoon baking powder

¾ cup granulated sugar

1 stick (8 tablespoons) salted butter, room temperature

1 yolk

RASPBERRY CRÉMEUX

2½ tablespoons cold water

2 teaspoons powdered gelatin

1 cup raspberry puree

½ cup granulated sugar

3 yolks

1 large egg

1 stick (8 tablespoons) unsalted butter, softened

Raspberry sorbet (homemade or store-bought)

Fresh raspberries for decorating

FOR RASPBERRY PUREE

COMBINE the raspberries, sugar, and juice over medium-high heat in a small heavy-bottomed saucepan. Bring to a simmer and cook, stirring constantly for about 3–5 minutes. Strain the mixture through a sieve into a small container and cool on the counter until it reaches room temperature. Cover and transfer to the refrigerator until needed.

FOR SABLÉ BRETON CRUST

IN a small bowl, whisk the flour and baking powder together and set aside. In the bowl of a stand mixer fitted with the paddle attachment, cream together the sugar and butter on medium-high speed until fluffy, about 5 minutes, scraping down the bowl as needed. Add the yolk and mix until combined. Reduce the speed to medium-low and add the dry ingredients, mixing until just combined.

TRANSFER the dough to a sheet of plastic wrap and, using the wrap, form the dough into a disc and wrap tightly. Alternatively, divide the dough into 5 pieces (use a scale for precision, or eyeball it), form each piece into a mini-disc, and wrap each disc in plastic wrap. Refrigerate the dough for at least 1 hour or overnight.

ONCE chilled, remove the dough from the refrigerator and let rest at room temperature for a few minutes. Once softened a bit, transfer the large disc to a 9-inch tart pan with a removable bottom, or the 5 small discs to five 4½-inch mini-tart pans with removable bottoms. Using your fingers, only press the dough evenly into the bottom(s) of the tart pan(s)—NOT the side(s). Return the dough-lined pans to the refrigerator and chill for an hour.

PREHEAT the oven to 375°F. Remove the tart pan(s) from the refrigerator, place the tart(s) on a baking sheet, and bake 15–18 minutes, rotating after 8 minutes, until the crust is nicely browned (tart(s) do not need pie weights or tin foil). The sides of the crust will rise up the edges of the tart pan due to the baking powder. When you remove the tart(s) from the oven, press down the bottom of the crust gently with the bottom of a dry measuring cup if it has puffed up at all, and lightly press against the edges and the sides of the tart pan(s) to secure them. Set aside to cool before filling.

(continued)

FOR RASPBERRY CRÉMEUX

POUR the cold water in a small bowl; sprinkle the gelatin over it and let sit for five minutes. Meanwhile, warm the puree and ¼ cup sugar in a medium-sized saucepan over medium heat, stirring until the sugar dissolves. In a medium-sized bowl, whisk ¼ cup sugar with the yolks and egg. When the puree is simmering, temper the egg-and-yolk mixture by adding a little of the warm puree to the mixture and whisking. Continue adding the puree to the eggs/yolks a little at a time until the temperature of the eggs/yolks has risen. Then, whisking constantly, carefully pour the tempered eggs/yolks into the saucepan of puree on the stove.

HEAT the mixture over medium heat, whisking constantly. Continue whisking until the cream coats the back of the spoon and has thickened considerably. Remove the mixture from the heat and add the gelatin. Stir to combine and add the butter. Stir again until the butter melts and is well combined. Scrape the crémeux into a small bowl and cover the surface with plastic wrap. Refrigerate until firm, about 2 hours or overnight. When ready to use, transfer to the bowl of a stand mixer fitted with the whisk attachment and whisk on medium to medium-high speed to loosen and lighten the crémeux.

TO ASSEMBLE

USING a small offset spatula, spread the whisked crémeux evenly over the bottom of the tart shell, or put ⅛ of the cream into each mini-tart. Decoratively press a few raspberries into the surface of the crémeux. Place in the refrigerator briefly to set, about 20 minutes.

TO PLATE

REMOVE the tart(s) from the pan(s), using a paring knife to ease the pan bottom and sides off if necessary. Place slices/mini-tarts on serving plates. Dust the tart(s) with confectioners' sugar, place a scoop of raspberry sorbet on each serving plate, and scatter a few raspberries over all.

BLUEBERRY TART WITH WHITE CHOCOLATE GANACHE

MAKES ONE 9-INCH TART OR FIVE 4½-INCH MINI-TARTS

This beautiful blueberry tart consists of a sweet-tart crust topped with a lightly spiced pastry cream, all covered with sweet white chocolate ganache that sets a layer of fresh blueberries in place on top. Pastry cream, or *crème pâtissière*, is a thick custard made with milk, sugar, and egg yolks (the custard's thinner cousin is *crème anglaise*, a sweet pouring sauce). The trick to cooking pastry cream just right is to add the hot milk to the egg yolks a little at a time; they'll scramble if they all go in at once. Ganache is made by pouring hot cream over chopped chocolate and stirring until smooth; it can serve as a filling, frosting, or sauce depending on how thick you make it. This dessert finishes the Light Summer Supper menu (page 246).

SWEET TART DOUGH

1½ cup all-purpose flour

⅓ cup sugar

¼ teaspoon salt

1 stick (8 tablespoons) unsalted butter, room temperature, cubed

1 egg, lightly beaten

LIGHTLY SPICED PASTRY CREAM

1⅓ cup whole milk

½ cup granulated sugar, divided

½ vanilla bean, scraped

4 yolks

3 tablespoons cornstarch

⅛ teaspoon nutmeg

¼ teaspoon cinnamon

1 tablespoon unsalted butter

1 tablespoon brandy, optional

WHITE CHOCOLATE GANACHE

½ cup chopped white chocolate

2 tablespoons heavy cream

¼ teaspoon pure vanilla extract

One pint of blueberries

Sifted confectioners' sugar, for decorating

FOR THE SWEET-TART DOUGH

PLACE flour, sugar, and salt in a food processor and process until combined. Add the cubed butter and pulse until pea-sized chunks form. Add the beaten egg and pulse until the dough begins to come together. Transfer the dough to a sheet of plastic wrap and, using the wrap, form the dough into a disc and wrap tightly. Alternatively, divide the dough into 5 pieces (use a scale for precision, or eyeball it), form each piece into a mini-disc, and wrap each disc in plastic wrap. Refrigerate the dough for at least 1 hour or overnight.

ONCE chilled, remove the dough from the refrigerator and let rest at room temperature for a few minutes. Once softened a bit, transfer the large disc to a 9-inch tart pan with a removable bottom, or the 5 small discs to five 4½-inch mini-tart pans with removable bottoms. Using your fingers, evenly press the dough into the bottom and sides of the tart pan(s). Return the dough-lined pans to the refrigerator and chill for an hour.

PREHEAT the oven to 375°F. Remove the tart pan(s) from the refrigerator and press tin foil over the bottom and sides of the dough (do not cover the top edge of the crust in foil), forming a tight seal. Place the tart(s) on a baking sheet and bake 18 minutes, rotating after 9 minutes, until the top of the edge of the crust begins to brown and the bottom no longer looks wet and shiny when you lift the tin foil. Remove the tin foil and bake for 10 minutes more, until the crust is nicely browned. Set aside to cool before filling.

FOR THE LIGHTLY SPICED PASTRY CREAM

IN a heavy-bottomed saucepan, combine the milk, ¼ cup sugar, and scraped vanilla bean. Place the pan on the stove over medium-high heat and bring just to a boil. In a medium bowl, combine the yolks, ¼ cup sugar, cornstarch, nutmeg, and cinnamon and whisk until thickened and smooth. Once the milk has boiled, reduce the heat and temper the yolk mixture by adding a little of the boiling milk to the yolk mixture and whisking. Continue adding

(continued)

the milk to the yolks a little at a time until the temperature of the yolks has risen. Then, whisking constantly, carefully pour the tempered yolks into the saucepan of milk on the stove.

BRING the mixture almost to a boil, whisking constantly. Continue whisking until the cream coats the back of the spoon and has thickened considerably. Remove the mixture from the heat and add butter and brandy (if using), and stir until the butter melts and is well combined. Scrape the cream into a medium-sized bowl and cover the surface of the cream with plastic wrap. Refrigerate about 2 hours until firm, or overnight. Whisk aggressively to loosen before using.

FOR THE WHITE CHOCOLATE GANACHE

PLACE the white chocolate and heavy cream in a small microwave-safe bowl and microwave on high for 10-second bursts, whisking after each burst, until the chocolate has melted. Alternatively, heat the chocolate and heavy cream in a small saucepan over low heat until the chocolate melts and the mixture is smooth. Add the vanilla and whisk to combine. Use immediately.

TO ASSEMBLE

USING a small offset spatula, spread a thin layer of ganache over the bottom and sides of the pre-baked 9-inch tart shell (you may have some left over). Or place 1 tablespoon of ganache into each prebaked mini-tart shell and, using a small offset spatula, spread a thin layer of ganache over the bottom and sides of the tart shell. Place in the refrigerator for at least 1 hour to set up. Once set, spread the whisked pastry cream evenly over the bottom of the tart shell, or put ⅛ of the cream into each mini-tart. Lightly press the blueberries into the pastry cream so that the entire pastry cream surface is covered in berries. Place in the refrigerator briefly to set, about 20 minutes.

TO PLATE

REMOVE the tart(s) from the pan, using a paring knife to ease the pan bottom and sides off if necessary. Dust the tart(s) with confectioners' sugar and decoratively drizzle any leftover ganache next to or on top of each slice/mini-tart.

MIXED BERRY PARFAIT WITH PASTRY CREAM AND SHORTBREAD COOKIES

MAKES FOUR 8-OUNCE PARFAITS

This dessert highlights four types of berries; feel free to swap in seasonal varieties or use just one, depending on what's available. The berries are set against simple pastry cream and fancied up with champagne syrup (a great use for champagne that's lost its fizz). You could skip the syrup for an any-night ending to a meal, or try making homemade walnut sablés (page 198) if you'd like to fancy the dish up further.

PASTRY CREAM

1⅓ cup whole milk

½ cup granulated sugar, divided

½ vanilla bean, scraped

4 yolks

3 tablespoons cornstarch

⅛ teaspoon nutmeg

¼ teaspoon cinnamon

1 tablespoon unsalted butter

1 tablespoon brandy, optional

MIXED BERRIES

½ cup sliced strawberries

½ cup blueberries

½ cup raspberries

½ cup blackberries

CHAMPAGNE SYRUP

1 cup champagne or dry white wine

6 tablespoons granulated sugar

½ teaspoon minced ginger

½ teaspoon pure vanilla extract

Store-bought shortbread cookies

Fresh mint leaves, for decorating

FOR THE PASTRY CREAM

IN a heavy-bottomed saucepan, combine the milk, ¼ cup sugar, and scraped vanilla bean. Place the pan on the stove over medium-high heat and bring to a boil. In a medium bowl, combine the yolks, ¼ cup sugar, cornstarch, nutmeg, and cinnamon and whisk until thickened and smooth. Once the milk has boiled, temper the yolk mixture by adding a little of the boiling milk to the yolk mixture and whisking. Continue adding the milk to the yolks a little at a time until the temperature of the yolks has risen. Then, whisking constantly, carefully pour the tempered yolks into the saucepan of milk on the stove.

BRING the mixture almost to a boil, whisking constantly. Continue whisking until the cream coats the back of the spoon and has thickened considerably. Remove the mixture from the heat, add butter and brandy (if using), and stir until the butter melts and is well combined. Scrape the cream into a medium-sized bowl and cover the surface of the cream with plastic wrap. Refrigerate about 2 hours until firm, or overnight. Whisk aggressively to loosen before using.

FOR THE BERRIES AND CHAMPAGNE SYRUP

RINSE and drain the berries and set aside. In a small saucepan over medium-high heat, add the champagne, sugar, ginger, and vanilla. Bring to a simmer and simmer constantly, until reduced to a syrupy consistency, about 10 minutes. Add the berries and simmer for 2–3 minutes. Remove from the heat and transfer the berries and syrup to a container, bring to room temperature on the counter, and then place in the refrigerator until ready to use.

TO ASSEMBLE

PLACE 3 tablespoons of pastry cream in the bottom of four 8-ounce glass serving vessels. Crush 4 shortbread cookies and place one broken cookie over the cream in each glass. Add 2 tablespoons of the berry/syrup mixture and continue layering in this order until you reach the top of the glass. Refrigerate at least 20 minutes or up to several hours before serving.

TO PLATE

PLACE the parfaits on serving plates. Decoratively place a mint leaf and a shortbread cookie on each parfait, and another cookie or two on each plate.

MENUS

CHAPTER SEVEN

FROM DATE NIGHT TO SURF AND TURF, ECLECTIC ETHNIC TO A FESTIVAL OF TRUFFLES, THESE MENUS GIVE YOU A CHANCE TO SHARE YOUR LOVE FOR FINE DINING WITH FRIENDS AND FAMILY. SOME ARE INSPIRED BY HELL'S KITCHEN CHALLENGES, SOME HAVE BEEN PUT TOGETHER FROM DINNER SERVICES, AND ALL ARE DRESSED TO IMPRESS AND DAZZLE YOUR GUESTS.

WELCOMING HOME A HERO

Based on the special service for a marine staff sergeant who had just come home from a year-plus tour of duty in Iraq. Serve this elevated comfort food menu to one of our nation's finest to celebrate their safe return.

STARTERS

Caesar Salad, Baby Gems, Pickled Red Onion, Parmesan Croutons

King Crab Capellini with Chili, Lime, and Green Onion

ENTRÉES

New York Strip, Truffle Polenta Fries, Tomato Jam, Sautéed Spinach, Red Wine Jus

Eight-Ounce Beef Burger with Caramelized Onion and Bacon Jam, Sharp Cheddar, and Special Sauce on a Brioche Bun with Sweet Potato Fries

Lemon and Thyme-Roasted Chicken Breast, Sweet Corn Polenta, Sautéed Spinach, and Chicken Jus

SIDE

Rainbow-Colored Carrots with Butter and Parsley

DESSERT

Vanilla Bean Cheesecake

STYLISH VERSIONS OF EVERYDAY DISHES

This menu turns comfort food into fine dining, a task well known to Hell's Kitchen contestants.

STARTER

Butter Lettuce Salad

ENTRÉE

Eight-Ounce Beef Burger with Caramelized Onion and Bacon Jam, Sharp Cheddar, and Special Sauce on a Brioche Bun with Sweet Potato Fries

SIDE

Truffle Mac and Cheese

DESSERT

Red Velvet Cake with Mascarpone Frosting

HELL'S KITCHEN CRAPS

In this challenge, each chef rolls a lettered die and quickly calls out an ingredient starting with that letter: P for potatoes, D for duck, L for lime, a second L for lemon, H for heirloom tomatoes, and P again for pine nuts was the roll of the die for one winning team. This is a fun one to try at home!

STARTERS

Trio of Oysters

Heirloom Tomato Salad with Burrata, Pine Nut Gremolata, and Pickled Red Onion

ENTRÉES

Creamy Asparagus Risotto with Lemon and Mascarpone

Duck Breast with Walnut-Grape Compote

SIDE

Dauphinoise Potatoes

DESSERT

Lemon Meringue Tart with Lemon Sorbet

Rainbow Colored Carrots with
Butter and Parsely, page 171

A GOLDEN WEDDING ANNIVERSARY

Based on a challenge to cook for a happy couple's fiftieth wedding anniversary: a revival of typical dishes of the era.

STARTER
Caesar Salad, Romaine Hearts, Pickled Red Onion, Parmesan Croutons

ENTRÉE
Duck Breast with Five-Spice Braised Endive and Parsnip Puree

SIDE
Rainbow-Colored Carrots with Butter and Parsley

DESSERT
Bananas Foster

DATE NIGHT

Based on a Date Night challenge that included a raw bar.

STARTERS
Seared Ahi Tuna Loin with Haricots Verts, Hard-Boiled QuailEggs, and Black Olive Dressing

Trio of Oysters

ENTRÉE
Filet of Beef au Gratin, Truffle Pommes Anna, Braised Salsify, and Pearl Onions

SIDE
Creamed Spinach

DESSERT
Chocolate Molten Cake with Malted Milk Ice Cream and Marcona Almond Brittle

BLACK-TIE CHARITY NIGHT

The most luxurious dishes make the menu black-tie-worthy and can really elevate your event. Based on the concept presented on a special Hell's Kitchen challenge.

STARTERS
Salad of Scallops with Truffle Vinaigrette

Lobster Spaghetti

ENTRÉES
Roasted Chicken Breasts and Kabocha Squash with Maple Jus

Beef Wellington

SIDES
Truffle Mac and Cheese

Ginger Caramelized Carrots

DESSERT
Pineapple Tarte Tatin

ECLECTIC ETHNIC

A tribute to world cuisine featuring an eclectic mix of Italian, Mexican, and Indian.

STARTER

Eggplant Involtini with Spicy Red Pepper Emulsion

ENTRÉE

Chicken Mole with Black Beans and Rice and Corn-Avocado Salsa

SIDES

Ginger Caramelized Carrots

Cauliflower-Stuffed Naan with Cilantro Chutney

DESSERT

Chocolate Empanadas with Macerated Strawberries

HELL'S KITCHEN CLASSIC

No season is complete without seared fish, scallops, Wellington, and brûlée on the menu. Here's a chance to try your hand at them all!

STARTERS

Pan-Fried Red Snapper with Roasted Beets and Pink Grapefruit Dressing

Salad of Scallops with Truffle Vinaigrette

ENTRÉE

Beef Wellington

SIDE

Creamed Spinach

DESSERT

Chai Crème Brûlée

CLASSIC FRENCH

Iconic French dishes in characteristic Hell's Kitchen style.

STARTER

Seared Foie Gras on Brioche French Toast with Caramelized Apples and Figs

ENTRÉE

Filet of Beef au Gratin, Truffle Pommes Anna, Braised Salsify, and Pearl Onions

SIDE

Rainbow-Colored Carrots with Butter and Parsley

DESSERT

Raspberry Crémeux Tart with a Sablé Breton Crust and Raspberry Sorbet

MODERN SOUTH

Based on a challenge where a Southern gospel choir made a guest appearance and contestants were tasked with recreating favorite Southern dishes.

STARTERS

Grilled Peach Salad

Butter Lettuce Salad

ENTRÉES

Pecan-Crusted Mahi Mahi with Edamame Succotash and Maple Brown Butter

Chicken Fried Rib-Eye with Yukon Mashed Potatoes and White Truffle Cream Gravy

SIDES

Creamed Corn

Creamed Spinach

DESSERT

Coconut Cake

Coconut Cake, page 205

QUINCEAÑERA

Based on a challenge celebrating a young lady's fifteenth birthday, the quinceañera is a Latin American tradition. There's no reason this menu couldn't be served at a Sweet Sixteen as well!

STARTERS
Pan-Seared Tuna Tataki with Green Tea Soba Noodles

Caesar Salad, Romaine Hearts, Pickled Red Onion, Parmesan Croutons

ENTRÉES
Lemon Tagliatelle with Toasted Pine Nuts and Arugula

Grilled Salmon with White Bean, Chorizo, and Lobster Ragù

DESSERT
Chocolate Caramel Tart with Caramelized Banana Ice Cream

Berry Pudding Panna Cotta

LIGHT SUMMER SUPPER

When it's hot as Hell's Kitchen outside, this menu offers light and breezy relief.

STARTER
Butter Lettuce Salad

ENTRÉE
Herb Oil–Poached Halibut with Potato-Fennel Puree, Roasted Tomatoes, and Lemon-Fennel Sauce

SIDE
Creamed Corn

DESSERTS
Mixed Berry Parfait

Blueberry Tart with White Chocolate Ganache

ASIAN FUSION

Celebrating the bold flavors of Asian cuisine from Japan to India.

STARTER
Crab-Shrimp Lettuce Cups with Black Bean Mango Salsa and Chili Vinaigrette

ENTRÉES
Miso-Sake Marinated Chilean Sea Bass with Seaweed Soba Salad

Crispy Pork Belly, Sushi Rice Cake, Long Beans with Shiso and Kimchi

SIDES
Tempura Broccolini with Lemon Aioli

Ginger Caramelized Carrots

Cauliflower-Stuffed Naan with Cilantro Chutney

DESSERT
Chai Crème Brûlée

VEGETARIAN

For vegetarians and omnivores alike.

STARTERS
Salad of Baby Gem Hearts, Toasted Walnuts, and Red Flame Grapes with Blue Cheese Dressing

Shallot and Caramelized Onion Tarte Tatin

ENTRÉES
Eggplant Involtini with Spicy Red Pepper Emulsion

Sheep's Milk Ricotta Gnudi

SIDES
Delicata Squash with Sage

DESSERT
Warm Raspberry Fritters

Salad of Baby Gem Hearts, page 65

Truffle Mac and Cheese, page 191

SURF AND TURF

Land and sea, **Hell's Kitchen** *style.*

STARTERS

Salad of Scallops with Truffle Vinaigrette

Lobster Spaghetti

Beef Carpaccio

ENTRÉES

John Dory with New Potatoes, Carrot Puree, Artichokes, and Fennel Velouté

Beef Wellington

DESSERTS

Fig Bread Pudding with White Pepper Ice Cream

Drunken Apple Pie

ITALIAN INSPIRED

A celebration of America's love affair with Italian food.

STARTERS

Cioppino

Sunchoke Risotto with Crispy Squid and Chili Oil

ENTRÉES

Homemade Pappardelle with Wild Mushrooms, Poached Egg, and Shaved Black Truffles

Roulade of Veal on Caramelized Onions

SIDES

Creamed Spinach

DESSERT

Crème Fraîche Panna Cotta with Honey Granita and Quince

A FESTIVAL OF TRUFFLES

A menu featuring truffles in every dish but dessert. Serve with copious champagne.

STARTERS

Salad of Baby Gem Hearts, Toasted Walnuts, and Red Flame Grapes with Blue Cheese Dressing

Salad of Scallops with Truffle Vinaigrette

ENTRÉES

Chicken Fried Rib-Eye with Yukon Mashed Potatoes and White Truffle Cream Gravy

SIDE

Truffle Mac and Cheese

DESSERT

Raspberry Crémeux Tart with a Sablé Breton Crust and Raspberry Sorbet

CATCH OF THE DAY

All things seafood.

STARTERS

Pan-Seared Grouper with Fennel Salad

Steamed Mussels with Tequila, Red Chili, Green Jalapeño, Coconut Milk, Lime, and Cilantro

ENTRÉES

Frutti di Mare

Halibut *en Papillote* with Purple Jasmine Rice and Island Salsa

SIDE

Rainbow-Colored Carrots with Butter and Parsley

COLD-WEATHER COMFORT FOOD

A menu to hunker down with for the night.

STARTERS

Sunchoke Risotto with Crispy Squid and Chili Oil

ENTRÉE

Oven-Roasted Pork Chops with Apple Butter, Cider-Braised Kale, and Pork Jus

SIDES

Delicata Squash with Sage

Potato-Leek Gratin

DESSERT

Drunken Apple Pie

JUST DESSERTS

All-out indulgent.

Passion Fruit Tart with Buttermilk Sherbet

Cinnamon Ice Cream, Caramelized Apples, and Walnut Sablé

Vanilla Bean Cheesecake

Red Velvet Cake

Chocolate Molten Cake with Malted Milk Ice Cream and Marcona Almond Brittle

MEAT LOVER'S MENU

To satisfy the carnivore in you. Lemon tart ends the meal on a lighter note, or go all-out gourmand with the caramel-filled molten cakes.

STARTER

Beef Carpaccio

ENTRÉES

Grilled Lamb Chops with Sautéed Linguine and Tomato Broth

Beef Wellington

Slow Braised Veal Cheeks with Smashed Red Bliss Potatoes and Garlic Confit

SIDES

Creamed Corn

Creamed Spinach

DESSERT

Lemon Meringue Tart

Caramel-Filled Chocolate Molten Cakes with Caramel Ice Cream

ON THE SIMPLE SIDE

An easy-to-put-together menu, perfect for weeknight fine dining.

STARTER

Grilled Jumbo Asparagus Salad with Fried Egg and Bacon-Shallot Vinaigrette

ENTRÉE

Brick Chicken with Herb Gremolata

SIDE

Roasted Delicata Squash

DESSERT

Mixed Berry Parfait

Grilled Jumbo Asparagus Salad with Fried Egg
and Bacon-Shallot Vinaigrette, page 63

LOOSELY LATIN

From tequila mussels to chicken mole and chocolate empanadas.

STARTER
Steamed Mussels with Tequila, Red Chili, Green Jalapeño, Coconut Milk, Lime, and Cilantro

ENTRÉES
Chicken Mole with Black Beans and Rice and Corn-Avocado Salsa

Elsie's Turkey Tacos

DESSERT
Chocolate Empanadas with Macerated Strawberries

PASTA PARTY

When all designs on dieting are thrown to the wind and enjoyment is the one and only mission of your meal!

STARTERS
King Crab Capellini with Chili, Lime, and Green Onion

Lobster Spaghetti

ENTRÉES
Frutti di Mare

Lemon Tagliatelle

Orecchietti with Broccoli and Italian Sausage

SIDE
Truffle Mac and Cheese

DESSERT
Vanilla Bean Cheesecake

ELEGANT DINNER PARTY

An epicure's delight.

STARTER
Seared Foie Gras on Brioche French Toast with Caramelized Apples and Figs

ENTRÉES
Halibut *en Papillote* with Purple Jasmine Rice and Island Salsa

Filet of Beef au Gratin, Dauphinoise Potatoes, Braised Salsify, and Pearl Onions

SIDE
Ginger Caramelized Carrots

DESSERTS
Coconut White Chocolate Panna Cotta with Champagne-Poached Fruit

Pineapple Tarte Tatin

Pineapple Tarte Tatin, page 225

CONCLUSION

IF YOU'VE SUCCESSFULLY MASTERED THESE ONE HUNDRED DISHES, you could be well on your way to becoming the next head chef at a five-star restaurant. *Hell's Kitchen* is calling your name if you're brave enough to give it a shot. Challenging yourself with this arsenal of *Hell's Kitchen* recipes is the best way to step up your game and approach the high standards you've seen on the show.

The more you practice, the closer you'll come to perfection and that coveted spot at the top. Practice starts with investing in a top-quality chef's knife that feels right in your hands. You'll be using it daily, so make it a top priority. Review your knife skills (pages 17 to 21) until you're chopping like a pro, and don't forget your mise-en-place (page 23). Prepping your ingredients in advance and having them at the ready when it's time to fire up your meal makes for a tightly run kitchen that puts out one successful dish after the next.

Keep cooking for gatherings both large and small. Create award-worthy meals with the menus on pages 240 to 253 and use special occasions to up your skills until they're *Hell's Kitchen*-worthy. Whether it's an intimate dinner party, inviting co-workers to your place, a boisterous group of friends, putting together a family reunion, or marking a milestone, these events can pave the way to new culinary heights.

Like anything, practice makes perfect. Perfection is what *Hell's Kitchen* demands, and it's what the show and the recipes in this book are designed to bring out in you. Get a jumpstart on your signature dish and make it over and over again until it meets the uncompromising standards of the show. That signature dish just may be your ticket to victory. Keep it up and you may be worthy to test your skills on a future season of *Hell's Kitchen*!

INDEX

A

Aioli
    Citrus, 76–77, *77*
    Lemon, 174, *175*
Almond(s)
    Marcona, Brittle, 217–218
    Toasted, 40, *41*
Apple(s)
    Caramelized, 198–199, *199*
    Caramelized Figs and, 69
    Pie, Drunken, *200*, 201
Artichoke(s)
    John Dory with, 108–109, *109*
    Shaved Baby, Slaw, 145–146, *147*
Asparagus
    Grilled Jumbo, Salad, with Fried Egg and Bacon-
        Shallot Vinaigrette, *62*, 63
    Risotto, Creamy, with Lemon and Mascarpone, 58,
        59
    Roasted, 156–157, *157*
Avocado-Corn Salsa, 158–159

B

Bacon
    and Caramelized Onion Jam, 134–136, *135*
    -Shallot Vinaigrette, *62*, 63
    Smoked, Collard Greens with, 160–161
Baked Cod with Green-Olive Crust, Marinated Bell
        Peppers, Caper-and-Raisin Puree, 92, *93*
Baked Oysters Rockefeller, 76–77, *77*
Bakeware, 10–11
Balsamic Vinaigrette, 42, *43*
Banana(s)
    Caramelized, Ice Cream, 229–231, *230*
    Foster, 202
Beef
    Burger, Eight-Ounce, with Caramelized Onion and
        Bacon Jam, Sharp Cheddar, and Special Sauce
        on a Brioche Bun with Sweet Potato Fries,
        134–136, *135*

Carpaccio, Pickled Radish, Fennel and Carrots, Yuzu
        (or Grapefruit) Vinaigrette, *52*, 53
    Filet of, au Gratin, Truffle Pommes Anna, Braised
        Salsify, and Pearl Onions, 96–97
    New York Strip with Truffle Polenta Fries, Tomato
        Jam, Sautéed Spinach, and Red Wine Jus,
        153–155, *154*
    Pepper-Crusted Steak with a Mushroom-Brandy
        Cream Sauce, Roasted Asparagus, and Sautéed
        Potatoes, 156–157, *157*
    Rib-Eye, Chicken-Fried, with Yukon Gold Mashed
        Potatoes and White Truffle Cream Gravy,
        94–95, *95*
    Short Ribs, White-Wine-Braised, 137
    Wellington, 84
    Wellington, Blackberry Sauce, Whipped Potatoes,
        Glazed Baby Carrots, 82–84, *83*
Beets, Roasted, *46*, 47
Bell Peppers, Marinated, 92, *93*
Berry. *See also specific types of berries*
    Compote, 212
    Mixed, Parfait, with Pastry Cream and Shortbread
        Cookies, *238*, 239
    Pudding Panna Cotta, 212–213, *213*
Black Bean(s)
    Mango Salsa, *56*, 57
    and Rice, 158–159
Blackberry Sauce, 82–84, *83*
Black-Olive Vinaigrette, 70, *71*
Bloody Mary Granita, 76–77, *77*
Blueberry Tart with White Chocolate Ganache, 235–
        236, *237*
Blue Cheese Dressing, *64*, 65
Bok Choy, *116*, 117
Bowls, 11, 13
Braised Pearl Onions and Salsify, 96–97
Branzino, Roasted Fennel, Caramelized Lemon, Olives,
        138, 139
Bread Pudding, Fig, with White Pepper Ice Cream,
        196–197, *197*
Brick Chicken with Herb Gremolata, *90*, 91

Brioche French Toast, 69
Broccoli, Orecchiette with Italian Sausage and, 132, *133*
Broccolini, Tempura, with Lemon Aioli, 174, *175*
Broth, Tomato, 100–102, *101, 102*
Brown Butter, 35, 74–75
Brown Butter Vinaigrette, 35
Brown Chicken Stock, 87
Brussels Sprouts
    Baby, Sautéed, 151–152
    Roasted, 98–99, *99*
Burger, Beef, 134–136, *135*
Butter
    Brown, 35, 74–75
    Maple, 88, *89*
Butter Lettuce Salad, 54, *55*
Buttermilk Sherbet, 221–222
Butternut Squash Puree, 151–152

C

Caesar Dressing, 48, *49*
Caesar Salad, Romaine Hearts, Pickled Red Onion,
    Parmesan Croutons, 48, *49*
Cake(s)
    Chocolate Molten, Caramel-Filled, 219–220, *220*
    Chocolate Molten, with Malted Milk Ice Cream and
        Marcona Almond Brittle, 217–218
    Coconut Layer, *204*, 205
    Red Velvet, with Mascarpone Frosting, 208, *209*
Candied Walnuts, 54, *55*
Capellini, King Crab, with Chili, Lime, and Green
    Onion, *32, 33*
Caper
    -and-Raisin Puree, 92, *93*
    -Red Onion-Tomato Relish, 114–115, *115*
Caramel, 219, 229–231, *230*
    -Filled Chocolate Molten Cakes, 219–220, *220*
Caramelized Apples, 198–199, *199*
    and Figs, 69
Caramelized Banana Ice Cream, 229–231, *230*
Caramelized Carrots, Ginger, *188*, 189
Caramelized Lemons, *138*, 139
Caramelized Onion(s), 121
    and Bacon Jam, 134–136, *135*
    Tarte Tatin, Shallot and, 72, *73*
Carbonara, 164, *165*

Carrot(s)
    Ginger Caramelized, *188*, 189
    Glazed Baby, 82–84, *83*
    Pickled Radish, Fennel and, *52, 53*
    Puree, 108–109, *109*
    Rainbow-Colored, with Butter and Parsley, *170*, 171
Cauliflower-Stuffed Naan with Cilantro Chutney,
        176–178, *177*
Chai Crème Brûlée, 194, *195*
Champagne
    -Poached Fruit, 210
    Syrup, 210, 239
Cheesecake, Vanilla Bean, 206, *207*
Chicken
    Breast, Lemon and Thyme Roasted, Sweet Corn
        Polenta, Sautéed Spinach, and Chicken Jus,
        110, *111*
    Breasts, Roasted, and Kabocha Squash with Maple
        Jus, *118*, 119–120, *120*
    Brick, with Herb Gremolata, *90*, 91
    Mole, with Black Beans and Rice and Corn-
        Avocado Salsa, 158–159
    Stock, Brown, 87
Chicken-Fried Rib-Eye with Yukon Gold Mashed
        Potatoes and White Truffle Cream Gravy,
        94–95, *95*
Chili Vinaigrette, *56*, 57
Chocolate
    Caramel Tart, with Caramelized Banana Ice Cream,
        229–231, *230*
    Empanadas, with Macerated Strawberries, 214–215,
        215
    Ganache, 229–231, *230*
    Molten Cake, with Malted Milk Ice Cream and
        Marcona Almond Brittle, 217–218
    Molten Cakes, Caramel-Filled, 219–220, *220*
    White, Coconut Panna Cotta, 210
    White, Ganache, 235–236, *237*
Chorizo Ragú, White Bean, Lobster, and, 124, *125*
Chutney, Cilantro, 176–178, *177*
Cider-Braised Kale, 85–86, *86*
Cilantro
    Chutney, 176–178, *177*
    Rice, *140*, 141–142, *142*
Cinnamon Ice Cream, Caramelized Apples, and
        Walnut Sablé, 198–199, *199*

Cioppino with Squid, Turbot, Salmon, Light Saffron Broth, Mussels and Clams, 36–37, *37*

Citrus. *See also* Grapefruit; Lemon(s)
Aioli, 76–77, *77*
Vinaigrette, 79

Clams
choosing and storing, 50
Cioppino with Squid, Turbot, Salmon, Light Saffron Broth, Mussels and, 36–37, *37*
Frutti di Mare, *128*, 129

Classic Vinaigrette, 92

Coconut
Frosting, *204*, 205
Layer Cake, *204*, 205
White Chocolate Panna Cotta, with Champagne-Poached Fruit and Mango Sorbet, 210

Cod, Baked, with Green-Olive Crust, Marinated Bell Peppers, Caper-and-Raisin Puree, 92, *93*

Collard Greens with Smoked Bacon, 160–161

Compote
Berry, 212
Walnut-Grape, *104*, 105

Confit Potatoes, 98–99, *99*

Cookies, Walnut Sablé, 198–199, *199*

Corn
-Avocado Salsa, 158–159
Creamed, 179, *179*
Polenta, Sweet Corn, 110, *111*
Roasted, Relish, *140*, 141–142, *142*

Crab
King Crab Capellini, 32, *33*
Shrimp Lettuce Cups with Black Bean Mango Salsa and Chili Vinaigrette, *56*, 57

Creamed Corn, 179, *179*

Creamed Spinach, *180*, 181

Creamy Asparagus Risotto with Lemon and Mascarpone, 58, *59*

Crème Brûlée, Chai, 194, *195*

Crème Fraîche
Panna Cotta, 212
Panna Cotta, with Honey Granita and Quince, 211
Spicy, *140*, 141–142, *142*

Crispy Pork Belly, Sushi Rice Cake, and Long Beans with Shiso and Kimchi, 143–144

Crispy Squid, 78

Crispy Zucchini Fries, 182, *183*

Croquette, Goat Cheese, 54, *55*

Crostini, 36

Croutons, Parmesan, 48, *49*

Crust. *See also* Pastry Dough
Graham Cracker, 206, 229
Green-Olive, 92, *93*
Sablé Breton, *232*, 233–234

Culinary education, 29

Cutting boards, 11

D

Dauphinoise Potatoes, 184, *185*

Delicata Squash with Sage, *172*, 173

Dressing. *See also* Vinaigrette
Blue Cheese, *64*, 65
Caesar, 48, *49*
Pink Grapefruit, *46*, 47
Sesame, 45
Truffle Blue Cheese, *64*, 65

Drunken Apple Pie, *200*, 201

Duck
Breast, with Five-Spice Braised Endive and Parsnip Puree, 103
Breast, with Walnut-Grape Compote, *104*, 105
Ragú Ravioli, and Pumpkin-Seed Puree with Brown Butter, 74–75

E

Edamame Succotash, 88, *89*

Eggplant Involtini with Spicy Red Pepper Emulsion, 60, *61*

Egg(s)
Fried, *62*, 63
Poached, 148–150, *149*
Quail, Hard-Boiled, 70, *71*

Eight-Ounce Beef Burger with Caramelized Onion and Bacon Jam, Sharp Cheddar, and Special Sauce on a Brioche Bun with Sweet Potato Fries, 134–136, *135*

Elsie's Turkey Tacos, 130, *131*

Empanadas, Chocolate, with Macerated Strawberries, 214–215, *215*

Endive, Five-Spice Braised, 103

Equipment. *See* Kitchen equipment

F

Fennel
    -Lemon Sauce, 106–107, *107*
    Pickled Radish, Carrots and, *52*, 53
    -Potato Puree, 106–107, *107*
    Roasted, *138*, 139
    Salad, *34*, 35
    Velouté, 108–109, *109*
Fig(s)
    Bread Pudding, with White Pepper Ice Cream,
        196–197, *197*
    Caramelized Apples and, 69
    Jam, 196
Filet of Beef au Gratin, Truffle Pommes Anna, Braised
        Salsify, and Pearl Onions, 96–97
Fish. *See also individual types of fish*
    Cioppino with Squid, Turbot, Salmon, Light Saffron
        Broth, Mussels and Clams, 36–37, *37*
    doneness test for, 124
Five-Spice Braised Endive, 103
Foie Gras, Seared, on Brioche French Toast with
        Caramelized Apples and Figs, 69
French Toast, Brioche, 69
Freshly Shucked Oysters with Bloody Mary Granita,
        76–77, *77*
Fried Eggs, *62*, 63
Frisée Salad, *72*, *73*
Fritters, Warm Raspberry, 203
Frosting
    Coconut, *204*, 205
    Mascarpone, 208, *209*
Frozen ingredients, 24, 27
Fruit, Champagne-Poached, 210
Frutti di Mare, *128*, 129

G

Ganache, 229–231, *230*
    White Chocolate, 235–236, *237*
Garlic Confit, 162–163, *163*
Ginger Caramelized Carrots, *188*, 189
Glazed Baby Carrots, 82–84, *83*
Gnudi, Sheep's Milk Ricotta, 122, *123*
Goat Cheese
    Croquette, 54, *55*
    Whipped, 40, *41*

Graham Cracker Crust, 206, 229
Granita
    Bloody Mary, 76–77, *77*
    Honey, 211
    Raspberry, 212
Grape
    Sauce, 151–152
    -Walnut Compote, *104*, 105
Grapefruit
    Pink, Dressing, *46*, 47
    Vinaigrette, *52*, 53
Gratin
    Potato Leek, *186*, 187
    Yam and Potato, 160–161
Gravy, White Truffle Cream, 94–95, *95*
Green-Olive Crust, 92, *93*
Green Tea Soba Noodles, *44*, 45
Gremolata, Herb, 90, 91
Grilled Jumbo Asparagus Salad with Fried Egg and
        Bacon-Shallot Vinaigrette, *62*, 63
Grilled Lamb Chops with Sautéed Linguine and
        Tomato Broth, 100–102, *101*, *102*
Grilled Peach Salad, Peppered Whipped Goat Cheese,
        Baby Arugula, Toasted Almonds, Sauvignon
        Blanc Honey Vinaigrette, 40, *41*
Grilled Pork Chop with Spinach Polenta and Shaved
        Baby Artichoke Slaw, 145–146, *147*
Grilled Salmon with White Bean, Chorizo, and Lobster
        Ragú, 124, *125*
Grouper, Pan-Seared, with Fennel Salad, *34*, 35

H

Halibut
    en Papillote, with Purple Jasmine Rice and Island
        Salsa, 166–167, *167*
    Herb Oil-Poached, with Potato-Fennel Puree,
        Roasted Tomatoes, and Lemon-Fennel Sauce,
        106–107, *107*
Haricots Verts, 70, *71*
    Sautéed, 114–115, *115*
Heirloom Tomato Salad with Burrata, Pine Nut
        Gremolata, and Pickled Red Pearl Onions, 42, *43*
Hell's Kitchen (TV show), 1–6
Herb-Crusted Rack of Lamb, Warm Sundried Tomato
        Tapenade, Brussels Sprouts, Confit Potatoes,
        98–99, *99*

Herb Gremolata, *90*, 91

Herb Oil-Poached Halibut with Potato-Fennel Puree, Roasted Tomatoes, and Lemon-Fennel Sauce, 106–107, *107*

Homemade Pappardelle with Wild Mushrooms, Poached Egg, and Shaved Black Truffles, 148–150, *149*

Honey

    Granita, 211

    -Grilled Shrimp with Roasted Corn Relish, Cilantro Rice, and Spicy Crème Fraîche, *140*, 141–142, *142*

I

Ice Cream

    Caramelized Banana, 229–231, *230*

    Cinnamon, 198–199, *199*

    Malted Milk, 217–218

    White Pepper, 196–197, *197*

Ingredients, 24, 26–27

Involtini, Eggplant, with Spicy Red Pepper Emulsion, 60, *61*

Island Salsa, 166–167, *167*

Italian Sausage, Orecchiette with Broccoli and, 132, *133*

J

Jam

    Caramelized Onion and Bacon, 134–136, *135*

    Fig, 196

    Tomato, 153–155, *154*

John Dory with New Potatoes, Carrot Puree, Artichokes, and Fennel Velouté, 108–109, *109*

K

Kabocha Squash, Roasted, *118*, 119–120, *120*

Kale, Cider-Braised, 85–86, *86*

King Crab Capellini with Chili, Lime, and Green Onion, *32*, *33*

"Kiss it and flip it" technique, 124

Kitchen equipment, 9–19

    bakeware, 10–11

    bowls, 11, 13

    cutting boards, 11

    knives, 17–19

    measuring devices, 14

    mixing machines, 13

    pots, pans, and skillets, 9–10

    stirring, flipping, whisking, and grabbing tools, 13–14

    straining tools, 15

Knife skills, 19–21

Knives, 17–19

L

Lamb

    Chops, Grilled, with Sautéed Linguine and Tomato Broth, 100–102, *101*, *102*

    Herb-Crusted Rack of, Warm Sundried Tomato Tapenade, Brussels Sprouts, Confit Potatoes, 98–99, *99*

Leek

    Potato Gratin, *186*, 187

    -Potato Puree, 114–115, *115*

Lemon(s)

    Aioli, 174, *175*

    Caramelized, *138*, 139

    -Fennel Sauce, 106–107, *107*

    Tagliatelle, with Toasted Pine Nuts and Arugula, *126*, 127

    Tart, Lemon Meringue, 226–228, *227*

    and Thyme Roasted Chicken Breast, Sweet Corn Polenta, Sautéed Spinach, and Chicken Jus, 110, *111*

    Vinaigrette, 54, *55*

Lightly Spiced Pastry Cream, 235–236, *237*

Linguine

    Carbonara, 164, *165*

    Sautéed, 100–102, *101*, *102*

Lobster

    Ragú, White Bean, Chorizo, and, 124, *125*

    Spaghetti, *38*, 39

Long Beans, 143–144

M

Mac and Cheese, Truffle, *190*, 191

Macerated Strawberries, 214–215, *215*

Mahi Mahi, Pecan-Crusted, with Edamame Succotash and Maple Butter, 88, *89*

Malted Milk Ice Cream, 217–218
Mango Black Bean Salsa, *56*, 57
Maple Butter, 88, *89*
Marcona Almond Brittle, 217–218
Marinated Bell Peppers, 92, *93*
Mascarpone Frosting, 208, *209*
Measuring devices, 14
Menus, 240–252
Meringue, 226–228, *227*
Mise-en-place, 23–24
Miso-Sake Marinated Chilean Sea Bass with Seaweed
    Soba Salad, 112, *113*
Mixed Berry Parfait with Pastry Cream and Shortbread
    Cookies, *238*, 239
Mixing machines, 13
Morels and Peas, 122, *123*
Mushroom
    -Brandy Cream Sauce, 156–157, *157*
    Duxelles, 82
    Sautéed Mixed Wild, Sauce, 148–150, *149*
Mussels
    choosing and storing, 50
    Cioppino with Squid, Turbot, Salmon, Light Saffron
        Broth, Clams and, 36–37, *37*
    Frutti di Mare, *128*, 129
    Steamed, with Tequila, Red Chili, Green Jalapeño,
        Coconut Milk, Lime, and Cilantro, 50, *51*
Mustard-Rubbed Veal Loin with Butternut Squash
    Puree, Sautéed Baby Brussels Sprouts, and
    Grape Sauce, 151–152

N

Naan, Cauliflower-Stuffed, with Cilantro Chutney,
    176–178, *177*
New York Strip with Truffle Polenta Fries, Tomato Jam,
    Sautéed Spinach, and Red Wine Jus, 153–155, *154*

O

Oil
    Saffron, 36
    truffle, 68
Onion(s)
    Braised Pearl, and Salsify, 96–97
    Caper-Red Onion-Tomato Relish, 114–115, *115*

    Caramelized, 121
    Caramelized, Tarte Tatin, Shallot and, 72, *73*
    Red Pearl, Pickled, 42, *43*, 48, *49*
Orecchiette with Broccoli and Italian Sausage, 132, *133*
Oven-Roasted Pork Chops with Apple Butter, Cider-
    Braised Kale, and Pork Jus, 85–86, *86*
Oysters
    choosing and storing, 50
    Freshly Shucked, with Bloody Mary Granita, 76–77,
        77
    Rockefeller, Baked, 76–77, *77*
    Tempura-Fried, with Citrus Aioli, 76–77, *77*

P

Pancetta, Carbonara, 164, *165*
Pan-Fried Red Snapper with Roasted Beets and Pink
    Grapefruit Dressing, *46*, 47
Panna Cotta
    Berry Pudding, 212–213, *213*
    Coconut White Chocolate, with Champagne-
        Poached Fruit and Mango Sorbet, 210
    Crème Fraîche, 212
    Crème Fraîche, with Honey Granita and Quince, 211
Pans, 9–10
Pan-Seared Grouper with Fennel Salad, *34*, 35
Pan-Seared Sea Bass, Potato-Leek Puree, Sautéed
    Haricots Verts, Caper-Red Onion-Tomato
    Relish, 114–115, *115*
Pan-Seared Tuna
    with Bok Choy and Wasabi Mashed Potatoes with
        a Soy Ginger Vinaigrette, *116*, 117
    Tataki, with Green Tea Soba Noodles, *44*, 45
Pantry ingredients, 24, 26–27
Pappardelle, Homemade, with Wild Mushrooms,
    Poached Egg, and Shaved Black Truffles,
    148–150, *149*
Parfait, Mixed Berry, with Pastry Cream and
    Shortbread Cookies, *238*, 239
Parmesan Croutons, 48, *49*
Parsnip Puree, 103
Passion Fruit Tart with Buttermilk Sherbet, 221–222
Pastry Cream
    Lightly Spiced, 235–236, *237*
    Mixed Berry Parfait with Shortbread Cookies and,
        238, 239

Pastry Dough, 201, 223
    Sablé Breton Crust, *232, 233*–234
    Sweet(-)Tart, 221–222, 226, 235–236, *237*
Peaches, Grilled, 40, *41*
Peas, Morels and, 122, *123*
Pea Shoot Salad, 79
Pecan-Crusted Mahi Mahi with Edamame Succotash
    and Maple Butter, 88, *89*
Pepper-Crusted Steak with a Mushroom-Brandy
    Cream Sauce, Roasted Asparagus, and
    Sautéed Potatoes, 156–157, *157*
Pickled Radish, Fennel and Carrots, *52*, 53
Pickled Red Pearl Onions, *42, 43*, 48, *49*
Pie crust, 223. *See also* Crust; Pastry Dough
Pineapple Tarte Tatin, *224, 225*
Pine Nut(s)
    Gremolata, *42, 43*
    Toasted, Lemon Tagliatelle with Arugula and, *126,*
        127
Pink Grapefruit Dressing, *46, 47*
Pistachios, Toasted, 79
Poached Egg, 148–150, *149*
Polenta, *104*, 105
    Fries, Truffle, 153–155, *154*
    Spinach, 145–146, *147*
    Sweet Corn, 110, *111*
Pommes Anna, 96–97
Pork
    Belly, Crispy, Sushi Rice Cake, and Long Beans with
        Shiso and Kimchi, 143–144
    Chop, Grilled, with Spinach Polenta and Shaved
        Baby Artichoke Slaw, 145–146, *147*
    Chops, Oven-Roasted, with Apple Butter, Cider-
        Braised Kale, and Pork Jus, 85–86, *86*
    Tenderloin, Roasted, Collard Greens with Smoked
        Bacon with Yam and Potato Gratin, 160–161
Potato(es)
    Confit, 98–99, *99*
    Dauphinoise, 184, *185*
    -Fennel Puree, 106–107, *107*
    Gratin, Yam and, 160–161
    Leek Gratin, *186*, 187
    -Leek Puree, 114–115, *115*
    New, 108–109, *109*
    Pommes Anna, 96–97
    Sautéed, 156–157, *157*

    Smashed Red Bliss, 162–163, *163*
    Wasabi Mashed, *116*, 117
    Whipped, 82–84, *83*
    Yukon Gold Mashed, 94–95, *95*
Pots, 9–10
Pumpkin-Seed Puree, 74–75
Puree
    Butternut Squash, 151–152
    Caper-and-Raisin, 92, *93*
    Carrot, 108–109, *109*
    Parsnip, 103
    Potato-Fennel, 106–107, *107*
    Potato-Leek, 114–115, *115*
    Pumpkin-Seed Puree, 74–75
    Quince, 211
    Raspberry, *232, 233*–234
    Sunchoke, 78
Purple Jasmine Rice, 166–167, *167*

Q

Quail Eggs, Hard-Boiled, 70, *71*
Quince Puree, 211

R

Radish, Pickled Fennel, Carrots and, *52*, 53
Ragú
    Duck, Ravioli and Pumpkin-Seed Puree with
        Brown Butter, 74–75
    White Bean, Chorizo, and Lobster, 124, *125*
Rainbow-Colored Carrots with Butter and Parsley, *170,*
    171
Raisin-and-Caper Puree, 92, *93*
Raspberry
    Crémeux, *232, 233*–234
    Crémeux Tart, with a Sablé Breton Crust and
        Raspberry Sorbet, *232, 233*–234
    Fritters, Warm, 203
    Granita, 212
    Puree, *232, 233*–234
Ravioli, Duck Ragú, and Pumpkin-Seed Puree with
    Brown Butter, 74–75
Red Pepper Emulsion, Spicy, 60, *61*
Red Snapper, Pan-Fried, with Roasted Beets and Pink
    Grapefruit Dressing, *46*, 47

Red Velvet Cake with Mascarpone Frosting, 208, *209*

Red Wine Jus, 153–155, *154*

Refrigerated ingredients, 24, 27

Relish

    Caper-Red Onion-Tomato, 114–115, *115*

    Roasted Corn, *140*, 141–142, *142*

Rice

    Black Beans and, 158–159

    Cilantro, *140*, 141–142, *142*

    Purple Jasmine, 166–167, *167*

    Sushi, Cake, 143–144

Ricotta Gnudi, Sheep's Milk, 122, *123*

Risotto

    cooking, 58

    Creamy Asparagus, with Lemon and Mascarpone, 58, *59*

    Sunchoke, with Crispy Squid and Chili Oil, 78

Roasted Asparagus, 156–157, *157*

Roasted Beets, *46*, 47

Roasted Brussels Sprouts, 98–99, *99*

Roasted Chicken Breasts and Kabocha Squash with Maple Jus, *118*, 119–120, *120*

Roasted Corn Relish, *140*, 141–142, *142*

Roasted Fennel, *138*, 139

Roasted Kabocha Squash, *118*, 119–120, *120*

Roasted Pork Tenderloin, Collard Greens with Smoked Bacon with Yam and Potato Gratin, 160–161

Roasted Tomatoes, 106–107, *107*

Roulade of Veal on Caramelized Onions, 121

S

Sablé Breton Crust, *232*, 233–234

Saffron oil, 36

Salad

    of Baby Gem Hearts, Toasted Walnuts, and Red Grapes with Blue Cheese Dressing, 64, 65

    Butter Lettuce, 54, *55*

    Caesar, Romaine Hearts, Pickled Red Onion, Parmesan Crouton, 48, *49*

    Fennel, *34*, 35

    Frisée, 72, *73*

    Grilled Jumbo Asparagus, with Fried Egg and Bacon-Shallot Vinaigrette, 62, *63*

    Grilled Peach, Peppered Whipped Goat Cheese, Baby Arugula, Toasted Almonds, Sauvignon Blanc Honey Vinaigrette, 40, *41*

Heirloom Tomato, with Burrata, Pine Nut Gremolata, and Pickled Red Pearl Onions, 42, *43*

    Pea Shoot, 79

    of Scallops, with Truffle Vinaigrette, *66*, 67

    Squab, with Blood Orange, Pea Shoots, and Citrus Vinaigrette, 79

    Wakame Seaweed Soba, 112, *113*

Salmon

    Cioppino with Squid, Turbot, Light Saffron Broth, Mussels, Clams and, 36–37, *37*

    Grilled, with White Bean, Chorizo, and Lobster Ragú, 124, *125*

Salsa

    Black Bean Mango, *56*, 57

    Corn-Avocado, 158–159

    Island, 166–167, *167*

Salsify, Braised Pearl Onions and, 96–97

Sauce

    Blackberry, 82–84, *83*

    Chicken Mole, with Black Beans and Rice and Corn-Avocado Salsa, 158–159

    Fennel Velouté, 108–109, *109*

    Grape, 151–152

    Lemon-Fennel, 106–107, *107*

    Mushroom-Brandy Cream, 156–157, *157*

    Sautéed Mixed Wild Mushroom, 148–150, *149*

Sautéed Linguine, 100–102, *101*, *102*

Sautéed Mixed Wild Mushroom Sauce, 148–150, *149*

Sautéed Potatoes, 156–157, *157*

Sautéed Spinach, 153–155, *154*

Sauvignon Blanc Honey Vinaigrette, 40, *41*

Scallops, Salad of, with Truffle Vinaigrette, *66*, 67

Sea Bass

    Chilean, Miso-Sake Marinated, with Seaweed Soba Salad, 112, *113*

    Pan-Seared, Potato-Leek Puree, Sautéed Haricots Verts, Caper-Red Onion-Tomato Relish, 114–115, *115*

Seafood. *See also individual types of seafood*

    choosing and storing bivalves, 50

    Cioppino with Squid, Turbot, Salmon, Light Saffron Broth, Mussels and Clams, 36–37, *37*

    Crab Shrimp Lettuce Cups with Black Bean Mango Salsa and Chili Vinaigrette, *56*, 57

    Seared Ahi Tuna Loin with Haricots Verts, Hard-Boiled Quail Eggs, and Black Olive Dressing, 70, *71*

Seared Foie Gras on Brioche French Toast with Caramelized Apples and Figs, 69
Sesame Dressing, 45
Shallot and Caramelized Onion Tarte Tatin, 72, *73*
Shaved Baby Artichoke Slaw, 145–146, *147*
Sheep's Milk Ricotta Gnudi, 122, *123*
Sherbet, Buttermilk, 221–222
Short Ribs, White-Wine-Braised, 137
Shrimp
    Crab Shrimp Lettuce Cups with Black Bean Mango Salsa and Chili Vinaigrette, *56*, 57
    Honey-Grilled, with Roasted Corn Relish, Cilantro Rice, and Spicy Crème Fraîche, *140*, 141–142, *142*
Skillets, 10
Slow-Braised Veal Cheeks with Smashed Red Bliss Potatoes and Garlic Confit, 162–163, *163*
Smashed Red Bliss Potatoes, 162–163, *163*
Soba (Noodles)
    Green Tea, *44*, 45
    Salad, Wakame Seaweed, 112, *113*
Soy Ginger Vinaigrette, *116*, 117
Spaghetti, Lobster, *38*, 39
Spicy Crème Fraîche, *140*, 141–142, *142*
Spicy Red Pepper Emulsion, 60, *61*
Spinach
    Creamed, *180*, 181
    Polenta, 145–146, *147*
    Sautéed, 110, *111*, 153–155, *154*
Squab Salad with Blood Orange, Pea Shoots, and Citrus Vinaigrette, 79
Squid
    Cioppino with Turbot, Salmon, Light Saffron Broth, Mussels, Clams and, 36–37, *37*
    Crispy, 78
Steamed Mussels with Tequila, Red Chili, Green Jalapeño, Coconut Milk, Lime, and Cilantro, 50, *51*
Stock, Brown Chicken, 87
Straining tools, 15
Strawberries, Macerated, 214–215, *215*
Succotash, Edamame, 88, *89*
Sunchoke
    Puree, 78
    Risotto, with Crispy Squid and Chili Oil, 78
Sundried Tomato Kalamata Olive Tapenade, 98–99, *99*
Sushi Rice Cake, 143–144
Sweet Corn Polenta, 110, *111*

Sweet Potato Fries, 134–136, *135*
Sweet(-)Tart Dough, 221–222, 226, 235–236, *237*
Syrup, Champagne, 210, 239

T

Tacos, Elsie's Turkey, 130, *131*
Tagliatelle, Lemon, with Toasted Pine Nuts and Arugula, *126*, 127
Tapenade, Sundried Tomato Kalamata Olive, 98–99, *99*
Tart
    Blueberry, with White Chocolate Ganache, 235–236, *237*
    Chocolate Caramel, with Caramelized Banana Ice Cream, 229–231, *230*
    Lemon Meringue, 226–228, *227*
    Passion Fruit, with Buttermilk Sherbet, 221–222
    Raspberry Crémeux, with a Sablé Breton Crust and Raspberry Sorbet, *232*, 233–234
Tarte Tatin
    Pineapple, *224*, 225
    Shallot and Caramelized Onion, 72, *73*
Tempura Broccolini with Lemon Aioli, 174, *175*
Tempura-Fried Oysters with Citrus Aioli, 76–77, *77*
Toasted Almonds, 40, *41*
Toasted Pistachios, 79
Toasted Walnuts, *64*, 65
Tomato(es)
    Broth, 100–102, *101*, *102*
    Caper-Red Onion-Tomato Relish, 114–115, *115*
    Heirloom, Salad, with Burrata, Pine Nut Gremolata, and Pickled Red Pearl Onions, *42*, *43*
    Jam, 153–155, *154*
    Roasted, 106–107, *107*
    Sundried, Kalamata Olive Tapenade, 98–99, *99*
A Trio of Oysters: Tempura-Fried Oysters with Citrus Aioli, Freshly Shucked Oysters with Bloody Mary Granita, Baked Oysters Rockefeller, 76–77, *77*
Truffle oil, 68
Truffle(s), 68
    Blue Cheese Dressing, *64*, 65
    Mac and Cheese, *190*, 191
    Polenta Fries, 153–155, *154*
    Shaved Black, Homemade Pappardelle with, 148–150, *149*
    Vinaigrette, *66*, 67
    White, Cream Gravy, 94–95, *95*

Tuna
    Loin, Seared Ahi, with Haricots Verts, Hard-Boiled
        Quail Eggs, and Black Olive Dressing, 70, *71*
    Pan-Seared, with Bok Choy and Wasabi Mashed
        Potatoes with a Soy Ginger Vinaigrette, *116*, 117
    Tataki, Pan-Seared, with Green Tea Soba Noodles,
        44, 45
    Turbot, Cioppino with Squid, Salmon, Light Saffron
        Broth, Mussels, Clams and, 36–37, *37*
    Turkey Tacos, Elsie's, 130, *131*

V

Vanilla Bean Cheesecake, 206, *207*
Veal
    Cheeks, Slow-Braised, with Smashed Red Bliss
        Potatoes and Garlic Confit, 162–163, *163*
    Loin, Mustard-Rubbed, with Butternut Squash
        Puree, Sautéed Baby Brussels Sprouts, and
        Grape Sauce, 151–152
    Roulade of, on Caramelized Onions, 121
Vinaigrette
    Bacon-Shallot, *62*, 63
    Balsamic, *42*, 43
    Black-Olive, 70, *71*
    Brown Butter, 35
    Chili, *56*, 57
    Citrus, 79
    Classic, 92
    Lemon, 54, *55*
    Sauvignon Blanc Honey, 40, *41*
    Soy Ginger, *116*, 117
    Truffle, *66*, 67
    Yuzu (or Grapefruit), *52*, 53

W

Wakame Seaweed Soba Salad, 112, *113*
Walnut(s)
    Candied, 54, *55*
    -Grape Compote, *104*, 105
    Sablé Cookies, 198–199, *199*
    Toasted, *64*, 65
Warm Raspberry Fritters, 203
Wasabi Mashed Potatoes, *116*, 117
Whipped Goat Cheese, 40, *41*
Whipped Potatoes, 82–84, *83*
White Bean, Chorizo, and Lobster Ragú, 124, *125*
White Chocolate
    Ganache, 235–236, *237*
    Panna Cotta, Coconut, with Champagne-Poached
        Fruit and Mango Sorbet, 210
White Pepper Ice Cream, 196–197, *197*
White Truffle Cream Gravy, 94–95, *95*
White-Wine-Braised Short Ribs, 137

Y

Yam and Potato Gratin, 160–161
Yukon Gold Mashed Potatoes, 94–95, *95*
Yuzu Vinaigrette, *52*, 53

Z

Zucchini Fries, Crispy, 182, *183*